The Romance of the Violet
and Other Wager Tales
from Medieval France

The Romance of the Violet
and Other Wager Tales from Medieval France

Translated by
NANCY VINE DURLING

McFarland & Company, Inc., Publishers
Jefferson, North Carolina

This book has undergone peer review.

ISBN (print) 978-1-4766-9437-5
ISBN (ebook) 978-1-4766-5400-3

LIBRARY OF CONGRESS AND BRITISH LIBRARY
CATALOGUING DATA ARE AVAILABLE

Library of Congress Control Number 2024030373

Front cover image: manuscript: Gérard de Nevers, prose version
of the *Roman de la Violette* by Gerbert de Montreuil. Liédet, Loyset,
Illuminator, Wavrin, Jean de, 1401–1500 (Library of France)

Printed in the United States of America

McFarland & Company, Inc., Publishers
Box 611, Jefferson, North Carolina 28640
www.mcfarlandpub.com

Table of Contents

Acknowledgments

Medieval wager tales have accompanied me for many years on a journey covering many miles. The adventure began in Paris in 1987, when I first examined Bibliothèque nationale de France manuscript fr. 24430. This late thirteenth-century collection of vernacular works includes the only extant copy of *Li Contes dou roi Flore et de la bielle Jehane*. To my surprise, a dramatic imperfection in the parchment on which the tale is transcribed was used by the scribe to "illustrate" a key scene. I presented this finding at Purdue in 1990 and published the paper, "La bielle Jehane and the Body of the Text," the following year.

At an earlier conference held at Purdue I met Patricia Terry, a superb translator of medieval French and Scandinavian texts. At her invitation, I gave a lecture about the wager tale tradition at UC San Diego, also in 1990. Soon after, Pat and I embarked on a translation of Jean Renart's acclaimed version of the story *Le Roman de la Rose ou de Guillaume de Dole*; it was published in 1993. This project prompted a visit to the Vatican Library where I consulted the unique manuscript version of Jean Renart's romance. In 1997, while living in Berkeley, I edited the first volume of essays devoted to *Guillaume de Dole*, to which Pat contributed an illuminating essay, "On the Untranslatable Surface of *Guillaume de Dole*." My collaboration with Pat taught me a great deal about the intricacies of translation, an often-misunderstood art. Our discussions eventually led to an experimental collaborative project, *The Finding of the Grail* (2000). Pat passed away in 2014 and I continue to miss her wise counsel and the great pleasure of working with her.

Over the decades, wager tales have continued to pique my interest. In 1992, I focused on an Italian version of the wager tale *Justa Victoria*, written by the fifteenth-century Veronese humanist Felice Feliciano, and published an analysis of it in 1993. That same year, a faculty grant from Florida Atlantic University, where I taught from 1991 to 1994, enabled me to travel to Florence to examine the original manuscript, written in Felice's own hand, and collate it with Giovanni Papanti's edition, published in 1871.

Frequent stays in Paris in the early 2000s allowed me to collate manuscripts BnF fr. 1374 and fr. 1533 (containing the *Le Roman de la Violette*) with Douglas Labaree Buffum's 1928 edition, and to collate Arsenal 3527 (*Le Comte de Poitiers*) with Bertil Malmberg's edition of 1940. In 2009, at the invitation of Danielle Bohler, I presented a second conference paper about *Flore et Jehane*, this time in Bordeaux; a revised version of the talk appeared in 2011. I am grateful to Danielle for her encouragement and steadfast friendship.

In 2018, I returned to Felice's version of the wager tale. Still little known, it presents a vivid portrait of the humanistic literary tastes of its time. I got to work and presented various drafts of a translation to my writing group here in Austin, Texas. To my fellow participants and good friends Susan Wan Dolling and Virginia Raymond, I extend my warmest thanks for lively discussions and ongoing, invaluable criticism. The translation, "*Justa Victoria*: A 15th-Century Wager Tale," was published in 2020. Having translated a second wager tale, I turned once again to the early French versions which have intrigued me for so many years. The volume at hand is the result. Here again, I thank Susan and Virginia for their perceptive comments. It is also a pleasure to thank Renate Blumenfeld-Kosinski, dear friend since our graduate school days, for her careful reading of the introduction and helpful advice. I am, in addition, grateful to an anonymous reader for McFarland, who made numerous useful suggestions.

NVD
Austin, January 2024

Preface

During the eleventh century, lives of saints (*Vitae Sanctorum*) and other devotional texts began to be translated from Latin into the vernacular languages of western Europe. Over time, other literary genres were explored, and by the second half of the twelfth century the corpus of works written directly in the vernacular had widened considerably. In France, lyric poetry, short narratives called *lais*, epic tales of military might and conquest (*chansons de geste*), and romance, all composed in French, began to proliferate. These tales were read aloud and were prized for their entertainment value. Of the various genres, romance was arguably the most popular, offering the enduring legends of Tristan and Iseut, King Arthur and the Round Table, and the Quest for the Holy Grail. These stories were frequently retold throughout the Middle Ages, just as they are today.

The basic structure of medieval romance is a simple one: a nobleman's reputation is threatened or lost. To reestablish his position in society, he must undertake a series of dangerous adventures and emerge victorious; only then can he reintegrate into courtly society.[1] The women in these works are typically portrayed as love interests, though they, too, may face daunting challenges. Often unjustly accused of infidelity or unchaste behavior, they must find a way to exonerate themselves.

The focus on female chastity in these works is unsurprising. Noblemen were frequently absent from home, sometimes in service to an overlord, at other times for more personal reasons. Whether attending tournaments, fighting in regional battles, or even traveling overseas to participate in a Crusade, these men were often away from home for weeks or even years at a time. Were their wives faithful during these long separations? Did their noble lineage remain "unsullied"? It is little wonder that the literature of the twelfth, thirteenth, and fourteenth centuries often reflected a pervasive social anxiety about female sexuality.

Nowhere is this anxiety explored to greater dramatic effect than in the medieval stories now known as "wager tales." These tales, classified by folklorists as "chastity wagers," circulated widely throughout the Middle

Ages.[2] Some forty versions, written in French, Italian, Spanish, German, Russian, Greek, and English were identified and discussed by the French medievalist Gaston Paris in an in-depth, albeit unfinished study published posthumously in 1903. Paris's study, a touchstone for future scholars, demonstrates that the tales were widely disseminated, transcending national and linguistic boundaries.[3] All of these stories follow a similar plot line: two men agree to a high-stakes wager concerning the virtue of a woman, usually a sister or a wife, though sometimes a sweetheart. When the lady proves to be above reproach, the man who has sworn to seduce her surreptitiously obtains knowledge about her of an intimate nature, often the existence of a birthmark on her breast or thigh. The woman is then unjustly accused and publicly disgraced. Eventually, despite daunting odds which she heroically confronts and overcomes, the lady is exonerated, her honor intact.

Wager tales enjoyed a particular vogue in France in the early thirteenth century. Male anxiety about the legitimacy of heirs was, no doubt, one reason for the popularity of the theme, but the increasingly important role played by women as patrons of the arts was another. The theme of female honor was likely of special interest to high-born women and the valor shown by wager tale heroines would have appealed greatly to a female audience. At the same time, these stories offered exciting and detailed depictions of battles and tournaments, highlighting the activities and interests of the noblemen of the time. Such scenes would have been particularly gratifying to male audience members.

No fewer than seven versions of the wager tale have survived in Old French, among them the lively romances of Jean Renart and Gerbert de Montreuil (*Le Roman de la Rose ou de Guillaume de Dole* and *Le Roman de la Violette*), the anonymous *Roman du Comte de Poitiers* and the short prose work, *Li Contes du roi Flore et de la bielle Jehane*. A fourteenth-century version, "Le Miracle d'Othon, roi d'Espagne," is included in the collection of dramatized Marian miracle tales, *Les Miracles de Notre Dame par Personnages*.[4] An additional short prose version, "Ysmarie de Voisines," dates from the fifteenth century.[5] A Latin version, *Guillermus Nivernensis*, was probably written in France and may have served as a source for Gerbert's romance, though the dating of it remains uncertain.[6] *Le Roman de la Violette* was rewritten as a prose narrative in the second half of the fifteenth century.[7]

Of these stories, only *Guillaume de Dole* and *Flore et Jehane* have been previously translated into English.[8] The present volume offers a new and accurate translation of the latter work, along with translations of *Le Comte de Poitiers* and of Gerbert de Montreuil's *Roman de la Violette*. As the reader will see, the three works translated here—two of them "romances," the third a kind of "mini-romance"—contain a wealth of information about aristocratic life in the first half of the thirteenth century. The *Roman de la Violette* offers an inside look at courtly entertainment and contains numerous song fragments, shown in performance. These songs are listed and identified in Appendix I. All three works offer detailed references to clothing, textiles, and armor. For many of these terms there is no readily available English equivalent. To help readers visualize these items, I have compiled a glossary and discussion of terms in Appendix II.

Information concerning manuscript sources and editions is given in the introduction to each work. Suggestions for further reading are provided at the end of the volume.

Introduction to
Le Roman de la Violette

Gerbert de Montreuil is one of the liveliest writers of medieval France, though one of the least known today. Only two of his works have survived: a continuation of Chrétien de Troyes's *Conte du graal* (ca. 1180) and *Le Roman de la Violette*, likely modeled on another romance, *Le Roman de la Rose ou de Guillaume de Dole*, written by Gerbert's close contemporary Jean Renart.[1] Because Gerbert's extant works are so clearly indebted to other writers, his reputation has chiefly been that of an epigone, albeit a very gifted one. Gerbert's pride in his own talent, given emphatic expression in the prologue to the *Roman de la Violette* is, however, entirely justified. His works are both entertaining and historically informative, and they richly deserve a wider audience.

Who was Gerbert de Montreuil? As with most twelfth- and thirteenth-century French writers, it is impossible to say. The sparse information we have about these authors is usually gleaned from the prologues and epilogues to their works, where they describe, sometimes disingenuously, their audiences, their patrons, and themselves. Their comments may be read with varying degrees of belief or skepticism, but the specificity of Gerbert's remarks in the *Violette* suggests that the information recorded here is accurate.

Gerbert dedicates the *Violette* to Countess Marie de Ponthieu, a niece of King Philippe Auguste (1165–1223) and the wife of Simon de Dammartin, one of the rebellious barons who opposed Philippe at the famous battle of Bouvines in 1214. As an enemy of the crown, Simon was subsequently exiled, and when Marie's father died in 1221, Philippe barred her accession to Ponthieu. Between 1223 and 1225, Marie made repeated appeals to Philippe's successor, her cousin King Louis VIII, to reinstate her hereditary right to the land. It is to this struggle, and to her ultimate success in 1225, that Gerbert refers in the concluding lines of the romance:

And so Gerbert de Montreuil
  brings to a close his story of the Violet...
  He has composed this work and put it
  into rhyme for the best lady who lives...
  Countess Marie de Ponthieu,
  who experienced great suffering
  before she regained her lands.
  She repeatedly applied for them,
  and by dint of her fidelity and loyalty
recovered her domain and inheritance [ll. 6634–6648].

Gerbert's comments identify him as a dependent of Marie's court; they also make it possible to date the *Violette* with exceptional precision: it was surely written between 1225, when Marie was allowed to return to Ponthieu, and 1231, when her husband was also permitted to return.[2]

This dating, further corroborated by the author's inclusion of historically identifiable characters, allows us to situate the romance in relation to other literary works of the period, notably those of Jean Renart, whose *Roman de la Rose* is a particularly elegant version of the wager tale. Although various thirteenth-century versions of the story survive, Jean Renart's has received the most attention from modern critics, largely because of an innovation he claims to introduce: the skillful interweaving of songs within the narrative.[3] This is a notable feature of Gerbert's romance as well, though he does not claim it as a novelty.

Gerbert's work differs from Jean Renart's in other significant ways. The plot itself more closely resembles two other contemporary versions of the wager tale, the anonymous *Roman du Comte de Poitiers* and, in Latin, *Guillermus Nivernensis*. In both works the loss of land and the resultant exile and suffering of the protagonists are critical to the unfolding of the drama. These features were ideally suited to Gerbert's purposes, allowing him to create a flattering mirror for his patroness, who triumphed over similar difficulties. Gerbert thus owes a great deal to other versions of the wager tale that were circulating in France in the early thirteenth century, but he emulates his models with discernment, creating out of preexisting themes and techniques something uniquely his own. He accomplishes this by making several shrewd choices.

First, Gerbert modifies the traditional wager tale scenario in a significant way. Instead of telling a story about a brother and sister or a husband and wife, Gerbert spins his tale around the emotions of two young lovers, cleverly exploiting the inherent ambiguities of *fin' amors,* or "courtly love," a form of devotion first celebrated in the troubadour lyrics of southern France that soon became a favorite topic for northern writers as well. A central feature of fin' amors is the necessity for absolute secrecy. This type of love was typically engaged in outside the boundaries of marriage; it was therefore essential for the male lover to protect the privacy, indeed the very identity of his lady.[4]

Gerbert makes sure that the details of Gerard and Euriaut's love affair remain tantalizingly vague. Early in the narrative, Euriaut reveals that she and Gerard have loved each other for seven years; soon after we are informed, this time "directly" by the narrator himself, that Euriaut is only fifteen years old.[5] We are not told Gerard's age, but Lisiart, the villain, refers to him deprecatingly as too young to understand the wiles of women. The parents of these two young persons are noticeably absent, although we learn quite late in the story that a concerned uncle of Euriaut's will soon arrive to help defend her reputation. This is all we ever learn about her family. Gerard's family is portrayed, albeit sketchily, as both large (some one hundred male relatives accompany him to court at one point) and geographically dispersed.

The depiction of the lovers and of their vaguely present families contributes to a general pattern of concealing and revealing information, a narrative game that finds graphic expression in Euriaut's floral birthmark, described as a secret sign shared by the young sweethearts. Just how Gerard learned of it is never explicitly stated. The violet birthmark is clearly a sign of Euriaut's singular beauty, but it is also a symbol of her sexuality, a euphemism for the "flower" of her virginity. Has the flower already been plucked? Gerbert, like the courtly lovers whose songs he quotes so frequently, remains discreet.

Gerard, in contrast, proves remarkably indiscreet, bragging about Euriaut's beauty and making her a topic of public debate. This infraction of the courtly code triggers Gerard's undoing; his is a moral failure that must be redeemed by suffering. Gerard must learn the value of humility and self-restraint; only then will he be allowed to reestablish himself in the world. Through no fault of her own, Euriaut must also undergo trials that test her character. Her vulnerability is the direct result of Gerard's arrogance, and it is therefore his duty to rescue her and restore social equilibrium.

The hardships endured by the young lovers are played out against a constantly shifting background in which fictional characters, sometimes accompanied by historically identifiable ones, move about to various locations in northern France and Germany. While it is difficult to assess the effect on contemporary audiences of this interweaving of fact and fiction, the innovation was likely viewed as daring.[6] Songs accompany the twists and turns of the plots, at times echoing a character's emotions, at other times serving as commentary.[7] As Maureen Boulton has observed, Gerbert, unlike Jean Renart, occasionally "alters songs to suit his purposes," a technique that calls attention to the complexity of the story.[8]

From a strictly technical point of view, the songs effectively break the rhythm of the octosyllabic rhymed couplets, altering the flow of the narrative in a way that can be only vaguely reproduced in translation. The length of the fragment quoted, the genre evoked, and the length of the lines would, no doubt, all have had a special resonance for contemporary audiences, though it is impossible to gauge the importance of these effects today. It is, however, clear that the songs served a more general purpose: the celebration of performance that is constantly alluded to in the author's praise of minstrels and of entertainment. This theme of entertainment is sustained throughout the romance both by the songs themselves and by the intrusions of the narrator, who frequently "interrupts" the narrative to comment on events or on his own role as storyteller.[9]

Gerbert is thus very present as the author of this work, demonstrating an admirable knowledge of the song repertory and showcasing his skill as a writer able to adapt the songs to suit his narrative purposes. He also exhibits a thorough familiarity with contemporary romances, which he evokes in ways similar to his citation of songs. His knowledge of Chrétien de Troyes is, of course, amply attested by his continuation of that writer's last, unfinished work, of which we find echoes in the *Violette* as well, notably in the description of the young noblewoman Aigline and her ruined lands, which closely resembles Chrétien's description of Blanchefleur and Beaurepaire in the *Conte du Graal*. The jealous bantering between two other female characters, Aiglente and Florentine, recalls the acrimonious exchange between two litigious sisters in that same work. These scenes highlight the author's easy familiarity with the domestic habits of the aristocracy and the literary tastes of noblewomen.[10]

Other romances are alluded to more directly. Euriaut's nurse Gondrée is said to know more about conniving (*engin*) than Thessala or Brangien, the magic-working attendants in Chrétien's *Cligès* and Thomas's *Tristan*. Aiglente's nurse follows the example of these literary predecessors by concocting a magic love potion. When Gerbert describes the magnificent clothes worn by Euriaut at King Louis's court, he refers to Queen Florence of Hungary, another unjustly accused heroine of romance who prevailed over daunting odds and regained her position in the world. This same passage evokes other faithful literary heroines, including the beautiful Aude, beloved of Charlemagne's nephew Roland, who dies when she learns that her betrothed has been killed at Roncevaux. Such references, woven into the fabric of the narrative, seem especially designed to appeal to the sentiments of female listeners or readers.

The descriptions of battles show a similar understanding of the interests of the noble men who would have been entertained by Gerbert's work. These are among the most vivid descriptions of fighting from this period,

remarkably fresh and energetic. Gerard's armor and weapons, like Euriaut's clothes and jewels, often possess a literary genealogy that enhances
their worth: at one point, Gerard dons a hauberk that belonged to the
emperor Alexander and a helmet once worn by Charlemagne. The story of
his sword constitutes a significant digression, a tale within the tale, probably based on a lost literary model.

The battle scenes, rather than serving in a perfunctory way to vary
the pace of the narrative, allow Gerbert to showcase his talent for gritty
realism and often startling detail. After one melee, the author describes
the excruciating pain experienced by Gerard, whose tunic has been deeply
embedded in his skin due to the pressure of the attached mail. In other
passages, sparks fly when swords hit helmets, and stars dance before the
eyes of stunned knights. Two men who lose their weapons wrap their arms
around one another, each attempting to crush the life out of his opponent.

Gerbert treats other standard romance themes with equal élan: generosity, hospitality, and knightly honor all figure importantly in this
tale, and his descriptions of loss, whether of love or of property, convey
a remarkable immediacy. It is, perhaps, because of these unusual qualities that the *Violette*, unique among wager tales dating from this period,
was "translated" into prose in the fifteenth century, when it became fash-
ionable to "de-rhyme" earlier verse romances.[11] Gerart's work was clearly
deemed worthy of preservation in the fifteenth century, an assessment that
remains equally valid today.

Four manuscript versions of *Le Roman de la Violette* are extant: two
date from the thirteenth century (Bibliothèque nationale de France ms.
1374 [ca. 1250] and fr. 1553 [ca. 1285]), and two from the fifteenth (one in
St. Petersburg, the other in the Pierpont Morgan Library in New York).
The fifteenth-century prose version of the work has also survived in two
copies, one in the Bibliothèque royale in Brussels, the other in the Bibliothèque nationale de France in Paris. Douglas L. Buffum chose BNF fr. 1553
as his base text and the present translation follows his edition.[12]

A Note on the Translation

All thirteenth-century French vernacular texts present challenges
for the modern translator, and *Le Roman de la Violette* is arguably more
challenging than many, precisely because of the vividness and immediacy
of Gerbert's language. The freshness of the work stems, in part, from the
author's use of somewhat unusual comparisons; although these may seem
quaint in translation, I have often retained them. The narrator's asides or
comments to the reader, though sometimes serving as "fillers" to round

out the syllable count of a line of verse, are also generally retained, as are his frequent invocations of God. Canonical hours (prime, terce, sext) are translated descriptively, according to the corresponding time of day (crack of dawn, early morning, noon). The names of characters are given in their Old French spelling, with one exception: Gerart is here spelled Gerard. It is one of the few names that has a clear, if differently spelled, equivalent in English.

Financial loss is an important theme in this work, and money is referred to repeatedly, both literally and metaphorically. Specific terms like marcs, sous, deniers have either been retained in their original form or else referred to generically as "money" or "coins." The term "livres" has been translated as "pounds." Tense switching, a common characteristic of medieval romance, is chiefly effective in oral delivery; to today's readers, the effect seems stilted and is often confusing. I have therefore regularized tenses following modern usage, a practice followed in all three of the texts translated here.

The forty-four song fragments, of different genres and syllable counts, present special challenges. For the sake of rhythm, I have adopted a relatively consistent syllable count within a given poem; the song fragments are also translated somewhat more loosely than the rest of the text. In this translation, the songs have been set off typographically to signal the shift from narrative to song. It should be noted that in both of the thirteenth-century manuscripts, the songs (unlike the rhymed octosyllabic couplets that make up the body of the text) are written out in prose format; i.e., line breaks are random, and do not correspond to the actual ends of verse lines. I have opted for a line-by-line translation with the goal of creating a fluid narrative that reads like prose, but which will allow interested readers to compare the English version to the original.

Because of the importance of the songs, I include an appendix in which the first line of each song is listed in translation, followed by the complete text as it appears in Buffum's edition, along with the name of the author, when known. Any additional information about the songs that might have been placed in endnotes appears there (Appendix I). As mentioned in the Preface, a second appendix offers information about clothing and armor as they appear in the three wager tales translated here.

The Romance of the Violet

Prologue
A poor man's wit is rarely prized;
those without money
lack standing in this world.
Even so, I value knowledge above wealth.   4
Possessions are easily lost!
A wealthy man soon falls into poverty
and when he does, he finds that doors
once open to him are now shut tight.   8
Should he come to court,
he'll be out of luck;
he won't gain entry there.
Poor people, you see,   12
are viewed with contempt
and scorned by the rich.
But a clever man has one great advantage:
people are quick to say: "He's very wise!"   16
That's why I'm putting into verse
a charming tale I've heard,
and since I have the necessary knowledge
and skill, I won't stop until   20
I've told an entertaining story.
If some scandalmonger hears me
and feels resentful and envious;
if he then badmouths me just because   24
I'm enjoying myself: well,
shame on him! Here's what I say:
my knowledge is mine alone,
so why should he care what I do with it?   28
If my efforts do annoy some people,
I hope an attack of gout
will rob them of their sight!
I'll keep at it, for as long as I'm able   32
and tell you a delightful tale.

Mind you, this isn't about
the Round Table and King Arthur
and his court, but it is, nonetheless,   36
a beautiful, noble story,
and one you can both read and sing.
The melody goes so well with the words
that anyone who hears it will,   40
I'm sure, believe it's a true story.
My talent means more to me
than wealth. I care nothing for money.
I'll now begin the tale   44
of The Romance of the Violet,
and before I'm done,
you'll have heard many fine songs.
I'm writing this for the most elegant lady   48
in the entire world,
one who is beyond reproach.
She is learned, honest and free of pride,
high-born and gracious.   52
All good qualities shine forth in her,
and above all, honor, which leads to magnanimity.
She has devoted herself to good works,
following the promptings of her heart.   56
I'm telling this tale
for the Countess of Ponthieu,
a most wise and admirable lady,
and that is why my own heart strives   60
to accomplish the task.
My lady is so very worthy that,
if it pleases God and her nobility,
she will surely reward my service well.[1]   64

Long ago in France there lived a king
who was most handsome, virtuous, and brave.
He was young, intelligent, courageous in battle,
and always eager to help others.   68
He held his knights in high esteem
and chose wise men as his counselors,
for he believed in good advice,
valued it, and never failed to follow it.   72
Well-schooled, sagacious,
and upright in his ways,
he honored noble ladies and maidens,
and granted them every courtesy.   76
This worthy king, so greatly admired,
was named Louis.

One April, on Easter Sunday,
he convened a magnificent court.   80
He invited dukes and counts,
I can't tell you how many,
the number was too great.
More than twenty countesses came,   84
along with chatelaines and duchesses,
all of them displaying great wealth.
They gathered at Pont-de-l'Arche,
and not since Noah built the ark   88
had so many assembled at court.
The handsome, noble king
graciously saw to the needs of his guests,
and after they had dined,   92
he invited them to sing and dance.
(You should have seen how the ladies
rushed to their rooms to get ready!)
To begin the entertainment,   96
each lady chose a knight.
The first to sing was my lady Nicole,
sister of the Bishop of Lincoln
and Countess of Besançon.   100
Without pretense or pride,
she began to sing:
    Go gently, for I am pained by love!
Afterwards, another lady sang,   104
her voice sweet and her song pleasing.
This was the Duchess of Burgundy.
Taking her companion by the hand,
she said to him,   108
"Sing, my friend!"
    Go sweetly and serenely,
    for love of me…
When she had finished,   112
a very clever maiden took her turn.
This was the Count of Blois's sister,
a charming, fun-loving girl
with hazel eyes and blond hair.   116
With a light heart,
she began to sing:
    Never will I marry, though
    my love will never vary!   120
Next was the Count of Saint-Pol's sister,
a most gracious and lovely lady,
with a sweet face and slender neck.
She began to sing in a steady,   124

clear voice, dancing all the while:
> If I love with a true heart,
> my joy is unbounded.
> Let gossipers be confounded!   128

The lady of Coucy,
may God have mercy on her,
was most graceful and comely.
She performed this new song,   132
for she was madly in love:
> All alone, I go to my lover's side,
> and I am utterly terrified.

The chatelaine of Niort,   136
a delightful, dark-haired lady
called Eleanor, then sang this ditty.
(*This* lady wasn't
the least bit afraid!)   140
> A good husband learn to be.
> Listen well, or you'll lose me!

A lady from Normandy, emboldened by love,
began to sing a different song.   144
She was so desperately in love
she didn't know what to do.
Everyone said it was the king she loved,
and that's why she was so elegantly dressed,   148
for she was his sweetheart.
She sang now,
and delivered her song quite admirably:
> Whatever my husband may think,   152
> my lover will have from me a wink.

When they had all amused themselves by singing,
everyone in the great hall fell silent.
Each man took a lady by the hand   156
and the couples lined up to dance.
The king rose and strolled about, singing.
He called out to a young man
who carried a falcon on his wrist;   160
the bird was in its third molt.[2]
When the lady from Normandy
caught sight of this young man,
the blood rushed through her veins.   164
How handsome he was—
his features, body, arms, and hands!
But these attributes were, to my mind,
trivial when compared to his complexion,   168
which was ruddier than a rose in May.[3]
One thing concerns me, however:

you might grow tired of hearing about him,
for even if I took all day, 172
I couldn't do justice to his good looks
and his courage.
So, let's just say that
he was the most accomplished singer 176
of his day, that he possessed much land
and that he had a beautiful sweetheart,
though she wasn't at court.
Gerard was the name of this knight, 180
and his reputation was great indeed.
Because he sang so beautifully,
he was urged by the chatelaine of Dijon
to take a turn. 184
"Gladly, my lady," he replied.
"To refuse a request from you
would be unworthy!
I therefore have no wish to remain silent." 188
In a clear, pure voice,
he began to sing:
    Since a lovely lady (Love her very self) asks me,
    I'm delighted to sing and do so gladly! 192
    I care not a whit what envious folk say—
    such people are unworthy and always behave badly!
    I care nothing for them, by night or by day.
    Whoever loves their kind 196
    is out of his mind,
    for jealous folk are wicked!
So ended his song.
But love, which never ends, 200
urged him to continue
with this little roundelay,
even though it might arouse envy.
    I have a love tailor-made for me, 204
    thus, of greater worth my life shall be!
"It certainly *should* be of greater worth,
for I can confidently boast
that my beloved is the most beautiful 208
woman who ever lived,
and the wisest, most elegant lady
from Metz to Pontoise!
And I would dare to claim 212
that a more loving woman can't be found.
My ship doesn't sail without a mast!
A man in love has no mast
when he entrusts his heart 216

to one of whose love he is uncertain.
Such a man is like a sailor
at sea who has no clue
how to make port   220
when he has no mast
to move his ship along
and no rudder to guide it.
That's how lovers come to grief   224
when their love is unrequited:
they've sown their seed on rocky soil,
where it can't take hold.
But rest assured,   228
I'm not one of them!
I dare to claim that the lady
of whom I've boasted
loves me above all else,   232
for she is both wise and true.
And since I'm thinking of her now,
I'll sing that song again.
Indeed, I will!"   236
    Have I not the right to stand tall,
      when my lady is the fairest of them all?
When the knight had finished singing,
and the assembled lords had listened to him,   240
there were some among them
who resented his happiness
and his good fortune.
He was having such a good time   244
that several of them became quite annoyed.
Indeed, they were so exasperated,
they felt ready to burst.
The most indignant of them all was Lisiart.   248
Treacherous and conniving,
he was more wicked than Ganelon.[4]
Long, lean, and hard featured,
he was also violent and unpredictable.   252
He was a count, and the lord of Forez.
To the others, he said: "I'm listening
to this knight who's having such a fine time.
What a spectacle he's made of himself today,   256
boasting about his lady!
She can't possibly love him as much as he claims.
That's absurd! Unless the king objects,
I'll willingly stake all my land against his,   260
if he agrees to the following terms.
If he allows me to approach the lady,

within eight days, provided he grants me
that much time and she's not forewarned,　　264
I'll have my way with her. That's *my* boast!"
The young knight quickly stepped forward.
He was so confident,
and had such great faith in his lady,　　268
that he wanted to stake
all his land against Lisiart's.
"You shouldn't start this," said the king.
"Let the matter drop.　　272
It could be costly for you both."
But Lisiart persisted, swearing
that he'd never back down from the wager.
The king reiterated his warning,　　276
stressing that things would turn out badly
for him if he didn't succeed.
"Lisiart, my friend," said the king,
"it's madness to boast　　280
of dishonoring another!
You'll pay for it in the end, and rightly so.
We often find that those
who want to dishonor others　　284
have dishonored themselves, instead.
Heed my advice and do not pursue
this matter any further."
"But Sire," said Gerard,　　288
"if my lord Lisiart
wants to make the wager,
I'm quite willing to accept!
He'll have conquered　　292
all of Germany singlehanded,
I think, before he wins this bet with me!
Let's let him continue to rant.
Each of us must now　　296
pledge his good faith."[5]
And so, the wager was made.
Each man asked the king to witness
his pledge, and he agreed to do so.　　300
Lisiart was then granted leave,
and he went straight to his lodgings
to prepare for the trip.
Now listen to what this wicked man did!　　304
He asked for pilgrim's clothes,
as though he were travelling to Saint Giles.
(What wicked guile![6])
He took with him ten knights,　　308

and before the week was out
the traitor had arrived in Nevers.
My lady Euriaut had gone up
into a high tower   312
where she sat at a window,
her elbows resting on the sill.
She was listening to the lovely,
sweet song of the birds.   316
When she thought of Gerard,
she sighed, moaned, and shivered.
After she had heaved many a sigh,
love prompted her to sing what are,   320
I believe, verses of a fine song
from Poitou
which had struck her fancy:
    There is no harm or sin,   324
    no baseness, so say I,
    save in one who slyly
    spies on those in love.
    Horrible man, what do you gain   328
    from inflicting so much pain?
    Everyone is out for himself.
    You've injured me but gained no wealth.
When she had finished singing,   332
she rested her cheek on her hand.
Lisiart heard her singing and,
looking up, saw her
sitting at the window.   336
He summoned a squire and told him:
"Go to the house and tell the steward,
lord Herbert, that he's to give us
lodging for the night."   340
The young man hurried off,
taking neither shield nor targe.
When he arrived at the front door,
he was fortunate enough to find the steward,   344
who was certainly no rustic.
The squire greeted him courteously
and, on behalf of his lord,
requested hospitality.   348
When the steward heard this,
I truly believe he wouldn't have been happier
had he been offered two hundred pounds!
"Young man," he replied, "your lord,   352
who sends this message,
must think me a difficult fellow!

Naturally, I'll order everything just as he asks.
My lord and my young lady,   356
who is so courteous and beautiful,
so wise and lovely, are never happier
than when unexpected guests arrive."
While they stood there talking,   360
the count approached,
accompanied by several of his knights.
They all went into the great hall,
where they were given a joyful welcome.   364
The lovely Euriaut, having heard
the news of their arrival, hurried down
from the tower and entered the room,
accompanied by her old nurse,   368
a most false and treacherous woman.
Euriaut welcomed the count, who replied,
"And may good fortune be yours."
Then they sat down. Lisiart, however,   372
was scheming all the while.
He drew a little closer to Euriaut,
believing he could seduce her.
"Have mercy, my lady!" he exclaimed.   376
"I've heard so much about you.
Your elegance, your beauty
and your nobility
are praised far and wide!   380
My heart urged me on,
compelling me to come here.
I have no choice
but to confess everything to you,   384
and recount the pain
that love makes me endure.
But I can't do justice to the agonies
I suffer for love of you!   388
They crush the heart in my chest
and chase the color from my cheeks.
I've been sick with love
ever since I heard about you!   392
I can't go anywhere
without seeing your image
before my eyes.
Your reputation, and even more,   396
your beauty, have wounded me,
for Love has taken aim
and pierced my heart with his arrow.
I beg you to be merciful   400

and believe what I say!"
"Ah, my lord, have pity, I implore you!
If I've allowed you to continue
and not yet rebuked you,   404
it was only out of courtesy!
You'll have seized the moon
up in the sky, before you get
what you've asked of me!   408
If you need anything else,
you have only to name it.
I'm not so proud
that I would refuse you lodging   412
and a proper welcome tonight
because of what you've just said.
But don't ask me again.
It would offend me,   416
and I wouldn't appreciate it at all."
"Ah, lovely lady, why not?
If you wish, I'll be quiet
and you'll hear me say no more.   420
But I'll die of sorrow
if I don't speak to you again!
Even if someone broke every bone
in my body, I couldn't stop!   424
Such passion cannot be so easily quelled!
I must speak plainly.
Do not think me impertinent
if I say what I must.   428
And may the one who told me
of your beauty and renown,
your worth and reputation,
be consumed by fire and flames!"   432
"My lord, it's a great mistake
for you to go on like this
when you know perfectly well
that it offends me.   436
If you have any sense at all,
you'll understand that I'm refusing you
when you hear the words of the song
I'm about to sing. Listen to me now: 440
    Love makes me joyful and makes me sing!
    Love transforms me, makes me more beautiful.
    Love makes me desire to love more truly,
    because of this madman who implores me!   444
    For I have a love, and I could not bear
    to be parted from his noble body.

I'll love him alone, for he loves me well.
And you? Leave me be, don't ask me again!   448
Accept that yours are wasted words.
When Lisiart had listened to the song
and pondered the words,
he wondered how he might trick the lady.   452
He sat down next to her on a chest
adorned with copper bands,
leaned close and softly said,
"Certainly, my lady, I'd stop if I could,   456
and if it were in my power to master my heart,
which ceaselessly urges me to love you.
But I think I'd rather die than remain alive
if you won't take pity on me.   460
And surely you know that one who
commits murder with forethought
assumes a heavy burden.
I've fallen low indeed if you send me away."   464
"Such talk is useless, my lord!
Do you really think
that because I'm listening to you
and not pushing you away,   468
you've persuaded me?
My heart isn't so easily won that,
merely because of your lament,
which is quite false and insincere,   472
I would do what you ask.
I'm not prepared to do any such thing.
I'd rather be driven from my own home!
You've lost your mind, asking such things of me.   476
Go look for a lady friend elsewhere
and try your flattery there.
I'll be very angry if you keep insisting.
Enough of your foolishness!   480
Any more of this talk would be tiresome.
Let's go have supper.
Evening grows nigh
and it's getting dark."   484
She rose and went to see her servants,
whom she ordered to prepare the tables.
Those whose job it was,
set them up and spread the cloths.[7]   488
The cooks prepared the food,
of which there was an abundance:
great platters of roast fowl
and venison and fresh fish.   492

The count was copiously served,
though he scarcely noticed.
He was thinking about the task ahead,
and how he would lose his land   496
if he didn't succeed.
He was so absorbed in his thoughts
that he almost seemed to be in a trance.
The old woman who was Euriaut's nurse   500
was sitting by the fire.
She had a dark and ugly face
and was truly an evil witch.
Gondrée was her name,   504
and she was the daughter
of the thief Gontacle,
who had begotten her
on a lapsed Beguine   508
who loved to lie on her back.
(I'm telling you this to demonstrate
that bad fruit comes from bad trees.[8])
This disloyal harridan   512
therefore came from malign stock.
She had murdered the two children
she had borne to Master Baudris,
a monk of the Charité   516
who was defrocked because of her.[9]
In my opinion, she knew more
about conniving than Thessala
and Brangien together ever did.[10]   520
She looked at the count's face
and saw how dejected
and downcast he was.
She was sure that her lady was the cause   524
and decided she'd sooner be a leper
than see the count deprived of his pleasure,
for "there's nothing I like better
than wreaking havoc.   528
Now I'll be able to do real harm!"
Nonetheless, she bided her time.
The cloths were removed from the tables
and basins of water were brought   532
for washing hands. Wine was served,
then everyone rose from the tables
and went upstairs to the galleries,
where they lounged by the windows.   536
The old woman approached the count,
who told her all about the love he bore her lady.

"If you're willing to help me," he said,
"I swear on my soul that there's nothing   540
you could wish for that I won't give you,
be it clothes, horses, or money.
Euriaut is the reason I came here,
and it will be a disaster for me   544
if I don't have my way with her,
for I've wagered all my land
that she'll be mine.
I'm asking you now, as a friend,   548
to do whatever it takes
for me to prevail."
"My lord," replied the disgusting old woman,
"since you've wagered your land,   552
would it be enough for you to win
if you could describe some mark on her body?"[11]
"That's all I'd need," said the count.
"If I could present such evidence,   556
it would certainly suffice."
"Excellent," replied the old woman.
"I know just what to do.
I guarantee that before noon tomorrow   560
you'll have what you need.
You'll be believed at court
and your status there will rise.
Go to bed now.   564
You have nothing to fear."
Two servants approached,
each one holding a lighted taper.
They led the count to his room,   568
and to an elegantly appointed bed.
His knights, who lay nearby,
whispered to one another
that they wished the maiden knew   572
the real reason why their lord had come:
it was for fear of losing his lands.
The old woman went to her lady,
whom she was planning to disgrace.   576
Hiding her ulterior motive,
she led her to her room
and prepared the bed.
When it was ready, she called Euriaut   580
and helped her into the bed.
The young lady wore only a chemise
over her bare skin, for never in her life
had this lovely, slender, golden-haired girl   584

wished to be seen naked.
The old woman approached the bed
and said to her, "May God help me, my lady,
but I've noticed something   588
that astonishes me.
I've never seen you completely unclothed,
even though I've looked after you
for seven years![12]   592
I've often seen you undressed,
but never without your chemise."
"Nurse," she replied, "I'll tell you why.
Seven and a half years ago, my dear Gerard   596
made me promise to do this
because I have a birthmark,
and no other man must see it.
No one knows about this except him,   600
and he made me swear to keep it a secret.
Otherwise, he said, if another man
knows about it, he'll believe
that man has lain with me   604
and he'll leave me.
He made me promise to do as he said."
The old woman replied: "God forbid
that fingers be pointed at you   608
in the public square! Believe me,
it's between the two of you.
Your sweetheart is the only man
who will ever know. It's time for bed now.   612
Let's get some sleep—and don't worry!"
The old woman left the room,
although she was extremely vexed
not to have learned what kind of mark   616
her lady had. The crone went to bed,
determined to do something wicked.
The next morning, she rose early,
had bathwater heated,   620
then let it cool. Afterwards,
she woke her mistress
and, after much persuading,
led her to the room with the waiting bath.   624
(Before the week is out,
Euriaut will have paid dearly for that bath.
She should have feared it!)
When she was about to enter the bath,   628
the maiden, not wanting to show herself naked,
ordered the old woman to leave the room.

She wanted no one to remain with her
while she bathed.   632
The old woman turned away
and left the room,
but she came back
to spy on her mistress.   636
Having seen that the door was intact,
she had pierced it with a drill,
creating a peephole through which
she could spy on her mistress.   640
(Alas, one cannot protect oneself
from betrayal. You know this very well!)
The old woman, who was cunning
and malevolent, as the book relates,   644
soon put her eye to the hole.[13]
She watched her lady in the bath
and soon perceived the mark:
a budding violet on her right breast,   648
purplish-blue against her white skin.
The old woman was astonished
by the form of the mark,
and hurried off to rouse the count   652
from his slumbers.
"Make haste, my lord! Get up!
You'll be able to win the wager
because I've done what you asked.   656
If you want to present evidence
of a mark on my lady,
you needn't consult anyone but me.
You won't even have to touch her.   660
Hurry! Get out of bed!"
With that the count rose.
The old woman grabbed hold of him
and led him to the peephole she had made.   664
The count put his eye to the hole
and saw the purplish-blue violet
on Euriaut's small right breast.[14]
"You've saved me!" he exclaimed.   668
"Henceforth, I'm yours to command,
I swear it by Saint Thomas!
You've delivered me from ruin,
there's no doubt about it.   672
Thanks to this mark, I'll win the wager
and make you mistress of all I have!"
They then returned to his room.
The count and his companions   676

got ready to ride back to court,
and the old woman hurried to Euriaut's room,
where she raised the iron ring and knocked.
The lovely girl was soon out of the bath   680
and sitting on her bed, drying off.
She dressed and adorned herself
and then opened the door to her room.
She was quite warm   684
and therefore wore no wimple.
In this simple and becoming attire,
she hurried to the great hall,
where she politely greeted the count   688
and all his knights. The count,
who was a smooth talker
and a double-crosser, said to her:
"May God protect you from all misfortune!"   692
He then took his leave,
mounted his horse and rode away.
Euriaut was left behind with her mortal enemy,
who had prepared for her a terrible misfortune.   696
The count rode for a long time,
and at last rejoined the king at Melun.
There was nary a nobleman at court
who didn't yearn to find out   700
which man would win the wager.
Gerard was sent for immediately,
and he didn't seek to be excused.
He soon arrived at court, along with   704
a hundred of his male relatives,
all young and good-looking.
His was a very great family.
The young men were smartly dressed   708
and each one wore on his head
a garland of roses and other flowers.
Great crowds lined the streets,
for everyone was eager to watch their arrival.   712
Heavens, how handsome they looked
as they rode along, two by two!
Gerard, as I recall, was singing this song,
so that all might hear it.   716
His pitch was sweet and high,
and his companions sang back to him:
"There goes one who loves well!"
"There he goes!"   720
Thus, they arrived at court,
where young and old alike

watched them admiringly.
King Louis was seated all alone   724
on a bright red cushion;
his advisors stood nearby.
When he saw Gerard arriving,
looking so fine, he was delighted.   728
It would please him greatly if Gerard prevailed!
The knights took their seats
around the perimeter of the room.
Count Lisiart then rose   732
and approached the king.
He spoke for himself, without a legal advocate.
"Hear me, my lords! You are aware,
for it is now widely known,   736
that a bet was placed the other day
between young Gerard and me.
A man is childish and naïve
to have such faith in a woman   740
that he would wager his land for her.
Now he'll learn the truth
about this sweetheart of his!
Have the lady summoned without delay   744
and I'll prove to him that I've won the bet."
"He has said enough," declared the King.
Gerard then came forward and responded:
"Sire, I want one of my nephews   748
to fetch her right away."
The nephew was summoned.
He was soon in the saddle and on his way,
just as Gerard had ordered.   752
When he arrived at Nevers,
his horse was in a lather,
overheated after galloping so hard.
This didn't concern the messenger,   756
who quickly dismounted,
ordered someone to hold the reins,
and asked where he might find his lady.
Euriaut, always a gracious hostess,   760
jumped up when she heard the news.
Ever courteous and attentive,
she felt her heart race with joy
as she opened the door   764
and entered the great hall
to greet the messenger.
She then eagerly asked for news
of the handsome Gerard,   768

"may he have joy and good fortune!"
"My lady, he sends you greetings
and asks you, by all you hold dear,
to come to him without delay."   772
"Of course! We'll leave immediately.
I'm eager to be on my way."
She made her servants hurry to get ready,
for she wanted to spend the night   776
at Bonny-sur-Loire,
no matter how difficult it might be
to travel that far.
Her servants received her orders   780
and hastened to ensure
that her palfrey had been saddled
and the reins attached.
Euriaut mounted her piebald horse,   784
and the messenger, Joifroi, rode next to her,
reluctantly urging her on.
Euriaut brought with her two young ladies
and three seasoned knights.   788
She was a practical young woman,
and left Nevers without a backward glance.
(This isn't the place for me to describe
her clothing and accoutrements.   792
You'll hear about them in a minute.)
They made good progress that day,
not stopping to rest until they arrived
that evening in Bonny, where they   796
spent the night. Early the next morning,
they were on their way again, hurrying
towards Melun. They didn't stop
until they arrived in that city,   800
and there they took lodging
for the night, close to the port.
Not even at the castle itself
would the maiden have been more comfortable.   804
(May God now protect her from harm!)
After supper they retired for the night.
I have no wish to describe the elegant
and sumptuous decor; suffice it to say   808
that they slept until daybreak,
then hurriedly rose from their beds.
The two maidens who accompanied
Euriaut unpacked a bliaut.   812
They woke their lady and dressed her
in this garment of violet hue,

sumptuously adorned and embroidered
with little gold crosses. At her neck, 816
they fastened a bejeweled brooch;
the story has it that the gems in it
were worth the entire town of Piacenza.
It had once belonged to Queen Florence, 820
who was empress of Rome;
whoever wears it at her neck
(and this is the salient point)
will never be dishonored by a man. 824
Euriaut had kept it carefully,
for a long time; her Aunt Marguerite,
who was Queen of Hungary,
had sent it to her.[15] 828
Over the bliaut, she tied on a silk belt.
No matter where I chance to be,
I would dare to claim that,
even with all his fortune, 832
the Count of Toulouse
couldn't have afforded this belt,
encrusted as it was with garnets,
rubies, and emeralds. 836
Roland sent this very belt to the beautiful Aude
when he left for Roncevaux,
where he suffered the agonies of death.[16]
On her head, Euriaut wore a circlet 840
adorned with many precious gems,
and around her neck was draped
an ermine-lined cloak,
darker green than a cabbage leaf. 844
The cloth had been finely embroidered
with little gold flowers,
and inside each one
a tiny bell had been sewn, 848
so that it was invisible.
When breezes blew, the little silver bells
made the sweetest sound imaginable.
I swear to you that no harp, 852
fiddle, or zither made a sound
as sweet as these tiny silver bells.[17]
After she had been so elegantly dressed,
everyone admired her clothes, 856
but I'm not exaggerating when I say
that her beauty was such
that they quickly forgot about her attire.
She was so very lovely to look at 860

that my heart prompts me to describe
her figure and her face.
This is understandable,
for her body was noble and straight,   864
her silhouette fine and slim,
her hips low beneath her belt,
and her height most pleasing.
Her wavy blond hair shone like gold,   868
and her forehead was white as polished glass.
Everyone agreed that her brown eyebrows
made her look even prettier.
Her eyes were bright and clear,   872
her nose well-formed
and slightly arched.
Neither Gaïté, the wife of Athis,
Polixena, nor the Lady Helen,   876
Queen Dido nor Ismene,
Antigone nor Iseut the Blonde,
Galienne nor Esclarmonde
had one-tenth her beauty.[18]   880
A summer rose, blossoming
in the morning light, couldn't compare
to the hue of her lips and face.
(I won't make you listen   884
to something that isn't true!)
Her complexion was whiter than silver or ivory,
and her cheeks were rosy.
But one thing truly amazes me: 888
her neck and her bosom
were whiter than lilies
or hawthorn flowers.
Her hands were white, her arms shapely.   892
The sweetheart of Carados Briebras
was not as comely as she.
She wasn't more than fifteen years old,
but even if I talked about her all day,   896
I wouldn't do justice
to her worth, goodness,
honor, and simplicity.
Her small, newly formed breasts   900
were firm and high.[19]
Everyone in town rushed to see
and admire her, and I can tell you truly
that whoever saw her that day,   904
unless he took great care, was smitten.
And one who loves

without being loved in return,
burns with the hottest fire!   908
A beautifully equipped palfrey was brought,
and Euriaut mounted.
I'm sure that the saddle and harness
cost more than a hundred marks.   912
You should have seen
how the inns emptied out!
Everyone was eager to follow her.
Many of the men who turned   916
to look at her that day,
fell right into the mud.
Euriaut rode along,
in cheerful company,   920
not stopping until she arrived at court.
Gerard, ever attentive and courteous,
ran to greet her, exclaiming,
"Welcome, my lady!"   924
He helped her down from her palfrey,
and she began to straighten her clothes.
Gerard took her by the right hand
and led her to the king;   928
all the members of his family
accompanied them.
When they entered the great hall,
everyone rushed to see Euriaut,   932
and Gerard began to sing
in a clear, high, and sweet voice:
    One who would love a lady like this
    would certainly have no cause for regret!   936
The king responded: "He surely wouldn't!
I swear to you that I've never seen
a more beautiful woman."
The king immediately summoned the count   940
who held the land of Forez,
and then, before one and all,
he recounted the details of the wager.
After he had his say   944
before the assembled court,
and after Euriaut had heard every word,
she said to Gerard: "My love,
the count who has challenged you   948
has, by law, forfeited his land."
The expression on Lisiart's face
didn't change.
He approached the king and said: 952

"Sire, I flatter myself
that I *did* have my way with her,
and you see me eager to prove it
here and now, with evidence I'll produce."   956
"Proceed," replied the king.
Euriaut, who stood next to the king,
looked straight at Lisiart.
"Sire," said the wicked man,   960
"I swear that there is a beautiful violet
on her right breast, and she told me
when I lay with her,
so I'm absolutely sure of what I say,   964
that her lover, the handsome Gerard,
had made her swear that if anyone
but he ever knew about this,
it would mean that another man   968
had enjoyed her favors.
I've told you the exact truth."
When Euriaut heard him, she crossed herself.
Stunned, she exclaimed, "Ah, holy Mary,   972
I've been wickedly betrayed!
How did he learn about the mark
when, as God is my witness,
no man ever knew of it,   976
except for my beloved."
Gerard heard what she said,
and was overcome with sorrow and rage.
"My God, there's no use denying it!   980
The proof is only too evident.
Your excuses aren't worth two straws!
You've robbed me of my lands,
But you'll soon get what's coming to you.   984
Get on your horse—*now!*"
She mounted her palfrey without delay,
only wishing that a sharp knife
could be plunged into her heart instead.   988
Everyone grieved for her,
and many were openly weeping.
Lisiart alone remained joyful,
for his perfidy had won for him   992
Nevers and all its lands.
The king appropriated Gerard's holdings,
for he was now free to take possession.
Later, the judgment would be made public   996
and recognized before the court,
so that everyone would know about it.

The members of Gerard's family
crowded around him, exclaiming, 1000
"What do you want to do?
Have the wretched woman killed!"
"Enough, my lords," said Gerard.
"If you care for me, say no more. 1004
I'll render justice as I see fit."
Tarrying no longer, he mounted his horse
and ordered Euriaut to do likewise.
She acquiesced without delay, 1008
her head bowed low.
Gerard's relatives also mounted
and came before him, swearing
that they would go with him 1012
and serve him anywhere.
"My lords," he replied,
"no one will come with us,
nor will anyone see what's to take place 1016
between the two of us."
The knights were unable
to hold back their tears while,
in misery, Gerard and Euriaut turned to go. 1020
I'm told that they rode for some time
before entering a forest.
The handsome Gerard dismounted
alongside a high hedge, then lifted 1024
the unjustly accused Euriaut from her horse.
He unsheathed his sword and,
taking hold of Euriaut,
pulled her close. 1028
Then he said, "Here you will die!
Your reckless behavior has ruined me."
While he was berating her,
she looked up and saw a dragon 1032
mere yards away from them!
I'm telling you the truth
when I say that fire and flames
were shooting from its maw 1036
as it advanced towards them!
The creature's eyes were huge and red
and it had a wide, curving tale,
long and sharp and forked. 1040
"Please, my lord!" said Euriaut.
"In the name of God, flee!
I see a demon approaching! It's true, I swear it!
If you don't protect yourself, you'll die!" 1044

Gerard then looked over his shoulder
and saw the giant dragon advancing.
No matter the outcome,
he won't fail to confront the beast   1048
and attack it with his sword!
He edged away from Euriaut,
and the creature rushed forward,
intending, I'm sure, to lunge at his face.   1052
Gerard folded his cloak and raised it.
The dragon struck, burning the cloth
to a cinder. Gerard then took aim
with his sword and thrust   1056
the steel blade into the dragon's maw,
forcing it all the way in,
right down to the guard,
slicing the beast's heart in two.   1060
The creature fell, dead, at Gerard's feet.
He then pulled out his sword
and wiped the blade on the green grass.
At precisely that moment,   1064
he remembered the laws of the just
and the wise. "Dear God," he said,
"what shall I do? How can I injure
the one who has saved my life?   1068
I don't know what to do. I'm confused!
But no matter how I feel, it's quite clear
that Euriaut should be spared.
Only a moment ago,   1072
I raised my sword
to cut off her head, and yet,
when she saw this beast approaching,
she warned me! I can't believe   1076
there is another woman in all the world,
not even as far as the most distant horizon,
who, seeing that her own death was nigh,
would tell the very one   1080
who intended to kill her
to save his own life.
Surely, she has earned a reprieve!
I do pity her. And so, I'll abandon her here   1084
and leave her all alone in this wood.
It would be wrong for me
to see her again,
though I'll always love her.   1088
That will remain my secret.
I'll leave her now

and do her no further harm.
May God, who alone is able, help her.   1092
Henceforth, she'll know
great suffering and fear!"
Then he said: "Beautiful Euriaut,
may God the Father, who reigns on high,   1096
help you. I'm leaving you now."
With that he turned and galloped off,
abandoning Euriaut. Grief-stricken
and in tears, she began to pull her hair   1100
and wring her hands.[20]
"Alas," she wailed, "how wrong
my beloved is to leave me!
Had he merely broken my heart,   1104
I'd feel so fortunate! My fate,
I know, was ordained long ago."
She scratched her face and tore her bliaut,
and her skin grew yellower than tallow.   1108
How she yearned for death!
Then she fainted and fell
at the foot of a white poplar tree.
She struggled mightily within herself,   1112
for death seemed preferable to life.
Her flesh, already pale,
now turned white.
As she was lying there like this,   1116
the Duke of Metz came riding along,
accompanied by twenty knights.
They were returning from Compostela.
When he caught sight of the clothes   1120
that Euriaut was wearing,
the duke halted immediately.
He looked at the lady,
at the dragon that was so enormous,   1124
and at the palfrey standing close by.
He reflected on the situation,
and feared that the dragon
had killed the girl who was lying there,   1128
although he couldn't imagine
how the beast itself had been killed.
He called out to his knights:
"My lords, this maiden   1132
has been killed by the dragon!
I think she had arranged to meet her lover
and was waiting for him here."
As the duke was speaking,   1136

Euriaut revived from her faint.
She was overcome with amazement
when she saw all these people,
and began to wipe her face and eyes,   1140
which were wet with tears.
She was astonished to see such a crowd!
When the duke saw
that she was alive and well,   1144
he wanted nothing more
than to learn what had happened.
He dismounted and greeted her,
but she didn't reply. She just sighed,   1148
then fainted again. When she came to,
she lamented being alive;
she'd much rather have been dead.
The duke comforted her most kindly,   1152
then said: "My dear, if it isn't too painful,
tell me what torments you so greatly
that you've become quite pale."
After a moment, she replied,   1156
unceasing in her grief:
"For the love of God,
my lord, leave me be!
Misfortune has made you stop here.   1160
I'm a lost woman, exiled and wretched.
You'll learn no more from me.
But if someone killed me,
it would truly be a worthy deed."   1164
The duke listened and was moved.
He looked closely at her face,
and it seemed to him
that he had never seen   1168
such a beautiful woman.
He decided that he would marry her.
He didn't think his people would criticize
or think less of him for this,   1172
for she seemed worthy of a king.
It was obvious from the garments she wore
that she was of high birth. With great pleasure,
the duke looked upon her fine body   1176
and soon was filled with desire.
He decided to tell her how he felt.
Quite abruptly, he ordered her to
"get on your horse, and no arguing!   1180
You'll come with us to my lands.
I'm glad I found you,

and want to make you my wife.
This shouldn't cause you sorrow,   1184
for it will bring you great honor.
You'll become a duchess that day,
thanks to me!" Euriaut listened,
and almost died of grief   1188
and anger and vexation.
She began to address the duke:
"Oh no, my lord, that's impossible!
I swear to you by my right hand   1192
that if you knew the truth about me,
you'd rather have me killed—
either buried alive or burned at the stake!
A more faithless creature   1196
than I have long been, has never lived!
Three years ago this summer,
I became a dissolute woman.
They call me "Easy Virtue"!   1200
I'm the daughter of a cart driver,[21]
but follow another line of work.
I went off with a grave robber
who clothed me in furs and silks   1204
he had stolen. He loved me, I think,
more than anything in the world,
so much so that the outfit
I'm wearing now is one he stole   1208
the other evening, by chance, in Coucy.
We were pursued for a long time,
and he was eventually seized in an ambush.
But I, who am equally guilty,   1212
managed to escape.
You should have nothing to do
with a woman like me!
I want to go back to this way of life."   1216
The duke replied: "By Saint Sicaut,
I care nothing about your past!
Just behave yourself from now on."
"You keep talking nonsense!"   1220
she replied. "I'd be very unhappy
to renounce my activities.
You're sadly mistaken if you think
that mere words from you   1224
can turn me into a different person!"
The duke was quite upset
by what she had said,
though the more she refused him,   1228

the more excited and inflamed he became.
He took her by the hand and said to her,
"My lady, get on your horse.
What you've told me   1232
makes no difference at all."
With that, she bowed her head.
Whether she wanted to or not,
the Duke of Metz made her mount   1236
and without further delay, they started off,
as Euriaut sighed and wept.
After a time, some of his knights
approached the duke   1240
and spoke to him harshly,
forbidding him to marry this woman,
for she wasn't of his high station in life,
and was, moreover, a strumpet.   1244
Everyone criticized him, saying he was a fool,
for there were women as beautiful,
and of better character, throughout the land.
He must let this loose woman go;   1248
they would find him a lady
who was equally beautiful.
"Leave me alone!" said the duke.
He forbade them to speak,   1252
and all conversation ceased.
The men turned their attention to the road,
while the duke continued to watch Euriaut.
The more he looked at her,   1256
the more he loved and desired her.
He became so enamored of her
as he rode along all day,
that he could scarcely take his eyes from her.   1260
She wept quietly and ceaselessly,
and the duke gently chided her for it.
To comfort her, he began to sing
in a strong, clear voice,   1264
opening wide his arms.
    He who counsels me on love,
    advising me to leave her,
    doesn't know why I can't sleep,   1268
    nor why I painfully sigh.
    How dull and dim is the man
    who wishes to chastise me.
    He has never been in love,   1272
    and makes a fool of himself
    interfering in matters

about which he knows nothing.
He took pleasure in singing,   1276
imagining he had chosen a sweetheart
to his liking and a true love.
And so, the duke rode on,
taking Euriaut with him.   1280
They traveled for a whole week,
until they came to Metz.

Now I'll tell you about Gerard,
who was wandering all alone in the woods.   1284
Losing his lands didn't matter to him
nearly as much as losing Euriaut.
He rode through the forest,
longing for his noble lady and repining: 1288
"Ah, lovely girl, you've made me so sad!
I thought I'd be your husband,
but now I understand how a woman
has been the downfall of so many men.   1292
Solomon, who was exceptionally wise,
suffered great harm due to a woman;
he was captured because of his wife.
Samson, renowned and greatly feared   1296
because of his strength,
was also deceived by his wife.
She sold him to his enemies,
had his hair shorn while he was sleeping,   1300
and then they put out his eyes.
The handsome lover Absalom,
died because of a woman.[22]
What fools men are   1304
when they're too confident in love,
and love beyond all reason.
No man should ever test his beloved.
He should leave her in peace   1308
and not try to tempt her.
I blame myself for what happened.
It's all my fault!
But I must try to console myself.   1312
I'll feel better if I sing."
In a strong, clear voice, he began:
    Dear God! What folly
    to test and try one's wife   1316
    or one's beloved!
    In loving your lady nobly,
    you must repress all jealousy.

Never pry into matters   1320
   you'd rather not discover.
And so, Gerard rode along,
singing all the while,
imagining he'd find comfort in song.   1324
But whenever he thought of Euriaut,
tears began to flow and he quietly wept,
for he missed her, and the sight of her beauty.
Be it foolish or wise,   1328
he decided to go to Nevers
and find out what Lisiart,
who wrongly held his land,
was doing there.   1332
He turned in that direction
and hurried through fields and woods
until he came to the River Loire
and arrived at the Chateau of Le Marche.   1336
He found quiet lodging
at the home of lady Marche.
Her husband was a minstrel
who detested hypocrisy.   1340
The minstrel happily greeted
and welcomed Gerard,
whom he was pleased to see.
Gerard had been very good to this man   1344
in the past and given him many fine gifts.
That night they ate and drank together;
after supper they all went to bed
and slept until the new day dawned.   1348
Gerard didn't tarry; he rose quickly,
put on old clothes, and then hung
a fiddle around his neck.
He was an accomplished performer,   1352
when he turned his hand to it.
There was nothing left to do but set forth,
for Gerard was now well disguised.
He approached Nevers   1356
at a leisurely pace,
dressed in ragged clothing.
It was raining that morning;
indeed, the weather was terrible.   1360
Gerard, who was travelling on foot,
was soon completely drenched.
He walked along, passing through fields
and valleys until he arrived at Nevers.   1364
A group of twenty or so townsfolk

observed his arrival and loudly proclaimed,
"This minstrel will be out of luck here!
He could sing all day long   1368
and no one would come listen to him.
Everyone is too sad about Euriaut,
who is dead, and about Gerard,
our young lord. Neither music   1372
nor birdsong will ever again
be appreciated here.
We'll be poorly provided for
by that traitor Lisiart!"   1376
Gerard, who clearly heard
what the townsfolk were saying,
continued walking in the direction of the tower.
He waited at the door until a knight   1380
who was passing through the courtyard
called out to him. The man then led Gerard
up into the great hall and invited him
to play his fiddle. But Gerard,   1384
who was very wet and tired
from his long walk, said,
"My lord, I would prefer to wait.
I'd gladly warm myself by the fire,   1388
and then, after I've eaten, I'll sing."
"To hell with your refusal,
and with your entertainment!" said Lisiart.
When Gerard heard this, he didn't delay.   1392
He jumped up, tuned his instrument,
and muttered to himself, "Alas, my arrival
is ill-timed since I must perform right away.
I now know it's true: a minstrel leads a hard life!   1396
Whenever he's coldest and most uncomfortable,
that's just when he's urged
to sit in some drafty spot and sing.
So be it, though what I plan to do   1400
is something I've never tried:
singing and playing an instrument at the same time."
Then, as I understand it, he began to sing
and play as skillfully as any professional,   1404
selections from *The Song of William Shortnose*.[23]
He sang the words clearly and played sweetly:
    Great was the gathering at the court of Laon;
    the tables were laden with fowl and venison.   1408
    Others dined on meat or fish,
    but these never touched William's lips;
    he ate, instead, plain bread and water.

When the noble knights had eaten their fill,   1412
servants and cupbearers removed the tables.
Count William then addressed the king:
"What say you, son of Charlemagne?
Will you help me fight the Saracen race?   1416
By now, the army should be at Châlons."
The king replied: "We shall confer about it.
Tomorrow morning I'll let you know
whether or not I've decided to go."   1420
William heard these words and grew red as coals.
"What the devil!" he exclaimed, "We'll *confer* about it?
This is the tale of the bull and the sheep."[24]
He bent over and grabbed a heavy stick,   1424
then said to the king: "We return your fief!
I'll no longer hold the slightest thing from you.
I'll be neither your friend nor your vassal.
But you'll come with us, whether you like it or not!"   1428
Gerard sang four stanzas of the story[25]
to entertain and amuse them,
and the count had tables set up
and delectable food was brought for them all.   1432
Gerard, however, wouldn't touch
any of the food that was served.
He'd sooner have beaten his head
against the wall!   1436
To judge by the small number of servers,
the court was practically deserted.
The shameless old woman,
Gondrée, dined with the count,   1440
reminding him reproachfully
that it was thanks to her
that he had won these lands,
for she had tricked her lady   1444
and her lord, stripping Euriaut
of her honor, even though
she had never done anything wrong.
Lisiart, who knew perfectly well   1448
that she was telling the truth,
swore to her on his honor
that she could rest assured
that everything he had, both land   1452
and possessions, belonged to her.
"It's due to you that I won Nevers.
The wager would have turned out
very differently if not for you.   1456
I'm sure I would have lost,

since I never touched that girl.
I almost died when I didn't
have my way with her,   1460
but I've taken care of her now!
The land and the county are mine!"
Gerard heard everything,
for Lisiart wasn't paying attention;   1464
he never imagined that Gerard was listening.
(His words, I'm afraid,
will cost him dearly!)
Gerard retrieved his fiddle;   1468
he had heard everything the count had said.
Wasting no time,
he ran down the stairs
without taking his leave.   1472
He passed through the main gate
and left the town,
his fiddle hanging from his neck.
He was so overjoyed by what he had heard   1476
that he didn't stop running,
neither sitting nor stopping to rest
until he was back at Le Marche,
where he was welcomed most warmly.   1480
His host jumped up to greet him
and exclaimed, "My lord, may God protect you!
How have you managed
to return so soon?"   1484
Gerard replied, "I can't tell you just yet,
but I hope to do so before long."
They sat down to supper;
no one else was present,   1488
it was just the three of them.
Afterwards, they cheerfully retired
for the night. His thoughts racing,
Gerard tossed and turned all night.   1492
At dawn he dressed and got ready,
and his host, eager to serve him,
saddled his horse. Gerard mounted,
took his leave, and was soon on his way.   1496
His thoughts, however, were in turmoil,
for he had no idea
where to look for his lady.
The magnitude of his suffering   1500
was very great; even more than
the repeated doubling
of squares on a chessboard!²⁶

He began to tremble with anger and grief, 1504
fiercely threatening Lisiart,
and swearing to make him pay
for his deception and his crime.
(The king will be to blame 1508
if Lisiart isn't burned at the stake!)
If only Gerard can find his lady,
he'll prove in single combat
that Lisiart lied like a traitor! 1512
Pensive and sad, he rode along,
searching throughout Burgundy
and asking everyone he encountered
for news of his lady Euriaut, 1516
though his quest was as pointless
as seeking Paris at Nivelles.
He inquired in vain, discovering no news
and finding nothing to bring him joy. 1520
He had been traveling for many days
when, early one evening,
he found himself riding towards a castle
situated on the banks of a river. 1524
As he studied the stronghold
and saw how heavily fortified it was,
he realized that war had occurred there.
The land had been burned 1528
for two leagues in every direction.
He caught sight of two knights,
both of them riding mares
and wearing armor, their helmets laced 1532
and their polished swords
positioned for fighting.
Four men followed them on foot,
three of them armed with spears, 1536
the fourth with a freshly ground battle axe.
Gerard rode to greet them, then asked
for their hospitality. They replied:
"You'll have such as we can provide, 1540
but you won't thank us for it,
for we live in great poverty.[27]
Everyone here is terrified.
Our castle is so battered 1544
that we've harvested no wheat
for more than three years.
But you mustn't think
we're looking for excuses 1548
not to receive you! Clearly,

you're no rustic shepherd."
"I thank you," replied Gerard.
They all rode over the water   1552
and the four servants raised the drawbridge.
The two knights rode ahead,
leading Gerard to the keep;
there wasn't a finer one   1556
from there to Dijon.
The servants led his horse to the stables,
where they removed the bridle
and gave it a little hay,   1560
for they had no barley or oats.
Gerard blanched when he saw
how poor the lodgings were.[28]
The knights invited him to sit on a low chest,   1564
then removed their armor.
They had worn it for so long
that it was now battered and rusty.
When they had finished,   1568
they looked about for some threadbare clothes.
Soon Gerard saw two groups of pale,
thin knights come into the hall.
They weren't dressed in silk,   1572
neither samite nor cendal,
but were raggedly attired.
With them came a maiden,
quite comely and attractive,   1576
though fasting had taken a toll,
making her face grow pallid and wan.
If the story holds true,
she was shabbily dressed.   1580
Her white tunic, old and tattered,
had a cloth belt; its little buckle
and tip weren't made of silver,
but of brass or copper.   1584
One could clearly see
that she possessed no great wealth.
Gerard, ever courteous and polite,
approached her and said,   1588
"Greetings, my lady," to which
she replied, "My lord, may God,
creator of the world,
send you honor and good fortune,   1592
for here you will find nothing,
and there is nothing at all
we can do about it. For this reason,

it saddens us deeply   1596
when a worthy man comes to visit.
It makes us even sadder
that I'm unable to honor him properly
when he asks to stay here with us.   1600
However, we haven't had this much food
in the castle for more than a week.
I have five loaves of bread
and three cakes, three partridges   1604
and four plovers—I wouldn't trade them
for Pithiviers—and a small cask,
full of wine. I must warn you
that there is nothing more,   1608
as God is my witness.
We expect to be attacked tomorrow
by foul and wicked folk.
I can't make peace with them   1612
unless I agree to marry their lord,
but he is so ugly and cruel,
I'd rather be hanged!
You've never seen a better swordsman,   1616
and he has sent word
that he'll lay siege tomorrow.
This man destroyed all my lands
and has reduced me to penury.   1620
He also killed two of my brothers,
and my father as well,
so there's every reason for me to grieve.
Do you imagine I'd willingly wed   1624
the man who has thus broken my heart?
No indeed! It would be very wrong of me."
With that, she began to weep
and wring her hands.   1628
Heaving great sighs, she repined,
"Alas, what paltry protection
I have against this enemy,
for I've no stalwart friend   1632
who would dare to fight him!
Dear God, will I never see his pride
and his treachery destroyed?
Please don't think ill of me,   1636
my lord, if I weep,
but I'm truly suffering.
However, I'll stop complaining now
and be comforted because   1640
you have taken shelter here."

"Thank you, my lady," replied Gerard,
"and may God, the true Father,
aid and comfort you. But in His name,   1644
dear friend, please tell me,
if it doesn't pain you too much,
whether this brave knight
who is so haughty and bold   1648
would be willing to fight for you
in single combat. If so, rest assured
that I would gladly offer my services
to defend you. In that case,   1652
it might be agreed that if he can conquer
and kill me, you and all your lands
would be his to command.
But if I conquer *him*,   1656
all the depredations and wicked deeds
he has committed against you
would be rectified as you saw fit—
except, of course, for those he has killed,   1660
since they can never be brought back to life.
The lady replied: "Dear God!
I seek nothing better, my lord,
but I'm so terrified of this cruel man   1664
that I dare not accept.
May God reward you for your offer,
and for the comfort you've given me."
At this point, an elderly knight,   1668
known for his probity and wisdom,
rose to his feet. "My lady," he said,
"thank the gentleman and do as he asks.
Let him fight! For I believe,   1672
indeed I'm quite sure,
that with his help we shall be saved."
With that, the maiden offered her glove
to Gerard and he took it.   1676
All her people were filled with joy
because of this decision.
Supper was prepared, and afterwards,
everyone stayed up late.   1680
The beds were then made ready,
and those who needed to sleep,
retired for the night.
The others, who were to keep watch,   1684
stood vigil and drank wine
until the new day dawned.
When the watchman blew his horn,

those who were abed wasted no time.   1688
They rose quickly, and the maiden,
who had awakened very early,
hurriedly got dressed
and made herself presentable.   1692
She had slept very little that night,
for she was so terrified of her enemy
that she couldn't fall asleep.
Throughout the castle,   1696
the knights were seized with fear.
Gerard's heart grew heavy
when he saw the maiden weeping.
In her terror, she had hurried to his bed.   1700
Very sweetly, she said to him,
"my lord, may the Father,
who made the Virgin his mother,
give you a good day and protect you,   1704
both life and limb." Then the lovely, slender
blonde girl sat down on the edge of the bed.
Gerard, however, felt no desire,
except for his beloved.   1708
When she saw that he was weeping,
the maiden was deeply saddened.
He rose as soon as he could,
and together they went to church   1712
to attend mass.
After leaving the service,
they hastened to the ramparts.
From there they saw the enemy forces,   1716
about which they had spoken,
some three thousand men-at-arms.
Grasping his shield by the straps,
their lord, fearless and cruel,   1720
rode before them all, carrying aloft
his banner of cendal silk.
He stopped at the foot of the drawbridge,
in front of the gate, and began to shout   1724
that he would have them all
cut to ribbons if they didn't
surrender the maiden to him.
When those inside heard him,   1728
they didn't know what to do.
"Allow me to settle this,"
said Gerard. "If it pleases God,
in whom I place my trust,   1732
you'll soon see this man

who is threatening you
repent of all the wicked deeds
he has inflicted on you.   1736
Have armor made ready for me.
I'm going out there to fight him.
If I'm able to humble this man,
and make him leave you in peace,   1740
I'll then be on my way
and commend you to God.
As you've said, you have in him
a formidable enemy.   1744
No arguing now!
Bring me some newly forged armor.
I don't care how it looks,
as long as it's strong and well made.   1748
They hastened to bring him
some beautiful, costly armor
that was very strong and light.
Then they laced on his chausses   1752
and attached them with strong
leather straps. A young knight
fastened golden spurs over the chausses.
There was an elegant hacqueton   1756
edged with bands of gold cloth,
and a woven mail hauberk
that had once belonged
to the emperor Alexander.   1760
Over his cuirass, he wore a cotte
made by a Scottish woman
from over the seas; her name was Rainse,
the mother of Taulas.[29]   1764
They then laced on a helmet with costly ties
(it had belonged to Charlemagne),
and girded on Gerard's own sword,
for there was none better.   1768
And if you'd like to know how it was found,
and how it was tested, I'll tell you the story.
It's all quite true.

The king of Baghdad had a nephew,   1772
a very handsome young man
who held the land of Salamis.
The king, however, hated his nephew
and desperately wanted him   1776
to be killed in a battle
so that he could acquire his land.

One day, the king tricked the young man
into declaring war against   1780
Esclamor of Baghdad.
The king, who had little love for his nephew,
had him provisioned with armor
of inferior make: a hauberk   1784
made of finely woven, light-weight tin,
and a helmet forged of iron,
though richly decorated
here and there with bands of gold.   1788
The written source, if reliable,
says that his sword had a gold cross
at the guard and a silver grip.
The scabbard was made of elegant   1792
cloth-of-gold, but the blade itself
was of burnished iron. Thus armed,
the young man mounted his swift horse
and was led to a little island   1796
where Esclamor was waiting
to do battle with him.
The two men lowered their lances
and began to joust, coming together   1800
so violently that both were knocked
to the ground. They jumped up
and renewed the fight. The king's nephew
drew his sword and struck Esclamor;   1804
as he pulled back, the sword,
so highly praised by the king, broke apart.
Esclamor rushed forward and seized
the young man, gripping him so tightly   1808
that he drew blood wherever he struck,
causing the boy to grow pale.
Seeing clearly that he had been betrayed,
the young man was overcome with fear.   1812
Not knowing where else to go,
he fled towards the river,
where he bent down to pick up some stones.
Suddenly, he felt the hilt of a steel sword   1816
pressing against his right hand.
As he stood up, he pulled the sword
from the riverbed, where it had lain
for more than sixty-one summers.   1820
The young man, graceful and strong,
leapt from the river, both feet together,
and confronted Esclamor,
striking him with such force   1824

that the sword lodged in the ground
after he had chopped off his head.
In memory of this blow,
the sword was known as "True War."   1828
And Gerard now has it at his side.

They brought Gerard's white horse,
which was draped in a silken cloth;
both sides were redder than madder.   1832
Gerard took the shield and the lance,
to which a banner was attached.
They opened the gate
and out he rode, over the bridge.   1836
With two bounds, he was off!
When Galeran, lord of the Gorgerans,
caught sight of Gerard,
he boldly approached   1840
and haughtily demanded:
"Tell me your name, knight!
I think you're very unwise
if you dare to oppose me!   1844
You're a fool, unless you're here
to surrender the castle to me."
Gerard replied: "I'm here to defend it,
and may God help me!   1848
The young lady, may God
protect her, has sent me."
"And do you love her so much
you would die for her?   1852
Because no one can save you
if you fight with me!"
"Enough of this game
and the one who's playing it!"   1856
retorted Gerard. "Let's make a deal.
If you're able to overcome and kill me,
you may enter this castle, take the lady,
and treat her people as you wish.   1860
But if I can conquer *you*,
you'll be her liegeman ever after
and make amends to her
by doing whatever she commands."   1864
"I ask for nothing better,"
said Galeran. "But now I ask
a favor of *you*. Here's what it is:
that you plant your banner   1868
right here in the ground

and wait while I summon
my men and bring them here.
To give you greater assurance   1872
of my intentions, I hereby pledge
and swear to you that they will honor
the terms of our agreement, and that three
or four of them will go to the castle   1876
as your hostages." "Agreed," replied Gerard.
Galeran spurred his horse and galloped off,
leaving Gerard behind.
He returned with his men   1880
and presented his seneschal,
who was made to swear an oath
to deliver the hostages.
The maiden climbed the stairs   1884
all the way up to the highest tower,
for she wished to watch the battle
between the two knights.
Not a soul remained indoors;   1888
everyone was leaning over the ramparts.
Galeran and Gerard unfurled their gonfalons
and drew away from one another
as far as an arrow could fly.   1892
Defiant, their lances raised on the felt,
they charged, each man sure of his strength.
They collided with such force
that their gold and azure shields shattered   1896
and their lances were reduced to splinters.
The very moment they came together,
they clashed so violently
(at least it seems this way to me),   1900
that their feet left the stirrups,
and both men sailed
over the hindquarters of their horses.
Great was the general distress and alarm   1904
when they lay there unconscious
for quite a long time.
When this battle was over,
they would both need medical attention,   1908
and whoever examined them would find
even the least of their wounds life-threatening.
They lay there, motionless,
for what seemed like hours.   1912
The knights were all talking about it,
swearing they had never witnessed such a joust.
At last, the two men regained consciousness

and stumbled to their feet.   1916
They retrieved their swords
and lunged at each other so violently
that, so help me God,
there was scarcely an inch of flesh   1920
where blood didn't flow. And so,
they began once again to fight.
Each man had a low opinion
of the other. (That's what I think).   1924
Blood and sweat dripped into their eyes;
they couldn't see a thing.
They dropped their shields,
lost them, then took hold of each other,   1928
pushing, pulling, and clawing so violently
that they tore the laces of their helmets.
Even the less tired of the two was exhausted,
but neither of them gave up.   1932
Each man retaliated
for the blows he received.
So tenaciously did they fight,
that they knocked each other to the ground,   1936
tumbling over one another
until they both lay flat on their backs,
unable to move, their faces pale
and wan from loss of blood.   1940
Everyone in the castle was distraught,
as were those on the field,
for they had lost their protector.
If their lord is dead,   1944
they'll be shown little mercy.
In dismay, those in the castle exclaimed,
"Alas! After all the suffering
we endured in April and May,   1948
we can't go on much longer."
They wandered about the castle, despairing.
As they lay on the field,
the two knights heard the noise   1952
and the tumult. They had no idea
what it was all about,
but were aware that everyone
was loudly singing their praises.   1956
Both knights continued to lie on the field
with no pillows for their heads,
until they had rested and caught their breath.
Then they got up and confronted   1960
each other, this time with swords.

Each man hammered away at the other's head,
striking great blows, parrying and lunging,
ripping apart the mail of his opponent's   1964
hauberk and splitting his helmet.
They hit one another's jaws and heads
with their fists and swords,
and when they came together,   1968
the blows resounded
like boards being crashed together!
Loss of blood and sweat made them
grow pale and blurred their vision,   1972
but they didn't stop.
Each man hit and struck the other
so that no one could tell
which of them had the advantage.   1976
Each man aimed at the other's chest,
just as he should, wielding his sharp blade.
Neither Roland nor Fernagus
ever experienced such a fight![30]   1980
Blood and sweat ran into their eyes,
making it hard to see where they were,
or what they were doing. But when
one of them brushed up against the other,   1984
his opponent was quick to strike.
They raised their swords
and bashed each other on the head
so hard that stars danced before their eyes.   1988
They often staggered, ready to fall,
but then propped each other up,
clinging stubbornly to one another.
They clashed so violently, striking, hitting,   1992
and shoving, that it was a wonder
they both weren't already dead.
In the end, utterly exhausted,
they collapsed to the ground.   1996
But Galeran was unlucky.
He fell with Gerard on top of him,
and at that very moment Gerard
thought of his dear sweet Euriaut.   2000
He raised aloft his steel blade
and cried out: "Ask for mercy!
It would be a pity for me to kill you."
"Foolish words!" replied Galeran.   2004
"You don't have the advantage,
as you think! With God's help,
I'll keep fighting."

"That would be a miracle!" Gerard replied.   2008
He gripped his bloodied sword,
sliced through the silk laces
woven with gold that fastened
Galeran's helmet and tore it off.   2012
Galeran saw no way to defend himself.
What could he do?
Even if he were able to get free,
he could neither escape nor fight.   2016
"If you want to be spared,"
said Gerard, "admit defeat."
"A scurrilous demand," retorted Galeran.
"I'll never be such a coward!   2020
Your mercy means nothing to me.
Go ahead and strike!
What are you waiting for?
I'm not afraid to die!   2024
I haven't yet found a knight
who could defeat me!"
Gerard would have willingly
spared him had he asked   2028
even once for mercy,
but Galeran wouldn't hear of it.
And so, Gerard raised his sword
and cut off Galeran's head.   2032
When the Gorgerans saw this,
they were overcome with grief.
But, true to their word,
they quickly came to Gerard   2036
and placed themselves, their possessions,
and their people at his mercy.
High in the tower, where
she had witnessed the fight,   2040
the lady wept tears of relief and joy.
I'm sure I've never heard such rejoicing
as filled the castle then,
to the music of flutes and pipes!   2044
No one tarried there;
they all passed through the gate
and over the bridge, led by their lady.
As she joyfully went along,   2048
she raised her voice in song:
    I've desired true love for so long,
    and now I'll have just what I want!
The maiden went forth singing,   2052
and was utterly charming,

though humbly dressed
in a plain white tunic.
However, when she saw Gerard,   2056
who was covered with blood,
she was terrified. "Ah, holy Mary,
how horribly wounded he is!
If he dies, I'll never be happy again,   2060
nor ever know delight or joy!"
She went to Gerard,
but he didn't see her.
Blood, sweat, and dust   2064
had shut the light from his eyes,
so that he saw nothing at all.
Weak from loss of blood,
he fell in a faint.   2068
When she saw him lose consciousness,
she became distraught,
and began to blame herself:
"Wretched, wicked girl!   2072
It's shameful for me to remain alive,
when this knight has died for me!
The fault is mine, I know,
for I allowed him to fight for me."   2076
Then she began to beat her fists together,
and tear out her hair.
She could hardly refrain from sobbing,
so great was her grief. As the girl wept,   2080
Gerard regained consciousness.
When he heard her lament,
he sighed and cried out.
So profound was his agony   2084
that he could scarcely open his mouth.
The maiden stretched her hand
to his face and wiped his eyes,
which were filled with blood.   2088
Her white tunic was soon bright red.
After she had cleaned his eyes,
he opened them a little
and then, with great difficulty,   2092
he spoke, his voice weak and broken:
"Have mercy, my lady!
In the name of God,
take me away from here!   2096
I need medicine, and someone
must remove my hauberk."
When the lady heard him speak,

she called her servants immediately.   2100
They lifted him onto a shield,
for he was unable to ride,
and quickly transported him
to the castle. Soon,   2104
all Galeran's men came to the lady
and became her liegemen.
When they had sworn fealty to her,
the lady, who knew what to do,   2108
unlaced Gerard's helmet
and removed his hauberk.
The bliaut and the chemise,
however, stuck to his skin,   2112
for the mail had pressed into his flesh,
leaving hundreds of marks.
They gently placed him in a bed
freshly made up with linen sheets,   2116
then prepared plasters and bandages
with a sweet-smelling ointment,
kept in a box. Clear as oil
and suffused with theriac,   2120
it had such wonder-working power
that when his wounds were anointed with it,
the less grievous ones knit together,
though the deeper ones remained open.   2124
With great difficulty,
the servants raised him to a sitting position,
and applied bandages.
Away from the crowds and the fire,   2128
they found a quiet place for him
and a very gracious young woman
to watch over his recovery.
(If the knight regains his health,   2132
he will reward her well!)
In no time at all,
the girl had so relieved his suffering
that he was able to drink and eat   2136
and speak to them all,
though she forbade him
to eat pepper or garlic.
She took such good care of him   2140
that all his wounds were healed
and he had completely recovered
before the month was out.
He rose as soon as he could,   2144
for being bedridden

was very disagreeable to him.
Thoughts of his lady returned,
and with them the desire and the need   2148
to take leave of his hostess
and search for his beloved.
"Lady," he began, "I'm well,
though I feared I'd die   2152
from these wounds.
Had I not received such good care,
I would never have regained my health.
It's clear that I must now be on my way,   2156
but should anyone ever trouble you again,
know that I am yours to command.
From this day forward,
whenever and wherever you have need,   2160
be it near or far,
I'll be ready to defend you.
But before I go, please tell me your name
and all about yourself."   2164
"My lord, as God the heavenly Father knows,
I'll most willingly and gladly
tell you everything.
My father's name was Turgis   2168
and this castle is known as Vergy.[31]
My name is Aigline,
and all of Beaune is under my authority,
for these lands belonged to my father.   2172
But this year, just before
the feast of Saint Peter,
Galeran, with his own hands, killed him,
along with two of my brothers,   2176
Clarembaut and Helie.
You have brought me great happiness
by avenging me, for Galeran
showed mercy to no one.   2180
Now I would like for you to tell me
your name and all about yourself.
Then we'll see whether
you wish to leave or to stay,   2184
for I will give you my land
and everything I have, including myself,
either as your sweetheart or your wife.
Pray God, do not refuse me,   2188
for I am indeed a noblewoman,
though I know perfectly well
that a lady shouldn't praise

or boast about herself."   2192
And so, a flame was sparked
that will never die, even though
Aigline can never have
the love she desires from Gerard.   2196
"My lady," he replied, "not for all the wealth
of Constantine, king of Rome,
would I abandon my chosen path,
and that's the truth."   2200
When the lady, who had fallen in love
with Gerard, heard him say
that he wished to leave without delay,
she became pensive and fell silent.   2204
Seeing how upset she was,
Gerard realized that she had
fallen in love with him,
so he quickly added: 2208
"Have mercy, my lady!
I swear on my honor that I cannot stay."
He reached for her hand
and continued, "It simply cannot be."   2212
Then he told her his name
and all about himself,
relating the whole story of his misfortune:
how he had lost his land   2216
and, even more painful to him,
the woman he loved.
The lady was heartbroken
when she heard him speak of his beloved;   2220
she had never experienced such grief.
"Alas," she said, "what shall I do?
How shall I bear the burden
I've placed on my own shoulders   2224
and the bad bargain I've made
by falling in love with this man?
I'll keep suffering the pains of love,
but all for naught.   2228
Although he has done me a great service,
having saved me from a terrible affliction,
he now brings me another, even greater grief.
But he's not to blame, I am.   2232
I'm a fool to have fallen in love with him.
No, no, that's not true!
Anyone can easily see
that if Gerard hadn't come here,   2236
I would never have thought of him."

And so, she made excuses for herself.
After a little while, she said:
"Of course, it's idiotic for me to blame him   2240
in order to exonerate myself!
It's not his fault!
My own heart makes me love,
and my own eyes have betrayed me.   2244
Alas! I thought I'd reached
the pinnacle of joy, but here I am,
in the valley of woe."
Gerard, who was ready to leave,   2248
asked for his horse, and a young servant,
to whom he had entrusted his sword,
hurriedly brought it to him.
Outside the hall with its carved stone walls,   2252
Gerard mounted, and took his leave
as a nobleman should,
then rode off without delay,
leaving everyone in tears.   2256
He hurried along, eager to find
his lost love, Euriaut, even though
he had no idea where to look for her.
For the next six days   2260
he traveled along, angry,
worried, and embittered.
He was unable to learn anything
of Euriaut's fate, and was overcome   2264
with anguish and woe.
Oppressed by grief, he fell ill,
and in the city of Châlons,
was forced to take to bed.   2268
The illness that overcame him was serious,
and he remained lodged
for quite some time with a townsman
called Guy the Grey-headed.   2272
He grew ever paler and thinner,
unable to eat or drink.
Nothing consoled him.
He forgot everything, cared about nothing,   2276
not valuing his own life one whit.
He truly felt ready to depart this world.
So great was his pain and grief,
that no one who knew him and saw him   2280
in this state would have recognized him.
He forgot who he was and where;
his body and all his limbs

turned greener than the leaves of an elder tree.   2284
He remembered nothing
about his beloved or himself.
His vital strength was ebbing away.
He languished for many days in this state,   2288
finding no relief in the home of Guy,
who became increasingly worried about him.
This man had a very charming daughter,
a lovely and gracious girl   2292
just on the verge of young womanhood.
She was very cheerful and sweet,
and her name was Marote.
One day, she sat in her father's chambers,   2296
delicately embroidering with gold and silken thread.
She was working on a stole and an amice,
onto which she carefully stitched
little gold crosses and stars.   2300
As she sewed, she sang this cloth song,[32]
acquitting herself quite well.
    Beautiful Euriaut sits alone, shut away,
    refusing to eat or drink, refusing to rest,   2304
    often lamenting her fate, berating herself
    for not daring to speak to her dearest Renaut.
        Often, she cries out these words:
        "Ah! God! Will I ever see   2308
        my darling Renaut again?"
Gerard listened as the girl sang,
and heard the name of his beloved.
Unable to get out of bed,   2312
he sat for a while, deep in thought.
"Alas!" he exclaimed,
"this illness has kept me lying here
for a very long time,   2316
far from my duty.
If I continue to lie here,
I'll never find my beloved!
I'm living proof that a man   2320
who forgets his lady
grows feeble in mind and body.
No wonder I've become so weak!
I've completely forgotten the lady   2324
whose love makes me a better man.
But I've neglected her long enough!
Now I must try to recover from this illness,
so that I can look for my dear Euriaut.   2328
I'll not delay:

I won't stop until I've found her!
Nothing will prevent me
from finding her,   2332
as long as she's still alive."
And so, gathering his strength,
he lamented. To console himself,
he began to sing this song,   2336
his voice clear,
loud, and strong:
> Love, when will this fierce pain end
> that makes me grieve and sorrow?   2340
> Often, I grow feverish,
> flush or grow pale,
> tremble, shake, sweat, or shiver.
> Often, I feel close to joy,   2344
> but then feel sure I'm dying.
The townsman's daughter, Marote,
heard Gerard singing these words
and listened to him in astonishment.   2348
She imagined, as was understandable,
that the knight had suddenly become delirious.
Kindly solicitous, as always,
she rose and went to his bedside,   2352
where she found him sitting up.
She pleaded with him,
for the love of God,
to lie down again   2356
and not upset himself,
for this would only
make his condition worse.
Gerard told her that   2360
he would willingly drink
some hot almond broth,
and she immediately ordered
one of her servants to prepare it.   2364
She forbade anyone to visit Gerard
before he had eaten.
"Young lady," said Gerard,
"I must ask you something.   2368
Have you ever seen or heard anyone
speak of a woman named Euriaut?"
"God help me, my lord, I have not.
I've never seen or known anyone   2372
by that name. But I must tell you
that I was greatly distressed just now,
when I heard you singing."

"That was to ease my pain," he replied,   2376
"for I remembered the one
who caused my illness
when I heard you name her in your song."
"My lord, is it lovesickness then,   2380
that has made you suffer for so long?"
Gerard then told her the whole story
about his anguish and his great loss,
recounting the complete truth about Euriaut   2384
and everything that had happened.
When the girl had heard his tale,
she replied: "Indeed, my lord,
no man should ever test his beloved.   2388
That's my opinion, and I know I'm right.
A well-born man can soon find a lover—
there's nothing easier.
It's the ability to hold on to her that counts.   2392
A man who decides to test his good lady,
shouldn't try it. Trust me!
Instead, he should always cherish her.
For any man who loves   2396
merely to satisfy his own desires,
conveniently forgetting to follow
the wishes of his lady, is a traitor to love.
A truly noble lover   2400
wants to serve his lady
ever more completely.
In that way, he may earn the prize
that Love can offer. I don't say this   2404
to instruct you; you are, I know,
well-informed on the subject.
Nevertheless, everyone should be
reminded from time-to-time   2408
of the correct way to behave."
"Ah, young lady, you speak the truth,"
exclaimed Gerard,
"and may God reward you for it!   2412
You've cured me of this illness
that has held me in its grip for so long,
giving me comfort
both with your words and your song."   2416
The servant who had prepared the broth
arrived just then; he hadn't stirred it as it cooked.
He held it carefully in his right hand,
and in his left, he carried a costly silver spoon.   2420
The shapely Marote took both the spoon

and the broth that she had had prepared,
and made Gerard drink some of it.
She didn't want to hurry him,   2424
so offered just a little at a time,
but often. She covered his head
to protect him from drafts
so that he wouldn't catch cold,   2428
and repeatedly bathed his face
and brow with rosewater.
She looked after him most attentively,
neither too much nor too little,   2432
bathing him to cool his fever
and encouraging him to such good effect
that he had soon regained his strength.
As soon as he had recovered,   2436
he began to think about
going to look for Euriaut.
(He won't give up until he has found her!)
He'll even go to England   2440
and look for her there, throughout the land,
for he'll never be happy until he succeeds.
He asked the maiden to tell him
what he owed her and her father.   2444
"My lord," she replied,
"I think that you
don't have much money,
so it wouldn't be right   2448
for me to accept payment.
You will honor your debts, I know.
But in the name of friendship,
I ask you to take my sparrow hawk   2452
when you leave.
It will amuse you
and make you think of your host.
I don't think there's a swifter   2456
or better hunting bird from here to Tôtes;
at least, that's what its trainer told me.
Please take it for your enjoyment."
She hurried off to fetch the hawk;   2460
I doubt that a faster one could be found
from there to Pithiviers, or even as far as Angers.
The hawk had elegant jesses,
beautiful and long,   2464
and you may rest assured
that the attachment ring
shone bright and clear,

thanks to a ruby that, to my mind,   2468
glowed redder than a live coal.
She gave the bird to Gerard,
and with it her purest
and most ardent love.   2472
"Lady, God has greatly blessed me!
You've treated me so well that,
from this day forward,
I'll be your faithful friend forever.   2476
Rest assured, I'm yours to command,
whenever and wherever you choose.
It will be an honor."
Gerard then turned to go.   2480
He had no other equipment
than that which he had brought with him,
but Marote gave him various garments
made of fine, soft linen,   2484
whiter than snow or hail,
a fur-lined set of clothes, and shoes.
He had no cause for complaint,
for he had everything he needed.   2488
His horse, still there, had become sleek
and fat from prolonged rest;
it had been very well cared for.
Gerard turned to his horse and,   2492
grasping his sword, mounted.
He took his leave and rode away,
enjoying the pure, sweet, clear air
of the early morning. And so,   2496
he left Châlons and headed off
to seek Euriaut, just as he had done before.
He travelled to many places,
seeking news but finding none.   2500
It grieved him greatly
to discover no trace of her.
He journeyed as far as the Ardennes,
and from there to Cologne.   2504
He wouldn't give up, no matter what!
He roamed through the streets of the city
until he came to the central marketplace.
There he took lodging with a townsman   2508
called Adam the Greek,
a most kind and courteous fellow.
Gerard dismounted in the courtyard
and Adam, who knew his business,   2512
ordered a servant to see to his horse.

Since Gerard was alone,
his host made a special effort
to welcome him warmly.   2416
The two men greeted each other cordially,
and Adam's good lady
welcomed Gerard, too.
They received him most happily,   2520
and Adam himself took care of Gerard,
placing his sparrow hawk on a perch,
and making sure his horse was stabled.
Afterwards, the three of them sat down to dinner.   2524
Pike and salmon and stuffed poussin
were served in abundance,
along with other dishes
too numerous to describe.   2528
But before they had finished,
they heard news that brought
confusion to the entire city:
Saxons were about to attack!   2532
In the countryside surrounding Cologne,
all the wheat and vines had been razed
to the ground. The Saxons had gathered
in greater number than ever before   2536
and had burned everything,
right up to the city gates.
Their own abundant supplies were stored
in ships that followed them on the river.   2540
The enemy troops were camped on the riverbanks,
before the Gate of the Three Kings.
So costly was their equipment,
that it lit up the whole countryside with gold   2544
and azure, whitest ermine, green and silver.
These were arrogant men,
who loved conquest.
They had taken many towns by force,   2548
and were now preparing to attack Cologne.
(Make no mistake,
if the army stays there,
the fighting will be fierce!)   2552
Inside the great tower of Cologne,
Duke Milon received the news,
and his blood boiled,
right down to his toes. Without delay,   2556
he had the alarm sounded,
and the citizens,
hearing the blast of the brass horn,

rushed to arm themselves. 2560
They all understood that Saxons were attacking!
Everyone climbed to the top of the castle walls
and made ready, filling the pathways below with rubble.
A great tumult spread throughout the city. 2564
Gerard heard the cry,
and saw the inhabitants rushing about.
He smiled with joy
when his host informed him 2568
that the Duke of Saxony
was preparing to attack,
bringing with him a great army.
Gerard ordered that the tables be removed, 2572
for time was of the essence.
He was worried that the army might decamp
and leave the city behind!
He called for his host right away, 2576
and politely asked to borrow weapons,
for he was eager to fight.
Adam listened to his request
and leapt to his feet. 2580
He brought a sturdy hauberk, tightly woven,
and shoulder protectors,
silk garters and laces,
iron leggings, a cuirass, 2584
a leather cotte covered with mail,
and helped Gerard into his gear.
The armor was bright red,
and his horse was draped in a saddlecloth 2588
of shimmering red samite.
Gerard waited no longer.
He mounted, sliding his feet
into the stirrups and stretching the straps. 2592
He took up his shield, lance, and pennant;
a crest of peacock feathers
adorned his helmet. Thus caparisoned,
he crossed himself and left the inn, 2596
his banner unfurled in the breeze.
His host also mounted,
intending to show Gerard the way,
but leading him along the wrong path, 2600
until they arrived at a gate close by cistern.
From there Gerard rode onto the embankment.
The Saxons had already pursued their quarry
and taken prisoners; 2604
ten of the enemy hid in a redoubt,

twenty more in another.
When Gerard got a good look
at those who were lying in wait,   2608
you may rest assured he was pleased.
With a defiant cry, he spurred his horse,
lowered his applewood lance
and struck the first man under the chin,   2612
thrusting the well-forged iron
right through his throat and knocking him,
head over heels, from his horse.
With a yell of triumph,   2616
he raised his shield to protect himself.
The other Saxons had retreated into a clearing,
and Gerard plunged into their midst.
You've never in all your life   2620
seen such beautiful jousting!
Before he had broken his lance,
Gerard brought down
two of his opponents in a single run;   2624
with the remaining stump of his weapon,
he went after a third and unhorsed him.
Duke Milon, who was at the gate,
saw Gerard but didn't recognize him.   2628
He cried out to his men:
"Get on your horses!
It will be a disgrace if this knight dies
because no one helped him."   2632
A hundred knights, en masse, rushed to his aid,
pounding through the gate
with Duke Milon close behind.
When they reached Gerard,   2636
he had already vanquished the first ten men,
but his shield was badly torn,
and twenty men had surrounded him.
They were about to take him prisoner,   2640
when reinforcements came rushing in.
The twenty Saxons gave a great cry,
for the sight of the duke's men
racing towards them   2644
struck fear into their hearts.
Should they stay and fight or flee?
Soon the men from Cologne
were upon them!   2648
Duke Milon lowered his lance;
made of oak, it was large and stiff.
With great force, he struck a Saxon

in the chest, right below the breastbone, 2652
knocking him from the saddle.
The Saxons, put to rout,
turned and fled. In hot pursuit,
Gerard and all the others chased them 2656
right into their encampment,
where they slashed the cords
of their tents and pulled them down.
The enemy sounded the alarm, 2660
and Duke Milon drew back,
along with Gerard and all the others.
The Saxons armed themselves at once
(there were more than twenty thousand of them, 2664
I believe), then poured out of their tents.
Duke Milon sent word throughout the city,
commanding his people
to come to his aid immediately, 2668
for he was determined to fight the enemy.
From the city, there soon rode forth soldiers,
townsmen, and knights,
some fifteen thousand strong. 2672
Duke Milon organized the troops.
Meanwhile, the ladies and young maidens
went up to the high windows,
for they wanted to watch the fighting. 2676
The Duke's daughter,
a lovely girl named Aiglente,
watched from the window in the tower.
Her attendant, Florentine, stood to her right. 2680
When Gerard saw the preparations,
both of those within and those without,
and understood that they were all
gathering their forces, he was so happy 2684
he hardly knew what to do!
He turned to his right and saw a knight
riding between the two ranks,
ready to do battle. 2688
This was Gontart of Coblenz.
His saddlecloth, lance, and shield
were fresh and new, his coat of arms
beautifully painted in rich gold 2692
and azure, vairy, quarter silver.
I honestly believe you couldn't
have purchased all this equipment
for a thousand marks. 2696
He was eager to start the fight.

When Gerard saw Gontart coming,
he couldn't get to him quickly enough.
Imbued with courage, he spurred his horse,   2700
and bore down on him as fast as he could.
Gontart rushed to meet him!
It so happened that both sides
had a clear view of the action.   2704
The moment the two men came together,
they exchanged such fierce blows
that their shields were worthless;
both of them split in two.   2708
Only their hauberks saved them from death,
and that's the truth.
Gerard dealt Gontart a brutal blow;
unable to avoid it, he was knocked off his horse,   2712
and hit the ground, breaking his arm.
This act of prowess by Gerard
was greatly admired by both sides.
The ladies of the town,   2716
gathered atop the walls,
were all talking about it, though Aiglente,
I believe, was the most voluble.
She called to Florentine,   2720
then took her by the hand:
"Tell me, my dear. Do you see that knight
who arrived here yesterday on horseback?
How well he fights!   2724
Did you see him just now,
jousting with that Saxon
whom he knocked to the ground?
May it please God,   2728
who doesn't disappoint us,
for this knight to fall in love with me,
for I would gladly love *him*!"
Florentine retorted: "I would willingly   2732
let him cut off one of my toes,
if I could only lie by his side for one night
and have what I desire from him!"
"Is that a fact?" said Aiglentine.   2736
"Are you so arrogant, lady Florentine,
that you've given your love to the man
I've fallen in love with?
He would sow his seed in poor soil   2740
if he chose *you* instead of *me*!
You're forgetting yourself
when you try to take precedence over me.

Remain loyal to me,   2744
and forget about this love of yours!
You've nothing to gain
by competing with me."
"Oh, hush," my lady!", Florentine replied.   2748
"I'm not 'competing' with you.
I just want to be loved by him!"
While the girls were arguing,
the Saxons dug in their spurs.   2752
They saw that Gontart was down,
but their help came too late.
Those from Cologne similarly
rushed to support Gerard.   2756
The two sides came together
with a great crashing of weapons,
the horses moving so fast that many banners
were driven through bodies.   2760
When he saw that the battle
was truly under way,
Gerard didn't hesitate.
Trembling with rage,   2764
he heaved a proud sigh
and spurred his dark-gray horse.
He grasped his shield, then drew his sword.
Into the crowded field he charged,   2768
wielding his blade so skillfully
that he cleared a wide path before him.
No one who saw him was brave enough
to wait and joust with him.   2772
Not stopping to rest,
he slashed his way through the Saxons
and penetrated the enemy camp.
After he had vanquished all the knights there,   2776
he plunged back into the fray.
He fought well and long,
striking with his sword and jousting.
After a while, he recognized, just next to him.   2780
the armor of Espaulart de Gormaise.
"Dear God!" said Gerard,
"I'll gladly fight this Saxon!
I've seen him vanquish all who oppose him!   2784
He has done well thus far,
but if I'm able, and with God's help,
he'll have to face me now!"
At that very moment,   2788
Gerard saw a Saxon galloping toward him,

eager to do harm, but he turned aside
and was unscathed, thanks be to God!
Gerard struck him as he passed.   2792
There would be no help for the man now,
for Gerard had split his head
right down to the teeth.
Gerard seized the dead man's lance,   2796
which had a pennant and a sharp steel tip.
He sheathed his sword, dug in his spurs,
and dashed through the valley,
racing toward Espaulart more swiftly   2800
than a deer darting from a clearing.
When the Saxon saw him coming,
his shield with quarter arms raised,
he spurred his horse   2804
and grasped his own shield,
which suited him admirably.
He well knew how to handle fine weapons.
But now I'd like to digress for a moment   2808
and describe his gear.
This Saxon was clothed
in bright red samite, and his shield,
saddlecloth, and even his cotte   2812
and hood, were costly and new.
Three lions, all embroidered
in gold thread, adorned his shield.
On his cotte were six more,   2816
and another six on the saddlecloth.
This man had won a great many battles
and hard-fought jousts,
but he'd have done better to stay in bed that day   2820
rather than confront Gerard!
The latter raced toward him,
furiously spurring his horse, and the Saxon,
enraged, rushed to meet him.   2824
They exchanged such fierce blows
that their shields were ripped to shreds
and both men were slightly wounded
in the chest, just above the stomach.   2828
The Saxon was tall and muscular,
Gerard strong and agile.
Gerard leaned to the side,
but the Saxon's blow   2832
came down on his neck.
(I'm sure this wound
will take a long time to heal.)

Gerard fought back so fiercely   2836
that he skewered Espaulart
with the banner on his lance.
What a ferocious battle it was!
His opponent was badly wounded   2840
and Gerard, as I recall,
was struck below the breastbone.
Both men were unhorsed, for neither
could withstand the other's blows.   2844
Blood, bright red and warm,
poured from their wounds.
Saxon reinforcements soon arrived,
as did Duke Milon.   2848
Before this battle is over,
there will be many more jousts
and many sturdy lances will be broken!
You could see shields splitting   2852
and hauberks being torn to shreds.
Knights were falling, wounded,
and many bodies had lost their heads.
Horses were fleeing, their reins in tatters.   2856
From various directions,
you could see knights coming together
and many pennants flying in the breeze,
many flags and banners of various kinds,   2860
many knights dying and crying out,
many sharp arrows being drawn.
The men from Cologne fought hard,
struggling so mightily   2864
that they were able to get Gerard
back into the saddle.
The Saxons, meanwhile,
were grieving loudly   2868
as they carried their dead from the field.
Duke Milon now rushed forward,
Gerard and all the others with him
(that's the way it seemed to me).   2872
His seneschal struck a Saxon
right in the center of his gold
and azure shield,
tearing and splitting it in two.   2876
Then he pierced the man's hauberk
and ran him through with his lance,
knocking him from his horse.
This terrified the Saxons,   2880
but Guinebaut, lord of Mayence,

soon had his revenge.
With his sword, which he greatly prized,
he struck the seneschal, whose helmet   2884
might as well have been made of brass,
for it gave him no protection at all.
The man's head was split to his teeth.
Gerard saw it happen; deeply grieved,   2888
he hastened to exact revenge.
His shining blade came down
near Guinebaut's ear
and severed his shoulder;   2892
he will never recover.
(I can vouch that he
died from this wound.)
He couldn't help but fall,   2896
for he had lost his good right arm.
The Saxons were stunned
when they saw that Guinebaut was dead.
Gerard now bore the brunt of their attack.   2900
Had he been less skillful,
they would have wounded him badly.
He split so many helmets,
slashed so many shields   2904
and killed so many Saxons,
that all those who remained
were sick at heart and terrified.
Suddenly, they rushed toward him!   2908
He would soon have been taken prisoner
and killed, had Duke Milon and his men
not come to his rescue.
The battle was fierce,   2912
for everyone wielded a weapon,
be it sword, lance, or mace.
But don't imagine for a moment
that God was not on Gerard's side!   2916
He had suffered greatly, and had given
and received so many blows
that he proved himself
the most valiant of them all.   2920
Gerard captured the Saxon leader
and turned him over to the duke.
When they saw that they had lost their leader
and finest warrior, the Saxons were distraught.   2924
As they grieved their loss,
the knights from Cologne,
led by Gerard, attacked again.

The Saxons, who realized that 2928
they were undone and utterly defeated,
threw down their shields and took to their heels.
They were terrified of the enemy
and fled toward the river. 2932
Gerard, I understand, slaughtered many of them
on the embankment. He didn't stay long
in one place, but chased after as many
as he could, fighting vigorously. 2936
He attacked them with such ferocity
that his wound reopened and the blood
ran down onto his horse's neck.
When Duke Milon saw this, 2940
he was greatly alarmed, so much so
that he halted his pursuit
and advanced no further.
The Saxons fled, not stopping 2944
to gather their belongings.
They were only too happy
to escape with their lives!
Duke Milon stayed where he was, 2948
ordering that the tents
be dismantled and the equipment
and other valuables seized
and transported into town. 2952
Everyone was saying that
the knight with the red shield
had been the bravest of them all.
Duke Milon then went to see Gerard. 2956
He was accompanied by more than
two thousand men, all of them wondering
if Gerard would recover.
Gerard assured them that he would. 2960
The duke was delighted to hear this
and said, "I'd like to learn about you—
who you are and where you're from."
This request didn't surprise Gerard at all. 2964
"My lord," he replied, "I've come from
a foreign land, to seek my fortune."
"And your name, good sir?" "Truly,
I have no great fame! I'm called Gerard 2968
in the place where I was born and raised."
Soon they were on their way into the city.
Ladies and maidens appeared at windows,
and stood there, two by two, looking out. 2972
The sound of church bells,

pealing in celebration, filled the air.
Gerard didn't stop along the way.
He went straight to his lodging and dismounted,   2976
feeling more dead than alive.
Duke Milon saw to it that his armor
was removed and his wounds examined
and carefully cleaned.   2980
He sent a physician who was
very knowledgeable about such injuries
and the best ways to treat them.
Aiglente was informed that   2984
the newly arrived knight had not fared well;
that he was, indeed, badly wounded.
On hearing this, her heart sank.
"Alas!" she said, "What shall I do?   2988
If he dies, I'll never have joy
from any man, nor love, nor happiness.
Alas! I had thought to make him mine,
but it was only a dream! The saying is true: 2992
Just when we think we've succeeded,
our hopes are dashed.
I've now fallen from the heights
to which my imagination had raised me."   2996
She went on like this at great length,
then burst into tears. Meanwhile,
Florentine was also suffering.
"Alas," she repined, "Why doesn't   3000
my heart break in two? If he dies,
I swear I'll never wear braids again!
I'll have all my hair cut off
and become a nun or a recluse   3004
in some wild forest! As God is my witness,
I'll never know the blessings of wedlock!"
When Aiglente heard her companion's lament,
her heart almost stopped beating.   3008
Then she said: "Why in the world
do you think he would care about you
and *your* love? How presumptuous you are
to imagine that he would marry *you*!   3012
If he chose you instead of me,
he'd be an utter fool!
What towns, castles, and money
would he get from *you*?   3016
What revenues?"
To which Florentine replied,
"Good heavens, lady Aiglente!

Don't be mad at me! 3020
If the knight recovers, go right ahead
and love him! I won't object.
But if he doesn't want *you*,
and would rather have *me*, 3024
I'd be so happy
I'd never feel sorrow again!"
Aiglente shot back: "I'd stab myself in the heart,
if he wanted to love you 3028
instead of me! From here to the sea,
I don't know of a single woman
who is more beautiful than I am!
Anyone who had to choose between us 3032
would have to be blind not to prefer me!"
"My lady," said Florentine,
let's not argue about it right now.
Let's just say this: if you're more beautiful 3036
and more elegant than I am,
but he nevertheless likes me better,
I'd be overjoyed if he chose me
and forgot all about you! 3040
It will be marvelous for me,
and just too bad for you,
if I have my way on this.
You could stay mad at me 3044
for the rest of my life if you wanted to.
I'd be delighted! I have no idea
what will happen, but if he decides to love me,
I'll do whatever he asks, and I don't think 3048
anyone would blame me for it."
"For heaven's sake," Aiglente angrily replied.
"You're driving me crazy,
daring to contradict everything I say! 3052
Let me ask you something.
Do you really think you're
of sufficiently high birth
to argue with me? 3056
I won't forget this!"
Just then she looked up and saw
her father and his knights approaching.
Aiglente was in no mood to smile, 3060
but she hid her feelings from her father
and rose to greet him, saying,
"How are you, Father?
Tell me, which man did the best 3064
in the battle today?"

Her father told her that there wasn't
a better or braver knight
in any kingdom anywhere than the one   3068
who had assured their success.
The duke then removed his armor
and his nobles dismounted
and hurriedly did the same.   3072
The duke and his men then went upstairs
to the great hall, where dinner awaited.
They washed their hands and took their seats.
More than six full courses were served,   3076
and many side dishes, too.
Aiglente was delighted to hear about
all the brave deeds accomplished by
the handsome Gerard.   3080
Everyone was singing his praises,
and the more they praised him, the more
the ardor of both young ladies increased.
They remained, however, wildly jealous   3084
of one another. After dinner,
all the guests washed their hands,
then rose from the tables.
They began to stroll about, enjoying themselves.   3088
Minstrels performed lais on their fiddles,
along with melodies, songs, and motets.
Everyone was having a wonderful time,
but Aiglente hardly noticed.   3092
Love had so pervaded her thoughts
that she cared nothing for such amusements.
She went to her room
and summoned her governess,   3096
who was entirely unaware of the girl's feelings.
Aiglente ordered that a coverlet
and a pillow be brought for her bed,
and then she laid down to rest.   3100
Her thoughts turned again to Gerard,
and soon she was lost in reverie.
Suddenly, she sat up and began
to wring her hands so vigorously   3104
that she tore the skin.
"I must be losing my mind," she said,
"wanting a knight in armor
I'd never even seen before today!   3108
I've been too hasty, that's for sure.
I swear I'll think about something else
and forget all about him!"

She then settled back into bed.   3112
Love, however, soon began to teach her a lesson,
making her (though it caused her pain)
think about Gerard and his noble body.
With Love overwhelming and inflaming her,   3116
her thoughts were such, that one minute
she was calm and the next she was shivering.
She wanted to conquer her feelings,
for Love was making her suffer,   3120
and so, she sang this song,
which has a pleasing melody:
    I swear to God, love's sweet pain
      will drive me insane,   3124
    unless he reassures me!
As for Florentine, she had stretched out
on an elegantly appointed bed
in another part of the room.   3128
She almost died when
she heard Aiglente's song!
She waited a bit,
then raised her head   3132
and looked at her lady,
who had sung the words so clearly.
She sat up and, resting her cheek
on her hand, thought about Gerard.   3136
Her reverie inspired her to sing;
she hoped this would bring her comfort.
In clear tones, she gave voice
to this sweet, melodious song: 3140
    You sing, and I die of love.
    Don't you care at all that I suffer?
Aiglente responded: "May God remember this:
you should die in agony,   3144
your face deathly pale!"
"My lady, please don't say that!
I don't deserve it!
I've never known another woman   3148
so prone to say mean things!
But enough about these young ladies.
I'll now return to Gerard.

Duke Milon visited him twice a day,   3152
without fail. Gerard's wounds
healed sufficiently to allow him
to rise from his bed and walk. Soon after,
he was able to go riding in the woods.   3156

The duke was delighted to have his company
and the first week Gerard was up
and about, asked for the favor
of his company at dinner.   3160
Gerard was pleased to accept.
The two men rode straight back
to the court, where the meal
was ready and waiting.   3164
The young ladies, however,
were still in their chambers, relaxing
and dressing in their best for dinner.
They left by separate doors   3168
and went into the great hall,
where they were delighted to see Gerard.
Aiglente gazed at him;
she didn't think that anyone   3172
would notice her watching him.
But God knows, it was obvious
to one and all that Love
now held her in his power,   3176
for she couldn't stop staring at him!
It was apparent to everyone
that she only had eyes for Gerard.
(I could report at length about her loving gazes!)   3180
Without delay, Gerard went to greet her,
and she replied very cordially,
without the slightest hesitation.
At his first words,   3184
she let escape such a deep sigh
that he would have understood her feelings
right away, had his desire
not been focused on another.   3188
Florentine, however, *was* paying attention.
"My lady," she exclaimed, "by Saint Gervaise,
you certainly are sighing a lot.
That last sigh was quite profound!"   3192
Aiglente heard what she said,
and was utterly mortified.
Even though she was furious,
she didn't respond.   3196
She feared her father,
and didn't dare react. And, of course,
Gerard was standing right there!
Soon the basins were passed.   3200
They all washed their hands and sat down.
During the meal, Gerard was preoccupied

with thoughts of Euriaut.
The duke noticed his silence, and was annoyed by it.   3204
They were served an abundant repast—
indeed, I've never seen such plenty
in a noble household,
except in that of my lady of Ponthieu,   3208
which, to my mind, surpasses all,
because her sweetness of demeanor,
her courtesy and conversation, nourish
and intoxicate all the members of her court.   3212
As for Gerard, I can confirm that
he was amply served
of every dish at this dinner,
and that everyone behaved   3216
most graciously towards him.
They had all the food they could wish for,
and were abundantly supplied
with un-peppered, spiced wine.[33]   3220
Immediately after dinner, the duke ordered
that the tables be removed;
he then rose and retired for the evening.
Some of the guests practiced fencing,   3224
some played backgammon or other enjoyable games.
Gerard, however, kept to himself.
He left the dining room
and wandered over to a window,   3228
thinking all the while of his beloved Euriaut.
His body grew weak and his limbs lost
their strength; he could hardly remain standing.
He vowed to look for his lady,   3232
though he might never succeed in finding her.
Amid all his suffering,
he remembered this song, and began to sing:
    Anguished, brooding, in dread I sing,   3236
    inflamed by a noble love.
    I pretend to be carefree,
    though I am oppressed by sorrow.
    My sweet lady has inflicted   3240
    wounds that cannot, and will not, heal.
    For her I endure the pain,
    ever her faithful lover.
Aiglente heard Gerard singing   3244
and listened carefully
to the words of his song.
The sound of his voice filled her with joy,
for she imagined the song was meant for her.   3248

She was delighted, and sent a message
to Gerard, saying that she
would gladly speak with him.
He went to her right away,   3252
accompanied by his host, Adam.
Into Aiglente's chambers they went,
where many noble maidens
and many high-born ladies were gathered.   3256
Gerard greeted her courteously,
as a nobleman should, and Aiglente
eagerly approached and welcomed him.
"May joy be yours,   3260
for that is my heart's desire!"
She tugged at his silk bliaut
and had him sit next to her.
Then she said: "My lord, God knows   3264
I've longed to see you and listen to you,
and find out who you are and whence you come.
I want to ask you, in the name of friendship,
to tell me the truth about all this.   3268
I'll then do whatever you ask,
from start to finish, without demur."
Gerard listened to her, then began
to tell this tall tale: "In truth, my lady,   3272
the other day I robbed a widow
who was very well-off.
Her lord had been an idiot.
He was a wealthy knight   3276
and quite a miser.
The riches he had amassed
wouldn't have fit into a simple oxcart.
I thought I'd scored a great coup   3280
when I abducted the lady
to get the money I coveted.
I took her as my wife and companion,
but as soon as she was able, she fled,   3284
and took the matter to court.
All my land was then seized
and I now have so little standing,
I dare not return." When the young lady   3288
heard him lament his poverty,
she thought she might be able
to tempt him with offers of her love
and riches, since he coveted wealth.   3292
And so, she said to him:
"My dear friend, the lady who caused you

to be banished from her lands
didn't love you very much   3296
if she lodged a complaint against you!
God knows, if I were your sweetheart,
I'd never do such a thing."
On the other side of the room,   3300
Florentine watched Gerard as he spoke to Aiglente.
Feeling deeply aggrieved, she exclaimed:
"Alas," poor me! She'll seduce him
with her conversation, and he'll be powerless   3304
to resist, for she's a wily creature!
Shameless, too, talking to him
for such a long time, and right in front of me!
She knows I can see what she's up to.   3308
But I'll try again,
and talk to him if I can.
With God's help, I'll make him
think about something else.   3312
There's no point
in my going over to him,
nor in warning him.
What a scourge that tongue of hers is!   3316
May God split it in two,
so the man can be left in peace!
I do notice that he's awfully quiet."
Such were the private thoughts   3320
of the lovely young woman,
who was almost overcome by sorrow.
Aiglente, meanwhile, was saying to Gerard:
"My lord, why don't you sing now,   3324
and console yourself with friendship?
That way you'll forget about your wife.
May she burn in Hell
for making you so unhappy!"   3328
Gerard then began to sing this song;
he wanted everyone to hear it:
    I do not see here the one
    from whom I await great joy.   3332
As Aiglente listened to the song,
she became increasingly upset
and angry, for she imagined
he had chosen it to spurn her   3336
and show that he didn't care for her.
Her face grew pale
from distress and anger.
"My lord, are you so faint-hearted,"   3340

said she, "that you dare not love
where you will be loved in return?
You are base indeed to reject me
when I've asked for your love!"   3344
"Please, my lady, don't say that!
I can neither reject nor accept you.
I tell you truly, as I should,
that I would be unfaithful to my wife.   3348
Surely you realize that I would be mad
to think of loving someone as high-born
as you are. People would rightly say
that I had lost my mind!   3352
I beg you to say no more about it,
my lady, since anyone who heard you
would think you were crazy yourself!"
Then he rose and took his leave.   3356
Aiglente was overwhelmed with sadness
when she saw him go and understood
that he no longer wished to speak with her.
She had her bed prepared   3360
and climbed into it.
The pains of love tormented her,
making her feel wistful, sad, and bleak.
Sighing and trembling, she tossed   3364
and turned, lamenting her fate.
(I believe she endured some twenty
or thirty such assaults, in rapid succession.)
Florentine went over to her and said: 3368
"How are you, my lady?
You had the knight all to yourself
for quite a while, I think.
If you've enjoyed him sufficiently,   3372
I ask you, as a friend, to let me
have a turn now." When she heard this,
Aiglente nearly lost her mind!
She was about to utter a most injudicious reply,   3376
when she saw her governess approaching.
She therefore suppressed the urge,
and cut short her sighs.
The quarrel was nipped in the bud.   3380
Her governess took one look at her,
came closer and asked:
"What's wrong, my lady?
Tell me the truth, as you should.   3384
Why are you so pale and wan?"
"A slight indisposition, madam.

I don't know what it is.
One minute I'm freezing   3388
and shaking all over,
but then I feel terribly hot,
perspiring so much that even if
a southerly breeze blew upon my face,   3392
it wouldn't relieve my suffering."
Her governess replied: "Now I understand!
Love is causing this 'illness.'
Tell me if you will: did the man you love   3396
ask you first for your love?"
"My lady, on my honor,
when I told him how I felt,
he didn't say a word.   3400
He left as quickly as he could,
causing me such grief
that I'm losing my mind."
"Oh dear, my lady, oh dear!"   3404
the governess replied.
"I'll make you a promise here and now,
for I see you have great need of it.
You'll soon have your way with him,   3408
and easily so. You'll never again
be troubled by this, but will soon
be happy and joyful, for I know
how to concoct a potion   3412
with which you can trick him
if you can make him drink some of it.
And if you drink some of it after he does,
no matter where he goes, near or far,   3416
he will love you above all others."
"Ah, madam, you've spoken well!
Go at once and prepare this drink."
But make sure that Florentine   3420
knows nothing about it."
"My lady," she replied, "she'll never know."
The governess opened the door
and went out to the orchard,   3424
where she hurriedly began
to search for various herbs.
Aiglente rose from her bed
and climbed up into the tower.   3428
Finding herself all alone,
she went to an isolated corner,
and to a window there.
She watched the people   3432

in the street below, hoping to see
the one she desired, but to no avail.
Not knowing what else to do,
she decided to sing so loudly   3436
that everyone would hear her.
That way, she reasoned,
her song would reach the ears
of her beloved.   3440
Then she decided not to sing,
and just keep on suffering.
"Suffering? Dear me,
why should I? If this illness   3444
lasts much longer, I'll die!
Since I've decided to sing,
I'll do it no matter what.
Nothing could stop me now,   3448
even if I were starving!"
        May the one who knows how to cure love's pain
        come to me right now, for I am dying!
While she was singing, her governess,   3452
who could hear her quite clearly,
returned from the orchard.
She had not been gone very long,
for she had quickly found what she sought.   3456
She went back into the room
and crushed and ground the herbs,
adding water to the brew,
which looked just like blackberry wine.   3460
A short time later, Gerard returned to court,
dressed in a short mantle of fine silk
and new ermine fur.
No queen or king had a better one.   3464
Under it he wore a pleated chemise
embroidered with gold thread.
He had chosen to wear it
because of the heat.   3468
He wanted to find Euriaut
and, not wishing to be discourteous,
he had come to take his leave.
His host, Adam, was with him   3472
and carried the items of clothing
that Gerard had cast off.
As they entered, they encountered
the daughter of the duke,   3476
who had just left her chambers.
When she saw Gerard,

she trembled all over, blanched,
then blushed and grew silent and still.   3480
Gerard observed her pallor,
and when she made no move
to welcome him, he went to greet her.
The maiden replied: "My friend, may God   3484
grant you joy and good fortune!
I wish to ask a favor of you.
Come to my chambers and take your ease.
I can accompany you there myself.   3488
Please come and go as you like.
I have something to say to you."
"With pleasure, my lady," he replied.
And so, the three of them went   3492
to her chambers and sat down to talk.
Aiglente spoke first. "My lord,
I'm consumed with sorrow and anger
because, no matter what I say,   3496
I cannot gain your love.
I very much want to know
the reason for this.
Can you not put aside your affection   3500
for a wife who hates you?"
"My lady," he replied, "No one knows
how my heart is governed.
Once inflamed, a loving heart   3504
is too powerful to be suppressed.
My own is so overwhelmed by love
for the one who makes me suffer,
that I'll never give her up."   3508
Aiglente heard his words
and waited a bit before replying.
"Truly," she said, I'm deeply hurt.
What a fool I was, to have asked for your love!   3512
Any woman who asks a man
for his love is out of her mind.
I've failed to capture my quarry
and must try my luck elsewhere,   3516
since you won't listen to me.
Why don't you join a monastic order?
I think you're afraid, or perhaps
you don't like women? I don't know   3520
what your inclinations may be."
Gerard listened to her scornful words,
then answered most judiciously:
"My lady, do not be downcast.   3524

As God is my witness,
I do have a sweetheart;
otherwise, I'd give my love to you,
if it would please you.   3528
I know beyond any doubt
that I would gain honor by doing so.
But you cannot wish for me
to grant you my love   3532
if I don't really love you.
It would be wicked, vile, and ignoble for me
to let you believe something that isn't true.
If I were unfaithful to my lady,   3536
whom I have loved for a very long time,
I would deserve to die in dishonor.
Shame on any man who betrays his beloved,
and on anyone mad enough to say   3540
he grants his love
if he doesn't really mean it!
But I want you to know that,
from this day forward,   3544
should you ever have need,
I'll be there to serve you, with all my heart.
Now I'll ask to take my leave of you,
for I must go look for my lady   3548
whom I have not seen in such a long time."
The maiden was devastated
when she heard that he wanted to leave.
She summoned her governess and asked her   3552
to bring something to drink. The old woman
hastened to pour the potion into a goblet.
(Alas, how great a sin is befalling
the one who wishes to trick Gerard!)   3556
First, she made sure that Gerard drank
from the beautiful goblet, and then Aiglente,
who drank it eagerly, knowing full well
what the potion would do.[34]   3560
The governess, who was very clever,
now took the goblet and poured out
what remained. To Adam,
she offered plain wine.   3564
When Gerard had drunk the potion,
it was as though he were reviving from a swoon.
He sat there, utterly silent.
For a long time,   3568
he remained lost in thought,
not remembering Euriaut at all,

but feeling an overwhelming desire
to look at the young lady,   3572
who seemed to him incredibly beautiful.
He didn't know what to say or do,
but he couldn't stop looking at her.
It was evident to Aiglente   3576
that the drink had confused him,
and she became a bit haughtier
and more condescending.
(Such behavior is typical   3580
of a capricious woman.
When she sees that a man is smitten
and has fallen in love with her,
she becomes a bit more standoffish   3584
and distinctly less friendly.)
"We must go now," said Aiglente.
"I don't want my father
to find you here."   3588
Gerard would most willingly have asked
for her love, but he didn't dare;
he was too afraid she would refuse him.
(Now the tables have turned!)   3592
The maiden didn't tarry:
"Truly, I dare not stay here any longer."
With that, she left them.
Gerard left as well, and before long   3596
he happened upon Florentine,
who was sitting on a counterpane,
skillfully embroidering an elegant
mail-clad tunic, designed for battle.   3600
The maiden, who was no fool,
quickly rose to welcome him.
"May great joy be yours,"
replied Gerard. "But please sit down,   3604
my lady, and continue sewing.
I'll keep you company."
"My lord, as God is my witness,
I desire your company   3608
and delight in it!
Nothing gives me more pleasure
than being with you.
If my company were equally pleasing to you,   3612
I feel sure no one could ever separate us!
But now I wish to ask something of you:
that you either grant me your love,
or else tell me right away   3616

if you already have a sweetheart,
for I wouldn't want to yearn for you
in vain. It would be too much to bear
if I loved you   3620
and were not loved in return.
I'm not accustomed, dear sir,
to throw myself at men,
nor is it my habit.   3624
I've never loved before,
and I feel quite frightened!"
Gerard replied: "Have mercy,
my lady! I find myself   3628
in a dilemma. I *am* in love,
of that I'm sure.
But I swear that I don't yet know
if the one I love shares my feelings.   3632
If she doesn't love me,
I don't know what I'll do!
Dear God! My lady's face
is so radiant and her lips so red!   3636
She's incredibly beautiful!
The mere thought of her
makes me want to sing."
Unable to remain silent, he began: 3640
   With one kiss alone, from a willing heart,
   she could ease my pain for many a day,
   but that kiss would bring death from desire!
     If such joy is not yet mine,   3644
     my suffering is fine,
     for from it springs sweetness,
     and comfort and delight.
Florentine listened to the song,   3648
and was overcome with dismay
and heartache. She had believed
she could make him love her,
but realized she'd failed.   3652
Trembling with sorrow
and vexation, she said:
"My lord, if I dared,
I'd willingly ask you   3656
where she is, this lady you love.
Be kind and tell me her name!"
"Oh no, my lady, I certainly won't!
But I'll continue to suffer   3660
until my tormentor takes pity on me.
This is my great misfortune."

Then he began once again to sing.
Rising to his feet, he continued: 3664
    You can guess who it is that I love,
    but you'll never find out from me!
When he had finished singing,
he took his leave, and Florentine,   3668
left behind, remained plunged in woe.
Gerard summoned his kind-hearted host
and they left together arm in arm.
The next day, Gerard went to court.   3672
He rose as early as possible,
which is to say, at the crack of dawn,
for he had heard the previous evening
that the duke intended to besiege   3676
a castle that had declared war on him.
He was determined to punish his enemies.
The duke was delighted to see Gerard,
who wished to accompany him.   3680
The duke mounted his horse
and his companions followed suit.
They set off, and rode without stopping
until they neared the castle.   3684
The duke and his men were armed,
and when they had taken their places,
more than sixty men formed the first rank.
Each one had a lance made of applewood   3688
with a banderole attached,
rich and varied saddlecloths,
a mail-clad cotte, and a brand-new shield.
Every man there was eager to carry the day!   3692
They were all certain
they would capture the castle
and vanquish those within,
and they vowed to hang the enemy's leader,   3696
who had behaved so wickedly towards the duke.
The lord of the castle was called Meliaduc.
Armed from head to toe,
his shield bearing corner arms,   3700
he appeared before the barbican,
holding a sturdy pike in his hand.
With him, I'm told,
were some ten Saxons,   3704
ten feet tall and greatly to be feared.
Even the timidest of them
was exceedingly brave.
Instead of lances and swords,   3708

they carried battle axes or iron mallets.
They looked like devils from Hell!
Duke Milon saw the men,
and was not at all pleased.   3712
His own men dared not begin the attack.
Gerard saw them bow their heads,
and said to himself: "God in heaven,
what shall I do? Shall I be the first to attack,   3716
or shall I wait for the others to begin?
Perhaps they won't even try.
How humiliating that would be for them!"
He said no more and let his horse race ahead.   3720
Meliaduc was eager to fight
when he saw Gerard pounding toward him.
The two men bore down on each other
and soon crashed together.   3724
Gerard had aimed his lance at Meliaduc's chest,
and ran him through,
killing him instantly.
He could inflict no greater harm.   3728
Brave and strong, Gerard
pulled his lance from Meliaduc's body,
then struck another opponent,
tearing through his armor   3732
and piercing the man's heart and entrails.
The dead man fell to the ground.
When the others saw their companion lying there,
his lips drawn back like a mastiff's,   3736
they all rushed towards Gerard.
They would have had him, too,
but Gerard turned his horse in the nick of time.
They didn't even touch him, praise God,   3740
except for glancing blow to his shield.
Gerard drew his sharp sword
and came back on them quickly.
Wielding the polished blade,   3744
he badly injured the first man,
striking him alongside his ear;
the man's armor didn't protect him at all.
Gerard sliced off his ear and half of his chin,   3748
which fell onto his chest.
He then thrust his sword into the man's shoulder,
cutting right through it.
He prepared to strike again.   3752
Dealing mighty blows,
he killed a third man, then a fourth.

The one who had been wounded in the face
bled so profusely that he fell face down 3756
into the filth below.
(I swear to you that this is true.)
The others were furious that they had been overcome
and put to rout by a single opponent. 3760
Each one thought he'd go mad
if he didn't avenge himself!
(May God protect Gerard!)
Duke Milon was watching it all, 3764
and said to his men: "Hurry, my lords!
Let's help this brave knight!
Shame on us if this noble, worthy
man dies or is taken prisoner." 3768
Hesitating no longer, the sixty men
rushed to Gerard's defense.
The Saxons saw them coming,
unsure what to do as they watched them advance. 3772
Gerard's assault became more ferocious
than ever, inspiring such fear
that the enemy fled before him
and took refuge in the fortress. 3776
Gerard spurred his horse
and dashed through the gate in hot pursuit.
He struck one man who was carrying
a battle axe, slicing off his arm. 3780
But he had been reckless,
and needed help right away,
for a Saxon was rushing towards him,
wielding an iron mace. 3784
He looked like a devil from Hell!
He charged ahead and hit Gerard hard
on his shield, splitting it in two.
The blow came down 3788
on the saddlebow with such force
that Gerard's fine Castilian charger,
feeling the weight of the blow,
staggered and fell. 3792
Thanks to God's protection,
Gerard was unharmed.
Duke Milon and his knights
rushed to the spot and encircled 3796
the enemy, attacking bravely.
Gerard jumped up,
welcoming the Saxons
with his sword. 3800

Soon the enemy lay injured or dead
and the castle was reclaimed!
But Gerard had all the glory that day.
Everyone declared that   3804
they had never seen anyone
wreak such havoc.
The duke hurried to embrace him,
congratulating and honoring him.   3808
He blessed a hundred times over
the hour when this knight
had come to his lands.
Thanks to him,   3812
the war was now at an end.
They began the journey home,
and as they rode along,
the duke consulted his nobles.   3816
They advised him to appoint Gerard
to oversee his lands.
The duke gave Gerard
complete control of its administration   3820
and court of justice,
and he fulfilled his duties most ably,
I believe, for quite some time.
He participated in many tournaments   3824
throughout Germany and the Hesbaye,[35]
never denigrating knights who
were worthy but poor.
Although he was renowned for his valor,   3828
he was neither proud nor vain,
but was gracious toward all.
Because of his wisdom, goodness,
and affability, he was loved by everyone,   3832
even the wicked and the arrogant.
The daughter of the duke loved him dearly,
and he loved her more than anything
in the world, so much so,   3836
that he never thought of Euriaut.
He forgot all about her;
it was as though she had never existed.
For an entire winter and summer   3840
Gerard stayed with the duke.
But now I will leave him,
and tell you about Euriaut,
for I'd like to get on with my story.   3844

Back in Metz, the lovely Euriaut

had just returned from the chapel,
where she had worshipped and prayed.
She hadn't lingered there,   3848
for everyone was watching her,
and she tried to shield herself from prying eyes.
The duke would have gladly wed her,
had no one objected,   3852
but his barons had forbidden it.
The duke was exceedingly vexed,
for he dared not defy them.
Wishing to reflect,   3856
Euriaut found a quiet room.
She thought about her home,
and about Gerard, whom she loved so dearly.
She greatly feared that,   3860
having lost his lands
and become an outcast,
he would fall victim to despair
and do himself harm.   3864
"Alas," she said, "when will I see the day
and find the place
where I'll see my true love again?
If only I had seen him one more time,   3868
how happy I'd be now!
Ah, Lisiart! God curse you
for having separated us!
My heart should truly break   3872
because you robbed me of the one man
in all the world who loved me best!
May God punish you for this!
You placed the bet with him,   3876
but I don't know how you found out
about my birthmark and thereby deceived him.
As surely as you cheated,
you should be burned alive!   3880
And may my beloved,
who, overcome by grief,
abandoned me, come back!
But how can he find me now?   3884
I could linger here for a long time
before hearing any news of him.
He might never come this way!"
And so Euriaut talked to herself,   3888
for she was suffering cruelly,
and nothing consoled her.
Just then, a young servant

brought her a lark   3892
that he had caught,
as pretty as it could be.
He presented the bird to her
and urged it to sing.   3896
Euriaut took the bird from the young man
and put it on her lap to feed it.
(But the lark will bring her
sadness and great sorrow,   3900
as you shall hear me tell.
She will heave many a sigh
because of this bird!)
The lovely maiden had a little ring,   3904
a gift from Gerard,
which she wore on her finger.
Without her realizing it,
the ring fell onto her lap.   3908
When the lark caught sight
of the sparkling stone,
it seized the valuable object in its beak
and shook it so vigorously   3912
that the ring slipped over its head
and around its neck![36]
Adorned with the ring,
the bird took flight   3916
and disappeared through a narrow window.
Euriaut was distraught
when she saw this happen.
In sorrow and dismay,   3920
she began to wail,
"Ah, holy Mary!
My heart is broken,
for I've lost the ring   3924
my sweetheart gave me!
Alas! Such grief, and all because of
that bird, may it burn in Hell!
Truly, I never imagined   3928
it would bring me grief,
though I know all too well
that joy flees from me,
abandoning me.   3932
Sorrows always come in pairs!
I had woes enough before,
but this bird has increased them.
Now my suffering will be even greater.   3936
How true it is that arrows keep on piercing

the one who is already wounded.
How I hate the lark that stole my ring!
Ah, beloved, your jewel   3940
is far away from me now.
My heartache and my sighs will never end."
Wailing piteously,
she plunged her fingers   3944
into her blond tresses
and pulled out her hair.
(But listen to what happened next!)
As Euriaut was agonizing,   3948
certain she would rather be dead,
a knight came into the room.
He was a treacherous, contemptible man
always eager to commit wicked deeds.   3952
Meliatir was his name,
and from there to Tyre,
no man was haughtier or more cruel.
(He should have been burned alive!   3956
Because of him, Euriaut endured
great suffering and pain.
Alas, it's all too true that one adversity
often brings with it another!)   3960
The traitor saw that Euriaut was all alone,
and asked her to satisfy his desire.
If she did, he would provide for her so well
that she would never again   3964
want for anything.
"Good heavens, my lord! It would be shameful
for a well-born man like you
to lie with me, and that's a fact,   3968
for I've never refused my body to any man!"
"You're crazy to refuse me!" he replied.
To which she retorted:
"For the love of God,   3972
my lord, you shouldn't say such things!
It simply cannot be."
He grabbed her by the left hand,
intending to drag her to a bed   3976
and have his way with her,
but she fought back, kicking so high
and so hard that she struck him in the jaw,
breaking three or four of his teeth.   3980
She then began to pound him with her fists
and after landing a blow to his chin,
managed to escape.

Hiking up her skirts, she fled the room.   3984
Furious and sick at heart,
she sought refuge in the great hall,
where she found the duke's sister,
a young lady named Ysmaine.   3988
Euriaut had taught her how to embroider silk
with a variety of stitches,
and the two young women
were extremely fond of each another.   3992
Now listen to what this traitor did.
He stayed behind in the chamber,
took a sharp knife
and, as malevolent men are wont to do,   3996
considered how he might wreak harm.
Making not the slightest sound,
he slipped behind a large chest,
where he remained until it grew dark.   4000
(Euriaut is in trouble now!)
The duke, who felt tired after dinner,
soon went off to bed.
He had shown great honor   4004
to Euriaut, allowing her,
out of love, to sleep in his
sister's room and share her bed.
When all was dark within,   4008
the traitor stood up and went
straight to Ysmaine's bed.
He pulled back the cover
and found the duke's sister,   4012
whom he believed to be Euriaut.
(But one whom God wishes to protect
cannot be harmed!)
The low-born traitor   4016
ran his hands over the maiden
until he found her heart,
just under her breast.
He aimed the sharp knife and plunged it in,   4020
right up to the grip, slaying her.
(May God curse this evil man!)
He then took Euriaut's hand,
thinking it was Ysmaine's, and raised it up,   4024
carefully drawing it to the knife.
Knowing full well what he was doing,
he wrapped her fingers around the handle.
Whoever finds the two women,   4028
and sees them lying there like this,

will naturally believe that the one
had killed the other.
He turned away from them   4032
and slipped from the room,
then quietly went to bed, staying there
until morning, when the household stirred
and the two girls were found,   4036
in such a way that it looked like
Euriaut had stabbed Ysmaine
with the knife and killed her,
for Euriaut's hand was still wrapped   4040
around the handle of the knife.
The duke remained at a distance,
transfixed by this incredible sight.
Euriaut now woke and saw   4044
the crowd of people standing before her.
Utterly bewildered, she began to tremble.
The duke looked at her and said,
"I was terribly mistaken   4048
about you but didn't realize it.
This is certainly cause to grieve,
and believe me, I do.
For having trusted you,   4052
I deserve whatever misfortune befalls me."
Euriaut, still unaware that the duke's sister
had been murdered, couldn't imagine why
he was speaking to her like this   4056
and was deeply pained by his words.
Then she raised her head slightly
and was horrified
to see the slain girl.   4060
Raising her hand to her cheek,
she cried out: "Ah, lovely, sweet maiden,
who has done this terrible thing to you?"
The duke grabbed her by the arm   4064
and ordered her to get dressed.
Then he handed her over to Meliatir,
saying: "You wicked madwoman!
Pray that I don't kill you here and now!   4068
But I won't—not until a judgment is reached.
You've committed a monstrous crime,
murdering my sister."
Euriaut didn't know what to say.   4072
Utterly petrified, she sank down
and sat on a marble bench.
The duke sent throughout the city

for his noblemen,   4076
commanding them to advise
how best to punish the one
who had murdered his sister,
and caused him such profound grief.   4080
"My lord," said Meliatir, "I'll speak frankly.
I don't know what judgment there can be,
other than to have her burned immediately.
Her guilt is evident.   4084
The circumstances in which
she was found clearly prove it."
But then a wise and well-spoken knight
stood up and appealed to the duke.   4088
"My lord, send to Bar-le-Duc
for your uncle, the count.
In my opinion,
there isn't a wiser man anywhere.   4092
The messenger will soon return.
In the meantime, have this woman
placed under guard.
This seems to me the best approach.   4096
Unless your advisors are informed,
she shall not be tortured."
Meliatir was fit to be tied when he heard
this man saving Euriaut from the pyre.   4100
Exceedingly vexed, he exclaimed:
"My lord, I don't see how anyone else
could have killed your sister!
She offers no evidence of her innocence,   4104
nor can she defend herself in any way.
Nonetheless, if someone wanted to claim
that she didn't commit this murder,
I'm prepared this very instant   4108
to prove that she should rightfully
be burned." The duke replied:
"I won't allow it.
I'll make no judgment   4112
before my uncle has arrived."
Meliatir became so angry
that he nearly lost his mind.
But the duke sent for his uncle,   4116
and had Euriaut locked up.

Now I'll gladly return to my account of young Gerard,
whose service to Cologne
had endeared him to all,   4120

both highborn and low.
He had no memory of Euriaut;
all thoughts of love were for Aiglente,
the daughter of Duke Milon, 4124
who had offered him the potion
that he had imbibed so thirstily.
Aiglente loved him
most passionately in return. 4128
Indeed, she was so besotted
that her father became aware of her feelings.
He found her behavior improper,
but decided that he would 4132
have them marry,
and resolve the situation in this way.
He felt sure he could never find
a worthier knight to whom to give her. 4136
His friends all advised him
to speak to Gerard and the two men
came to an understanding,
The marriage was arranged, 4140
though Gerard suffered greatly,
as the wedding day seemed very far off.
Although his yearning
made him melancholy, 4144
he continued to live quite comfortably.
One day, he decided to go hunting,
both to cheer himself up
and to better train his sparrow hawk 4148
to hunt larks and quail;
it was already an excellent hunter
of magpies, teals, and plovers.
Astride his rapid steed, 4152
his hawk on his fist,
Gerard rode through the gates of Cologne
with Adam, his host, riding to his right.
Aiglente was at the window 4156
of the highest stone tower,
with Florentine next to her.
She was chastising Florentine
for loving Gerard and for believing 4160
that he could be hers.
When Gerard caught sight of Aiglente,
he laughed and said to Adam: "Dear friend,
tell me honestly what you think. 4164
Hasn't the sun just risen at that window?
The balcony looks more beautiful now,

because I can see the one woman
in the world I most desire.   4168
I'm going to sing something now,
for I'm sure she'll hear me."
In a clear, powerful voice, he began:
    I await my joy from her,   4172
    but dear God, shall I have it?
Gerard finished his song
as he rode along the banks of the Rhine.
He reined in his horse   4176
when he heard the song of a lark
that had spread it wings in flight.
Panting, it flew along
as it sweetly sang.   4180
When Gerard heard the sound,
he stretched his feet in the stirrups
out of pure joy.
Remembering his noble love,   4184
he felt inspired to sing for Aiglente
some of this song from Poitou:
    When I see the lark joyfully lift
    its wings against the light of the sun   4188
    and, forgetting all, let itself fall,
    its heart suffused with sweetness—
    dear God, how envious I am
    when I behold such utter bliss!   4192
    I'm amazed its song doesn't melt my heart,
    so great is my yearning and desire.
And so Gerard rode along,
but before he had finished the song,   4196
the lark drew in its wings and alighted.
Gerard spurred his horse, untied the straps
that restrained his hawk
and handed them to Adam.   4200
The hawk, who saw the lark from afar,
crouched on his fist and launched.
It was a splendid sight!
The lark rose into the air   4204
but the hawk gained speed.
It was well-trained and knew
how to capture its prey
It seized the lark,   4208
gripping it tight with its talons.
Gerard, pleased with this flight,
hurried over and nimbly dismounted.
He let the hawk pull out   4212

some of the lark's feathers
and enjoy its prey,
then separated the two birds,
lest the hawk be deemed a thief. 4216
He fed the brains of the lark to the hawk,
making sure to keep the birds apart.
As he pulled the lark away,
he noticed a little ring around its neck. 4220
He slipped it off at once
and called to his friend, who hurried over.
Gerard showed him the ring;
it was set with a bright red gemstone, 4224
and was extraordinarily beautiful.
Gerard stared at the ring
and suddenly realized
that it belonged to his beloved Euriaut. 4228
You could have travelled
a league and a half
before Gerard moved a muscle.
When he remembered Euriaut, 4232
he was overcome with grief and anguish.
His face grew ashen
and he fell in a faint.
When he revived, 4236
he began to berate himself:
"Alas! How shameful that I still live,
when I've lost my true love."
So miserable was he, so plunged in woe, 4240
that he seemed to have lost his mind.
Abruptly, he jumped up, crying out
and beating his palms together.
His hawk, though calm by nature 4244
and well-trained, flew off and perched
in a laburnum bush on the riverbank.
Unnerved and overwhelmed,
Gerard gave way to his grief. 4248
"Alas," he repined,
"why don't I kill myself,
wicked wretch that I am?"
His anguish was so intense 4252
that he almost went mad.
Adam, astonished, had no idea
what had caused this outburst.
He dismounted, approached Gerard, 4256
and began to reason with him:
"My lord, this is crazy!

Your distress is so great that
you've turned white as a sheet!   4260
What has happened to you?"
"Dear friend, I've remembered the lady
I love so dearly!
That's why I call myself wretched,   4264
for I lost her long ago." So acute
was his anguish that he began to rake his nails
across his face and tear his bliaut.
Adam tried to reason with him: 4268
"Noble lord, forgive me for asking,
but are you saying that you have
a sweetheart other than the lady Aiglente?"
"Yes, and as God is my witness,   4272
she's a hundred thousand times more beautiful,"
replied Gerard. "But the sin I've committed
made me forget her for a very long time.
I vow I'll never spend   4276
more than two nights anywhere,
until I have news of her.
I'll search far and wide!"
"My lord," Adam replied,   4280
"my lady will go mad from grief.
She'll never marry another."
When he heard his friend speak of Aiglente,
Gerard didn't know what to do,   4284
or how he could possibly leave her.
Love is offering him two alternatives:
he may choose whichever he wants,
though either choice will cause him pain.   4288
Now we shall see which one wins the day,
and it will be revealed whether
magic and sorcery can better inspire
devotion, and of a finer kind,   4292
than noble, loyal love.
If Gerard remains in Cologne,
distancing himself from Euriaut,
then without a doubt,   4296
sorcery and enchantments
will be shown to be more powerful
than love that comes naturally.
But if right and reason do not lie,   4300
love that springs from true desire
has greater power, is finer and
worthier. Of course, Gerard
will go in search of Euriaut!   4304

He'll not fail to do so!
And Aiglente will be left behind.
He mounted his spirited horse and
slipped onto his finger the ring   4308
that belonged to the one he loved so dearly.
He summoned his sparrow hawk,
which swiftly responded.
"Good host, please take this hawk   4312
as a most sincere gift to the lady I have loved.
Tell her I pray that God
may bless her and her father
for the many kindnesses they've shown me.   4316
And may He one day give me the opportunity
to repay you for this service."
Then he took his leave, asking Adam
to greet Aiglente on his behalf.   4320
Adam watched as Gerard rode away
and was sorely tempted to follow him.
He kept watch until
Gerard was out of sight,   4324
then commended him to God's care.
He mounted, and with the sparrow hawk
on his fist, soon found himself
riding through the gates of Cologne.   4328
Aiglente was still at the window,
observing the activity below;
she hadn't budged. When she saw Adam,
returning alone, she grew very pale.   4332
She didn't know what to think
when she saw that Gerard wasn't with him,
and was greatly distressed
by his long absence.   4336
Little did she know that Gerard
was leaving her behind
and going in search of his beloved Euriaut.
And so, expecting his return,   4340
she continued to keep watch.
She thought of a song,
which love inspired her to sing:
    Dear God, my heart will break!   4344
    How I yearn to see him.
No sooner had she finished this song,
which was admirably suited to her voice,
than Adam strode into the great hall.   4348
Everyone ran to greet him,
and Aiglente asked him right away

for news of Gerard. Adam,
who was almost dying of sadness,   4352
pain, and grief, replied:
"My lady, let there be no sorrow now."
Then he told her how Gerard
had found the ring   4356
around the bird's neck
and how he had recognized it.
He continued, telling her
all about the grief   4360
that Gerard had shown for his lady.
"He said that I must swear
to convey his greetings to you
and give you his sparrow hawk.   4364
Here it is—he sends it to you."
Aiglente almost lost her mind
when she heard these words.
She stretched out her left hand   4368
and seized the sparrow hawk.
She would have killed it, had her father,
with a severe reprimand,
not taken it from her.   4372
"Daughter, this would have been
poor revenge on your part!
The hawk has done no wrong."
"Yes, it has, Father!   4376
It caught the bird that brought news
to Gerard of the woman
for whom he has left me."
She then gave way to her grief.   4380
Nothing could comfort her, though her father
offered such strong reassurances
that she began to hope.
He said he'd send someone to search   4384
for Gerard, "no matter how inhospitable
the land or distant the place.
And if he's not found, I swear
I'll find another to take his place."   4388
"May God help me, Father!
I swear to you that I wouldn't have
the emperor of Germany
and all his wealth   4392
in exchange for Gerard.
Hurry! Send at once
for a messenger
to bring him back!   4396

For as God in heaven is my witness,
I'll never be given to another man,
even were I to gain a crown.
I'll marry Gerard or no one!"   4400
The duke had his messenger
prepare immediately
to go in search of Gerard.
Aiglente was overjoyed   4404
when she saw him ready to depart,
and further consoled herself
by singing this song
in a clear, sweet voice: 4408
    You who go, for God's sake, let him know
    he leads me to death unless he shows mercy!
Before she had finished her song,
the messenger turned and rode off,   4412
beginning his search for Gerard.
He followed his trail and before long,
found the hoofprints of Gerard's horse.

Now I'll tell you about Gerard,   4416
who had left, all alone, in such haste.
He looked everywhere for Euriaut,
for he was determined to find her.
After passing through deep forests,   4420
he at last emerged into open country;
there was none finer from there to Ireland.
In the middle of the plain was a tree,
and beneath it, lying on a marble mounting block,   4424
was a knight whose face
had been horribly lacerated.
Bright red blood poured
from a deep wound in his body.   4428
Gerard rode over to him and asked
who had injured him so grievously.
The knight raised his head
very slightly and replied: 4432
"The one who did this to me
has abducted my wife,
whom I married this very day.
We were returning home—   4436
only two other men were with us—
when that double-crosser,
the lord of Durlus, seized her.
He governs the Ardennes,   4440
and used to live here in this forest.

He is my mortal enemy,
but had granted me a truce.
Now he has abducted my wife,   4444
for our party was outnumbered.
I'm more concerned about her
than about my injuries."
"My friend," replied Gerard,   4448
"I'm not made of iron or steel,
and I have no weapon, save my sword.
It's a good one, and well-tempered.
But rest assured,   4452
I'd go after him if I had armor.
He'd have to fight with me
if he didn't agree
to return your wife!"   4456
"My lord," the knight replied,
"take the armor of the knight
who lies dead over there,
under the laurel tree.   4460
He was killed in the attack."
Gerard rode over to take a look.
He dismounted, and in no time
had removed all the dead man's armor,   4464
which he hastened to don.
He then remounted and set off,
leaving behind the wounded knight,
who had told him which way to go   4468
to follow the men who had abducted his wife.
(If he rides fast, he'll surely
catch up with them!)
As he raced through the woods,   4472
he thought of Euriaut,
and the joy he felt inspired him to sing.
Without hesitation, he began,
and soon the woods rang   4476
with the sound of his voice:
    How glad I'd be if I could see
    my lady, my beloved!
    May God lead me, full of joy, to her side!   4480
He rode along, singing,
until he caught up with the knight
who had abducted the lady.
She was wailing and sobbing,   4484
for the wicked man
had dragged her to the ground,
and had her stripped to her chemise.

Three knights held her tightly by the arms,   4488
while their leader beat her so viciously
with a hawthorn branch
that scarcely an inch
of her skin remained intact.   4492
She was loudly imploring Christ to help her.
Gerard saw clearly what was happening,
and galloped that way,
shouting words of encouragement to her.   4496
He told the men to leave her in peace,
and for the love of God,
to stop torturing her.
Durlus heard what he said and paused.   4500
With a smirk, he turned his head
to look at Gerard and sneered:
"Audigier, is that you,
come to avenge her?[37]   4504
When you've left us,
I think you'll carry off a reward
like the one she's just received."
Gerard replied: "Politeness is pointless,   4508
that much is clear. But trust me:
when we're done, it won't take long
for you and your men
to divide up *your* spoils!   4512
Leave the lady alone!
I won't allow this abuse to continue.
If you persist, we must fight."
The men heard Gerard and didn't hestitate.   4516
Each man went straight to his horse,
thrust his foot into the stirrup and mounted.
They left the lady behind,
in the middle of the path,   4520
as they spurred their horses
and raced toward Gerard,
who rushed to meet them!
They swore on Christ's death   4524
and on their very own eyes,
to tear him to shreds.
(But as the saying goes,
a threatened man isn't dead yet!)   4528
Ever alert, Gerard seized his shield,
lowered his lance, and struck
the broad targe of their leader,
who was so deceitful and bold.   4532
He sliced straight through the man's shield.

A pig at slaughter isn't split more neatly
than that awful man was
from Gerard's blow!   4536
His soul departed, and his body fell.
All three of his companions yelled
"Traitor! By God, you'll die for this!"
Gerard, accustomed to fighting   4540
and battle-hardened, rushed to face them,
his sword at the ready.
He struck one who was retreating,
cutting off his arm; the man fell   4544
right there, in the meadow.
But this blow cost Gerard dear,
for two of his adversaries
had wounded him badly   4548
in the thigh and in the side.
Gerard bravely attacked them once again,
splitting open the head of one;
the other man then turned and fled.   4552
Gerard returned to the lady,
had her get dressed
and then mount one of the horses.
They rode off, not stopping   4556
until they reached
the wounded knight,
who was still lying there, motionless.
When he saw his wife,   4560
his face was transformed by joy.
The happiness he felt
made him forget all about his pain.
Gerard dismounted and bandaged   4564
the man's head and side
with a wimple that the fair lady
had removed from her head.
Gerard then asked him   4568
if he felt able to ride:
"I'll carry you on my own horse,
which I greatly prize, until I find
a town where I can leave you,   4572
for you need a doctor."
"My lord, may God reward you for that!
In his name, I thank you.
But I have a manor house nearby,   4576
about a league from here, or less.
One of my cousins is looking after the property.
If you take me there, I'll be in good hands.

And if I recover, 4580
you'll never lack for help
should you have need of me."
Gerard got him onto the horse,
then (of course!) he himself mounted. 4584
The three of them rode along together,
the lady in front, and the two men following.
As they left the woods,
they came upon Monglai, the castle 4588
that belonged to the wounded knight.
It was situated in a field, alongside a lake.
They rode over the bridge and through
the gate, then halted in the courtyard. 4592
Everyone who heard them came running.
When they saw that their lord
was wounded, they were distraught,
though they found comfort 4596
in Gerard's presence.
They soon carried their lord inside
and put him to bed. Afterwards,
they returned to welcome Gerard properly 4600
and keep him company.
They served him well
throughout the evening
and until the following day dawned. 4604
Gerard, however, had no wish to linger there.
He rose early and donned proper gear,
then took his leave
of the wounded knight. 4608
Pleas and prayers
couldn't change his mind.
Astride his horse,
he resumed his wanderings, 4612
travelling over plains
and through forests filled with wild beasts.
He rode for several days,
never staying long in one place, 4616
looking high and low for Euriaut,
asking, day in and day out,
for news of his beloved.
He was grieved by his lack of success, 4620
and yet, the mere thought of Euriaut
brought with it the desire to sing.
This he did, and with a will:
    Oh God! Oh Love! It's so hard to forgo 4624
    the sweet comfort of her company and

the loving words she would say to me,
my lady, my companion, my adored.
When I reflect on her nobility,   4628
her sweet looks and radiant visage,
how does my heart continue beating?
Why does it not break? What torment this is!
Thus, Gerard rode along singing.   4632
He travelled a great distance that day,
eventually finding himself in lands
that were utterly barren.
No crops had been sown;   4636
vast fields and abundant woods
were all that remained.
The most beautiful vineyard
from there to Constantinople grew   4640
along the banks of the great river,
which was broader
than a bolt could fly,
when shot from a crossbow.   4644
A bridge spanned it and, truth to tell,
a finer one has never been seen.
At the foot of the bridge was a castle,
the most secure and well-situated   4648
anyone could ever hope to see,
with towers, ramparts, and opulent rooms.
No emperor or prince ever possessed
a more delightful abode, nor I imagine,   4652
will there ever be another
as sumptuous, imposing, and secure.
But Gerard saw no outlying structures:
no cottages, houses, or manors.   4656
Beyond the castle walls, nothing remained,
for everything had been burned to the ground
or demolished, and no ships or barges
sailed along the swift-flowing river.   4660
Gerard was astonished to find
the entire region so devastated,
for it had obviously once been prosperous.
He caught sight of a noble-looking squire   4664
mounted on a large, dark-grey hunter.
The man was riding rapidly in his direction
and Gerard rode to meet him.
After they had exchanged greetings,   4668
Gerard asked the name of this castle
that was so imposing and so fine.
The squire made haste to reply,

exclaiming, "Take care, my lord! 4672
In the name of God, flee this place at once!
No man, however brave,
is safe around here!"
"Why is that, my friend? 4676
I don't see why a man
should be afraid to stop here.
Tell me the reason!
And tell me why 4680
all the surrounding land
has been laid waste."
"My lord," the squire replied, "listen.
The chateau you see here, 4684
whose walls are so high,
used to be called 'Happily Situated'.
But just over six years ago,
its name was changed due to events 4688
that occurred at that time.
Within the chateau, once filled
with all good things, nothing remains.
A giant named Brudaligan has destroyed it all. 4692
He set fire to everything,
wreaking utter havoc and reducing the land
to such a sorry state that every house
outside the chateau walls 4696
was burned to a cinder.
For obvious reasons,
everyone now calls it
'The Chateau of the Lost Isles'. 4700
Unless you have a solid guarantee
of safe conduct, go no further, noble lord!
But if you absolutely must ride this way,
turn to the left to avoid danger. 4704
The giant, may God punish him,
spares no one;
he seizes everyone
and throws them into prison. 4708
And I'll tell you why
he keeps them locked up.
Every three years,
a ghastly illness wracks him; 4712
he would die in such agony
that anyone who witnessed it
would be appalled. Do you know how
he alleviates the pain? By eating men! 4716
That's the way his illness,

which lasts for forty days, is cured.
It's unwise to linger here.
If he finds you, you'll be taken prisoner.   4720
I've now told you all there is to know."
The squire had gone on at great length,
and when Gerard looked up,
he saw a knight riding forth   4724
from the castle,
his head enveloped in a cloak.
Gerard rode to meet him,
and as he got closer, he saw   4728
a lady ride out after the knight;
behind her rode a beautiful maiden.
I don't think a lovelier,
nobler one ever lived,   4732
though she was extremely unhappy
and was quietly weeping.
Her father and mother
made her ride between them;   4736
they, too, were crying.
Folk from the castle came
running after them, weeping
and wailing so pitifully   4740
that anyone who saw them,
unless they were made of stone,
would have been compelled
to grieve as well.   4744
Wasting no time, Gerard
galloped to meet them
and found both the knight
and the lady in tears.   4748
The maiden, sighing
and sobbing most pitifully,
bewailed her grief.
Gerard saw that their people   4752
were also suffering cruelly.
He greeted the knight courteously
and was given as cordial a reply
as the knight could muster.   4756
When Gerard asked
what had caused such anguish
to everyone there,
the knight, full of sorrow   4760
and grief, began to explain.
"My lord, it's a long story,
but if you wish to hear it,

I'll tell it all to you.   4764
There is a fearsome giant in these parts
who seizes whatever he wants.
No one he captures can escape!
He has already seized   4768
more than two thousand men.
I have seven sons, all of them knights,
and the giant has taken them all.
But I've reached an agreement with him.   4772
I've made peace,
though I hated to do it,
for I must give him my daughter.
She's to wait for him by that tree   4776
until he brings back my sons.
Then the giant will take her away,
may God punish him for it!"
Gerard replied: "I swear to you, my lord,   4780
this won't happen without a fight!
But I need armor and equipment.
Send someone to find gear for me!"
"It's no use, my lord," said the knight,   4784
"for God help me, he fears neither battle
nor assault. His strength is so great
that he's afraid of nothing.
He could vanquish an entire army!"   4788
Gerard replied, "It pains me
that you reject my offer.
Only loan me some armor
and I'll go with the girl.   4792
God willing, I'll protect her
from this evil, brutal giant."
And so, the knight sent a squire
to get the armor.   4796
There was none better
or sturdier, handsomer
or more suitable, from there to Parma.
The men brought weapons, too,   4800
and armed Gerard magnificently,
as was appropriate for battle.
His aventail, however, remained open,
and he rode off with his helmet unlaced.   4804
Soon the whole party drew close to the tree.
The knight, filled with grief
and anger, led his daughter there,
commending her to Gerard's care.   4808
Compelled to leave her,

he tearfully kissed her goodbye.
Her mother, distraught, fainted repeatedly.
Her heart nearly broke.   4812
when she left the girl.
The knight and all his people
returned to the castle, and then Gerard
and the lovely girl rode swiftly to the tree.   4816
When they came to a marble mounting block,
they dismounted and sat down on it.
Gerard was troubled
when he saw the lady's deep distress: 4820
"Ah, sweet, noble friend,
cease your grieving and take comfort!
For if God, the sovereign king,
wills it, the giant   4824
will soon be dead and gone."
As they were conversing,
they looked up and saw the giant
who was laying waste to the land.   4828
He was stomping towards them,
leading the sons of the lord,
all seven of them in chains.
When the maiden saw the giant,   4832
her heart nearly stopped beating,
such was the terror, grief, and despair she felt.
Surely death would be preferable to this!
Waiting no longer, Gerard jumped up.   4836
Valor coursed through his veins
as he fastened his aventail.
The maiden handed him his helmet,
which he strapped on; then he mounted.   4840
"Don't worry, my lady!
Hand me the shield and lance.
Not even for the city of Valence
would I fail to fight this giant!   4844
I'll destroy his pride
or perish in the attempt!
One of us must die.
Please pray that God will help us."   4848
(You should have seen the giant
bounding toward Gerard!
What a fierce battle it will be
between these two!)   4852
When the giant saw that Gerard
dared to wait for him, he seethed with rage,
though he was not the least bit afraid.

Iron and steel didn't faze him at all! 4856
He was protected by a fine leather garment
made of dragon skin.
Gerard drew back some distance
for the giant was indeed huge. 4860
When Brudaligan saw this,
he grasped his club and prepared to attack.
(Now the battle will begin!)
Gerard galloped toward him, 4864
rapidly spurring his horse.
When he got close, he lowered his lance
and with a well-aimed blow
struck the giant in the chest. 4868
The sharp steel ripped through the leather,
leaving a wide tear.
With his mace, the giant whacked
the broad surface of Gerard's shield. 4872
The blow would have caused great harm
had Gerard not swerved aside just in time,
for the weapon was made of heavy wood.
The mace came down with a thud, 4876
narrowly missing the neck of Gerard's horse,
and lodging a foot deep in the ground.
The giant was furious
that he hadn't slain Gerard! 4880
Gerard sped toward him,
spurring on his horse.
He struck the giant in the same place
where he had hit him before, 4884
but this time the steel of his lance
pierced the giant's spine.
The giant quickly retaliated,
hitting Gerard's helmet and shattering it. 4888
(This was not child's play.
Whatever Brudaligan hit,
hit the ground!)
He struck the pommel of Gerard's saddle, 4892
shattering it. Had Gerard received the blow,
he would have been a dead man.
When he found himself on the ground
and his horse dead, 4896
Gerard's face darkened with rage.
He jumped up and seized his shield.
Guillaume Fierebras himself
never clasped one better or more beautiful![38] 4900
Not since the time of Abel

has anyone seen a knight
wield a shield so skillfully
to protect himself in a fight.   4904
Gerard had good reason
to fear his adversary,
who was advancing toward him,
but he was ready. Sword drawn,   4908
he rushed ahead,
drawing back his weapon.
He stabbed the giant's dragonskin garb,
plunging his sword a whole foot into his side.   4912
Brudaligan struck back,
landing a hard blow with his club,
but then he fell face down on the hill
and the great mace   4916
escaped his grasp.
Gerard ran over to him
and pinned him down.
Before he could rise,   4920
Gerard hurt him badly,
inflicting three grievous head wounds
from which the blood ran down
into the giant's eyes.   4924
Gerard took the mace, then sheathed his sword.
Suddenly, the giant jumped up
and lunged at Gerard!
With his bare fist, he landed such a blow   4928
that he almost knocked Gerard senseless.
He bore down on Gerard anew,
taking hold of his shield
and ripping it from his neck.   4932
He swung the shield
and hit Gerard in the chest,
landing such a powerful blow
that he was knocked flat.   4936
The giant's eyes were so filled with blood
that he couldn't see, but he fought on.
The maiden and all her brothers
keeled over in a swoon,   4940
for they were quite sure
that Gerard had been killed.
But Gerard jumped up, eager
to avenge himself if he could.   4944
He moved toward the giant,
raised the mace with both hands
and made his move,

hitting with such force   4948
that he cracked the giant's skull,
spilling his brains. Mortally wounded,
Brudaligan fell to the ground, dead.
As he collapsed, he emitted such a roar   4952
that it could be heard
more than a league away.
A gigantic litter, some twelve feet long,
would be needed to cart him away.   4956
The seven knights,
along with their sister,
were overjoyed to see the giant dead
and didn't hesitate to show their happiness,   4960
though they were grieved to see
how badly Gerard had been wounded.
The lovely, sweet maiden wept for pity,
and they all feared for his life.   4964
They helped Gerard onto a palfrey,
then rode toward the castle.
When those within
saw them approaching,   4968
they rushed out,
their elation a wonder to behold.
Everyone was overcome with joy,
welcoming Gerard with open arms,   4972
as well they should!
The lord of the castle
was particularly solicitous.
He had Gerard brought into the great hall,   4976
where his armor was carefully removed.
Then they placed around his neck
a short cloak of silk, lined with squirrel fur.
He remained indoors for three full days,   4980
during which time they had him bathe
and saw to his every need.
The lord of the castle
was the most attentive of all.   4984
After a time, Gerard made a request of him;
he wished to be on his way
and asked for the loan of a horse.
The lord replied: "You shall have one right away,   4988
large and swift, powerful and strong.
But first let me ask you to stay.
The horse is yours, and by the holy paternoster,
I ask nothing else of you!"   4992
Gerard quickly replied:

"My lord, do not take it amiss
that I cannot stay any longer.
I've undertaken a mission   4996
and would be greatly to blame
if I neglected to accomplish it."
The lord replied: "Then I'll do as you ask."
They went downstairs and the lord sent for a horse,   5000
a fine one, darker than blackberries.
Gerard wasted no time.
Girding on his sword, he mounted
and sat astride the horse.   5004
The daughter of the lord came running,
for she had just heard the news.
The lovely girl wore only her bliaut.
It was unbelted, and her head was bare,   5008
save for a simple circlet of gold.
(Here I'd like to say again that her hair
was blonder and shone more brightly
than the golden circlet on her head.   5012
That, at least, is my opinion!)
The fresh color of her cheeks
was more luminous than a rose
on a May morning, setting off   5016
the whiteness of her skin.
Her eyes were large and grey green.
When she appeared before them,
the very air sparkled with her beauty.   5020
Her body was well proportioned,
as were her hands and arms.
She had raised her skirt a bit,
and you could see her little feet,   5024
small and white, nicely formed,
and clean. One toe was scraped
and bleeding; she had injured it
while hurrying to see Gerard.   5028
She was beside herself when she found him
already on his horse, and rushed forward,
for Love held her in its power.
Grabbing hold of the reins, she pleaded: 5032
"Have pity, my lord!
Be merciful and do not kill me!
I love you and yearn for you,
but I dared not speak   5036
until you were healed!
I thought you would be
staying with us for a long time."

Gerard replied: "I swear to you   5040
that I can remain here no longer,
and so I ask your leave to go."
He asked everyone to grant him leave,
and they all commended him to God,   5044
except for the young lady, who hesitated.
To hide her distress,
she began to sing in a pure voice,
as though for her own amusement.   5048
It was an attempt
to divert attention from herself:
   Alas, however shall I survive?
   How on earth can I remain alive,   5052
   when the very one I wished to love
   spurns me and won't listen to a word
   I say? I find no comfort anywhere,
   but must bear the pain that torments me.   5056
   It conquers me and makes me tremble,
   yet I'll derive no joy from another!
Gerard heard her song,
but did not delay his departure.   5060
He rode swiftly through the gate
and over the bridge,
thinking all the while of Euriaut.
Because of the maiden's song,   5064
which was so beautiful,
he himself felt an urge to sing.
And so, he lifted his voice, strong and pure:
   I would have had some fun with love,   5068
   had I chosen to stay behind!
Before he had finished the song,
he caught sight of the chateau
of Pont-à-Mousson, situated on   5072
the banks of a wide and deep river.
He rode over the bridge
and through the gate, thinking to himself
that he would stay in town to see   5076
if there were any news of Euriaut,
whom he had been seeking for so long.
He asked a widowed lady
for lodging that night.   5080
"Most willingly, my lord,"
she replied. "By Saint Herbert!
You'll have all you need
of good food and a good bed.   5084
Everything will be the way you like it."

Gerard dismounted and thanked her.
Servants led his horse to the stable
and gave it oats and hay,   5088
while the lady, who knew
how to welcome a guest,
led Gerard upstairs,
to a very pleasant room.   5092
There she told him stories
and entertained him until supper was ready.
An abundance of delicious roast fowl
and fresh fish was served.   5096
Later, the beds were prepared
and everyone retired for the evening.
Gerard's thoughts, in turmoil,
kept him awake all night.   5100
In the morning, he rose early,
for he couldn't bear
to remain there any longer.
As soon as his horse was saddled   5104
and made ready, he took his leave
of the lady, as a courteous,
well-mannered person should do.
He mounted and rode swiftly   5108
through the city gate,
praying that God would set him
on the path that led to his lady.
He repeated this prayer   5112
as he rode through wide, open fields,
the terrain beautiful and even.
After a time, he saw a great company
of knights riding along.   5116
He rode their way to greet them
and they returned his salutation most cordially,
for they saw that he was both handsome
and well-equipped.   5120
They began to ride together,
but before they had gone very far,
Gerard asked where they were going.
(If they're willing to tell him,   5124
he'd certainly like to know!)
"My lord," said one of the knights,
a most courteous and well-spoken man,
"we've no wish to hide the information.   5128
The truth is, we're going to Metz
to render a verdict. I'll tell you all about it,
just as it was told to me.

It's a true story.   5132
Two years ago, the Duke of Metz
was returning home from Compostela.
Quite by chance, as he was traveling
through the wilds of Burgundy, he found,   5136
deep in the woods, the most beautiful creature
ever fashioned by Nature.
The duke took her with him,
but never enjoyed her favors,   5140
because his men forbade it.
They were quite upset about
his infatuation with her.
I think he would have married the woman   5144
despite their objections,
had she not viciously murdered his sister.
Today a verdict is to be rendered.
She'll be tortured, burned at the stake,   5148
her ashes scattered to the winds."
When Gerard heard these words
he was, on the one hand, overjoyed,
for he knew this had to be Euriaut;   5152
but on the other, he was deeply distressed,
for he knew how cruelly she had suffered.
He vowed to let himself
be drawn and quartered   5156
if he didn't rescue her!
If she died, he'd no longer want to live.
They rode along in silence,
until Metz came clearly into view.   5160
Outside the city, in the middle of a field,
they saw the flames of a great pyre.
The duke and his noblemen were all there.
They had brought Euriaut,   5164
who was to be burned in the fire,
and had made her stand on a cloth,
stripped to her chemise.
She saw the punishment that awaited her,   5168
but little did she suspect
that help was close at hand.
(Such amazing good fortune
will never befall another woman!)   5172
Here came Gerard,
galloping across the field
ahead of all the other knights,
hurtling towards the pyre!   5176
He reached Euriaut

just as she was saying a prayer,
imploring Jesus Christ.
She prayed aloud,   5180
so that all could hear:[39]
"True God, who created the world
and caused the air of the earth to rise,
you put angels in heaven,   5184
fashioning them as spiritual beings,
marvelously beautiful. But Lucifer,
enamored of his own beauty,
grew proud, and for this reason   5188
you deprived them of your glory, dear God.
You cast out the proud ones,
consigned them to Hell and filled it up.
To carry out your law,   5192
you fashioned other angels,
more beautiful than Lucifer once was,
and with your own hands you created
Adam and then Eve, his wife,   5196
and commanded them
to watch over Paradise.
You gave them everything
except the fruit of an apple tree,   5200
which you forbade them to eat.
But at wicked Satan's urging,
Eve made Adam eat of it, and then,
dear Lord, their eyes were opened   5204
and they saw that they were naked.
An angel came swiftly and drew a sword,
banishing them from Paradise,
and barring their return.   5208
You brought them a spade, a staff,
and a spindle for work, Lord,
and later they had to endure
great suffering in Hell   5212
with the devil, Lucifer.
When souls were parted from bodies,
they used to go straight to Hell.
Not once, Lord, in five thousand years,   5216
did anyone die who did not suffer
the torments of Hell until, true God,
you at last took pity on them.
Sweet Lord, by the holy angel Gabriel,   5220
you sent word to the Virgin in the sanctuary,
that you would hide yourself in her,
taking on humanity there.

When Mary heard the news,   5224
she was both joyful and troubled.
She carried you, almighty God,
for nine months and gave birth
on Christmas day.   5228
When you were born, a lady came,
an excellent woman named Onestasse.
She had no hands, only stumps,[40]
but when she was to hold you, dear Lord,   5232
you instantly made her whole,
with hands as beautiful and white as linen.
In Bethlehem, a star appeared,
and when the three kings saw it,   5236
they left their far-away lands
and came to search for you, dear Lord.
They arrived in Herod's land,
and he gave them lodging.   5240
Each of the kings told him
they were searching for a child;
they knew not where, but in the East.
A star was leading them, guiding their way: 5244
"We're certain he is the Lord of the world."
Filled with anger, wicked Herod
told the kings they should go
and adore this child, then return to him.   5248
The kings departed and followed
the star until they found you,
dear Lord, in Bethlehem,
outside he walls of Jerusalem.   5252
They offered you gold,
myrrh, and frankincense,
and then began their journey home.
You saved them from Herod's power,   5256
leading them back by different paths.
When the wicked man found out,
he was enraged, and ordered that
all the baby boys in his lands   5260
be beheaded.[41] Sweet Lord,
for thirty-two years you went
throughout the country preaching.
One day, on Palm Sunday   5264
(thus Scripture relates it to us),
you came to the holy city.
Overcome by pity, sweet Lord,
you wept; this is what we read.   5268
When you arrived, riding a donkey,

the gates opened before you.
The people followed you,
true God, some hoping for food,   5272
others to hear you preach,
yet others to mock you.
Wicked Judas sold you
to the infidels, who arrested you.   5276
On holy Friday, dear Lord,
you were hung on the Cross;
on it your limbs were stretched out
and nailed. With sharp thorns,   5280
worthy King, your head
was crowned on the Cross.
Longinus, a blind man, was brought to you,
sweet Lord. He struck you, opening   5284
your side and piercing your heart.
Your bright blood flowed
down the lance and onto his hands.
He wiped his eyes with it,   5288
then saw you clearly.
He begged for mercy and was pardoned.
To your right, a thief had been hung
who begged you for mercy;   5292
Lord, his reward for this is great,
for his soul is now in Paradise.
There was another thief to your left,
but he didn't deign to ask for mercy.   5296
Now he has a most terrible reward,
for the devil made off with his soul.
Joseph, who had served Pilate
for seven years, wanted no other recompense   5300
than to take your body down and lay it
in the sepulcher, where you were to be placed.
On the third day you rose from the dead.
You descended straight into Hell,   5304
sweet Lord, where you broke down the gates
and brought forth your friends.
The devil had placed them there,
and they had suffered most cruelly.   5308
Lord, you first appeared
to Mary Magdalene and then
to your beloved apostles.
But Saint Thomas, who doubted,   5312
put his finger in your side
before he would believe it was you.
By this act he made our faith greater,

Lord, for those who truly seek you, 5316
though they see you not,
will receive your blessing.
On the Thursday of your Ascension,
Lord, you appeared to your apostles, 5320
then rose to holy Paradise
with your blessed angels.
On Pentecost you came
to comfort your apostles 5324
when they were afraid.
Lord God, as I have told the truth,
may you receive my soul, for I swear
that Ysmaine did not suffer death, 5328
injury, or pain by my hand!
Have mercy on my soul, Lord,
for my bodily life will now end."
Then she said the Lord's Prayer. 5332
Gerard, who was close by,
now approached the fire.
When he saw his beloved weeping,
his heart was filled with sorrow. 5336
He went straight to the duke
and said to him: "Hear me, my lord!
Tell me the reason why
you are holding this lady here." 5340
"In truth, my lord, she is accused
of a most brutal murder," replied the duke.
"It isn't right to let her go,
for she has killed my sister." 5344
Gerard replied: "If anyone claims
that she is guilty of this crime,
I'm ready right now to prove them wrong!
Hear what I say!" 5348
Meliatir approached and said:
"Sir, we care nothing
for your proposed defense.
Word of this crime has spread so widely 5352
that this woman will not be helped by you,
nor will any combat for her be fought.
She's to be burned
and put to death here and now! 5356
That said, I'm not the least bit afraid to fight you.
Your threats aren't worth a counterfeit coin![42]
You are foolish and perverse
to make such a boast." 5360
"Silence, my lord," said the duke.

"I want to settle this according to the law.
I'll not have her killed
before a judgment has been reached."   5364
He summoned his advisors and told them
to "confer together and render a just verdict.
I don't want to commit a sin."
His twelve advisors, all elegantly attired,   5368
then withdrew to take counsel
and reach a decision.
After many fine words and speeches,
they at last agreed that two of them   5372
would pronounce the judgment,
and whatever those two should decide
would be upheld by them all.
The two men who were chosen   5376
accepted the responsibility.
One of them was the lord of Lansi,
the other was the lord of Aspremont.
No other knight in all the world   5380
knew more about legal procedure
than Aspremont; he was a handsome man,
and very able. The lord of Lansi,
who was also very learned,   5384
leaned on his staff, and began:
"My lords, listen to me now.
This woman, who was discovered
in the act, was taken as she was found,   5388
still holding the knife with which
she had killed the maiden.
What's more, witnesses attest that
the blade was in the girl's body,   5392
and that this woman's hand
was wrapped around the handle.
Who would not judge that,
having been found like this,   5396
she had not committed the murder?
These facts and this visual evidence
clearly prove that anyone discovered
in such circumstances cannot be defended   5400
in combat or under law. I stand by the opinion
that, for justice to be served,
she must be found guilty,
condemned to torture and burned.   5404
If anyone thinks otherwise, I won't object.
I'm quite willing to hear him out.
It isn't fitting for us

to quarrel or fight.   5408
You may rest assured
that I won't tolerate any maliciousness
in these deliberations.
I swear by Saint Jacques of Compostela   5412
that I wouldn't pronounce a false judgment
for all of Metz—or even half of it!"
He was a clever speaker
and knew how to provoke debate.   5416
He was also a relative of Meliatir's.
When he had finished speaking,
he fell silent, and I'll tell you why:
he didn't want anyone to think   5420
he was being partial to Meliatir.
The lord of Aspremont
then rose to his feet.
"My lords," he said, "listen now   5424
to what I have to say.
A man who judges a case
acts badly when he wrongs someone,
for it is a sin to lie   5428
or to condemn someone
to death without just cause.
You have heard the arguments
made by the lord of Lansi: 5432
the woman was found
still holding the knife
that had been plunged into Ysmaine's breast,
right up to the handle.   5436
Here's what I think.
Had this woman stabbed her,
she would have fled immediately.
Do you believe she'd have fallen asleep?   5440
Surely, she would never
have done anything so reckless!
It is perfectly clear that,
had she committed such an act,   5444
she would have run away,
and yet she was found right there,
sleeping soundly. You can be sure
she didn't stab her while she herself was asleep,   5448
and I have absolutely no doubt that
had she stabbed her while she was awake,
she would have run away immediately.
I'd be utterly astonished   5452
had she remained there!

The law requires us to go to her
and ask her whether she committed this murder.
If she says she's innocent, let Meliatir,   5456
whom I just heard boasting about his prowess,
take up his shield and lance,
for she already has a champion.
I readily concede that the responsibility   5460
for deciding the outcome of this case
should rest with him.
And may God exonerate
the young woman if she's innocent!"   5464
They all swore by the heavenly king
that they accepted this decision,
and then approached the duke
to apprise him of it.   5468
When the duke had heard them,
he sent for Euriaut,
and began to question her,
asking her to tell them why   5472
she had so wantonly dared
to kill his sister. Euriaut,
whom distress had turned
yellower than tallow, replied: 5476
"My lord, if you will permit it,
I offer to undergo trial by ordeal."
Gerard said, "I won't allow her,
my lord, to undergo such a trial.   5480
But if anyone feels brave enough
to fight for her,
let him come forward!
I'm ready and able to defend the lady."   5484
"I'll certainly not fail to fight you,"
replied Meliatir,
"and may the best man win!
I ask for nothing better!   5488
If someone offered me twice
the silver in the exchequer to stay
my sword, I wouldn't take it.
You'll all see how well I fight!"   5492
"What a braggart you are!"
exclaimed Gerard.
"Before this day is over,
you'll find yourself in very hot water!   5496
I'm ready for combat,
if someone will loan me armor."
The lord of Aspremont replied,

"By heaven, I'll loan you 5500
the weapons myself!"
Gerard dismounted
and quickly donned the armor.
Euriaut, who was calling on Jesus, 5504
had not yet recognized Gerard.
Meliatir was also getting ready.
He was furious that Euriaut
hadn't yet been burned! 5508
The spectators drew to one side
of the beautiful meadow,
which was now surrounded by knights.
Euriaut stood next to the pyre. 5512
Gerard, deeply pained by the sight,
called out to Meliatir:
"Knight, be it known:
I'm challenging you! 5516
We'll soon see which of us will win!"
Unimpressed, Meliatir clutched
the strap of his shield.
Then, the two men spurred their horses, 5520
lowered the iron tips of their lances,
and came together with such force
that their lances splintered like bark
and fell to pieces. 5524
Bodies and shields collided,
shields snapped and shattered,
but the riders held their seats.
Each man unsheathed his sword. 5528
(If I spent all today and tomorrow, too,
I still wouldn't have time
to describe every blow!)
Wielding their well-honed blades, 5532
they rushed forward,
each man eagerly striking
his opponent's gleaming helmet.
The blows they exchanged 5536
continued hard and fast, for both men
were completely intent on the fight.
Meliatir, brave and proud,
smoldered with rage and fury. 5540
He struck Gerard's helmet,
tearing off a good quarter of it.
Had the blow not been deflected,
nothing could have saved him. 5544
The sword came down on Gerard's left side,

slicing his shield in two,
but he escaped, his flesh untouched.
Meliatir, certain he had dealt   5548
a mortal blow, cried out:
"I'll show you how foolish it is
to risk your life for another!"
Gerard heard every word,   5552
but remained silent;
he had no wish to argue.
He gripped his steel sword
and struck a powerful blow   5556
to the traitor's helmet,
tearing through the visor.
His sword kept moving,
for the stroke had been well aimed: 5560
Meliatir's chin and half of his nose
were sliced away.[43] The blow came down
in front of the pommel,
chopping the horse's neck   5564
like a cabbage leaf.
The beast fell, throwing its rider to the ground.
In a ringing voice, Gerard called out to Meliatir:
"Sir knight, curb your anger now!   5568
Loose talk is dangerous,
or so I've heard! It's base to quarrel,
and madness to make threats!
Surely you can see   5572
which of us is going to win."
Meliatir was distraught;
he almost lost his mind
when he realized how disfigured he was,   5576
and swore by all the nails in the Cross
that he'd soon be avenged.
Gerard rode a short distance away
and dismounted. It wouldn't be right for him   5580
to confront his opponent while he was still riding.
When he thought of his sweetheart,
his strength intensified.
He moved toward Meliatir,   5584
who was edging toward him,
and then the swordplay began.
Neither man spared the other.
They cracked helmets and shattered shields,   5588
and with their steel blades tore holes
in each other's cuirasses,
hauberks, and padded vests.

Both men were cut to the bone, 5592
but both were brave and strong.
They continued to slash away, ripping through
one another's shields and helmets.
(No one had ever seen such a fight!) 5596
They made sparks fly from helmets,
and tore through the laces.
So great was the suffering on both sides
that those who were watching them 5600
said it was a miracle they were still alive.
Meliatir, though seriously wounded,
pulled back as far as he could,
then lunged at Gerard, 5604
hitting his helmet with such force
that Gerard was stunned and fell to his knees.
The knights all said
that Meliatir was truly valiant, 5608
for he had seriously injured Gerard.
Furious, Gerard jumped up
and raised his shield.
He knew how to wield a sword! 5612
He landed a skillful blow
between Meliatir's shield and his side,
slicing off his adversary's arm.
Meliatir staggered, and Gerard, 5616
putting all his strength behind the blow,
hit him with his shield, knocking him flat.
He jumped on top of his foe and
pounded him so vigorously with his sword 5620
that he knocked off Meliatir's helmet
and then yanked down his coif.
Meliatir didn't remain silent,
but instead cried out: "Wait, vassal! 5624
Call the duke, so that he may listen,
and I'll confess the truth."
The guards heard him, and had
the duke and the Count of Bar-le-Duc 5628
summoned at once.
Meliatir told them everything,
omitting not one word:
how he had gone after Euriaut, 5632
and how he had murdered
the duke's sister as she slept.
When he heard these words,
the duke swore by Saint Amand 5636
that he would have the count

dragged by horses and hanged.
He made sure that Gerard was helped to his feet,
then had Meliatir tied to the tale of a mare   5640
and shamefully dragged to the gallows.
There he was hanged and
received his just reward.
The duke then rode over to Gerard,   5644
dismounted, and extended
his heartiest congratulations.
Euriaut's clothes were brought
and she put them back on.   5648
The duke and Gerard mounted,
along with Euriaut and the barons,
and they all hurried back to Metz,
straight to the great palace.   5652
They soon helped Gerard to remove
his armor, and then his wounds
were examined and bandaged.
After the servants had taken away his gear,   5656
they dressed him elegantly in a fine cotte
and cloak, a belt, hat, and clasp,
with a garland of bright red roses for his head.
Euriaut looked at him in wonder.   5660
Trembling with astonishment,
she recognized Gerard at last.
All color drained from her face.
Then she said: "Heavenly Father,   5664
what shall I do? Shall I go to him,
or shall I wait and see if he comes to me?
But I'm sure he never will.
He cares nothing for me."   5668
She abruptly rose, went to him,
and knelt. Her face wet with tears,
she begged him to be merciful.
Deeply pained to see her weeping   5672
so piteously, Gerard raised her up,
and gave her a hundred kisses.
The duke, along with all the others,
were dumbfounded by what they saw,   5676
for they knew nothing about
what these two had endured.
Then, Gerard said to his beloved:
"Beautiful one, don't cry anymore!   5680
You have my love! Lisiart tricked you,
and therefore wrongly holds my land.
But I'll get it back, God willing,

and if I live long enough."   5684
The duke, eager to learn the truth
about what had happened,
immediately sat down
next to Gerard and asked him,   5688
if he was willing and able,
to tell him his name
and to what family he belonged.
Gerard told him the whole story,   5692
and when the duke had heard it,
he was delighted to learn
that he and Gerard were related.
Gerard was his nephew, his sister's son.[44]   5696
Euriaut, who had suffered so greatly
and for so long, joyfully began
to sing this song,
her voice sweet and pure: 5700
    I have regained my joy by loving well!
As soon as she had finished,
she told Gerard the story
of how she lost his ring.   5704
"Sweetheart," he replied,
"I have good news for you!
The ring will once again be yours."
Then he told her all about   5708
the difficulty and the hardships
he had endured while searching for her,
and how he had travelled through many lands
without learning anything about her,   5712
until he caught the lark.
Then he showed her the ring.
At that very moment,
a young man rushed into the room,   5716
lustily singing in a strong, clear voice:
    No one should have a sweetheart,
    or be allowed to love, unless
    it makes him a better man.   5720
When he had finished his song,
he proclaimed: "May God bless
and protect the duke and all his knights!"
The duke didn't stand on ceremony,   5724
and quickly replied: "God be with you,
my friend! Please tell us where you're
from. Do you bring a message for me?"
"Yes, my lord, and it will be welcome   5728
news for all who love fame and glory!

The Count of Alost, who is on his way here,
asks you to find horses and armor
and prepare yourselves right away   5732
to participate in a tournament
that is about to take place in Montgargis.
This is what I've been told.
He has solemnly sworn to be there   5736
to support two well-known noblemen.
The Count of Montfort has enlisted
his aid against the Count of Forez,
coward and traitor that he is!   5740
Forez has done him great wrong,
for he has dishonored Montfort's niece,
who lived in Nevers, causing her
to be banished from the land.   5744
Her lover has taken her away,
and they've been wandering ever since,
wherever fate might lead them.
Now the count, overcome by grief,   5748
has sent a message to all his friends,
urging them to attend the tournament.
It will certainly grieve and shame all those
who are well-disposed toward Montfort,   5752
if their efforts at this tournament
aren't enough to avenge the dishonor,
shame, and pain that Forez
has visited upon Euriaut."   5756
When he heard these words,
Gerard jumped for joy.
The entire court rejoiced and the duke
threw his arms around his nephew's neck.   5760
He summoned his seneschal, lord Nicholas,
and made him swear that the duke
had never succeeded in seducing Euriaut.
Even the promise of great riches   5764
couldn't inspire in her
the desire to be his wife.
Though it had often caused him great suffering,
she steadfastly refused, consistently claiming   5768
that she was a loose woman.
"And I had such a great desire
to marry her," said the duke,
"that I couldn't even look at another!"   5772
When Gerard heard this, he began to laugh.
He forgot all the hardship he had endured,
now that he had found his sweetheart

and she had proven herself so true. 5776
"Dear one," said Euriaut, "by separating us,
that man caused you great suffering.
But your burden will be lifted,
now that you have found me. 5780
Because of the trust you have in me,
and because of my love for you,
you have found solace.
Won't you sing for me now?" 5784
Gerard replied: "Truly, my dearest love,
I would never refuse a request from you,
even if I were offered great riches!"
In a robust voice, he sang this song 5788
straight through to the end:
    I have no need to sing about
    gardens, shady groves, or woodlands.
    When my lady wishes to command, 5792
    I need no better reason to sing!
    I happily relate her worth,
    her radiance and dazzling beauty,
    given her in abundance by God, 5796
    making me forget all others.
Before he had sung this song
through to the end,
the Count of Alost and his retinue 5800
arrived in great splendor.
Their joy was all the greater
when they heard that Gerard was there,
and that he had rescued Euriaut. 5804
The count, also a relative of Gerard's,
took hold of his left hand
and said: "We will all go
to the tournament and fight against 5808
the Count of Forez.
Your prowess means nothing
if you don't avenge yourself
and reclaim your lands from him." 5812
Gerard replied:
"No good ever came
from threats or arguments.
If we attend this gathering, 5816
it will be obvious to all
which of us is in the right.
It irks me that we haven't
already begun to fight! 5820
It's past time for me to avenge myself.

If I have any worth at all,
I'll make him pay for all the anguish
he has made me suffer."   5824
When they had finished talking,
the duke and all the other noblemen
sat down to dine
with Gerard and Euriaut.   5828
The whole court was filled with joy!
Afterwards, they all retired for the night.
The beds in which they were to lie
were most elegantly appointed.   5832
Unable to sleep, Gerard continued thinking
about the tournament until daybreak,
when everyone in the castle began to get ready.
They mounted and soon were on their way,   5836
a hundred knights of tremendous valor,
riding along until (trust me on this!)
they at last reached the home
of the Count of Bar-le-Duc.   5840
He was well acquainted with Gerard's story
and all the suffering the young knight had endured.
The count said: "If Gerard takes my advice,
he will avenge himself at this tournament.   5844
Shame on him if he doesn't make Lisiart suffer
just as he has done!"
To which Gerard replied,
"You needn't worry about that!"   5848
The count ordered his knights
to prepare immediately
to travel to the tournament.
They mounted and set off,   5852
keeping on the road
and hurrying along
until they arrived at Chateau Landon,
where their squires secured lodging for them.   5856
Gerard, who knew how to behave,
offered generous hospitality to all.
The knights gathered in the town
and countryside. That night,   5860
many of the squires had trouble
finding a place to stay and little wonder!
Everyone dressed and adorned
himself as elegantly as he knew how.   5864
The valets, in charge of the weapons,
and the heralds were not idle; they rose
the next morning at the crack of dawn,

crying out, as was their duty: 5868
"Sir knights, it's time for church!
Attend the Mass of the Holy Spirit,
so that God will protect you from harm!
Then lace up your leggings,   5872
for as you well know,
it will then be time to head to the field.
The lark raises its song,
for the sweet season makes it eager,   5876
and the path to the field is long."
When the knights heard these words,
they hurried to get dressed
and head to the church for services.   5880
Afterwards, Gerard's friends suggested
that he leave Euriaut behind, in town.
"Most willingly," he agreed.
Anyone who saw them running to their horses,   5884
lacing up their leggings
and donning their hauberks,
all to the sound of flutes and drums,
would have had a heart of stone   5888
not to feel elated by this thrilling sight.
Gerard wanted to disguise himself
so that no one would recognize him.[45]
He dressed in silk garments,   5892
whiter than snow and patterned
with little flowers,
and around his head he wrapped
the wimple of fair Euriaut.   5896
Then (just for the fun of it, I think),
he attached her ribbon to the border
of his shield. His companions all wore
white battle tunics under their mail,   5900
and their horses had white breastplates.
Thus caparisoned, they sallied forth.
The entire countryside thrummed and roared
with the sound of the forces that were gathering.   5904
The approaching knights looked
just like winged angels!
Even if I talked all day,
I couldn't do justice to the scene,   5908
but I hope you won't mind
if I describe the appearance of those
who came to support each contingent.
On one side, there was the Count of Montfort,   5912
and with him many powerful fighters:

the lords of Brittany and Brienne were there,
and the lord of Rouci,
eager to garner praise   5916
for his skill at arms. There was,
as well, a very rich count
of high and noble birth, generous,
brave and true, and devoid of malice.   5920
This was the Count and lord of Boulogne.
The Count of Ponthieu was also there,
ever worthy and magnanimous.
He was liberality itself.[46]   5924
The lord of Bar came,
along with the lord of Garland,
ever eager to do battle.
The Count of Saint-Pol was there, too.   5928
Whoever wished to oppose these men
would have been a fool,
unless he had powerful reinforcements!
Gerard joined them on the road,   5932
riding ahead of them
farther than an arrow could fly.
They rode along, in orderly fashion,
their lances raised high on the felt supports.   5936
(I'll tell you more about these men in a moment.)
On the opposing side came the Count of Forez,
leading a great and well-armed company.
There was the lord of Bourbon,   5940
and with him many good knights;
also, the lord of Beaujeu, whose prowess,
so they say, couldn't be matched
from there to the Great Saint-Bernard Pass.   5944
The Count of Châlons came,
as well as the count from Beyond-the-Saône,
who never sought excuses when honor was at stake.
The Count of Auvergne was there;   5948
he was a young man, his hair not yet grey.
The Dauphin of Montferrand came,
his large retinue astride grey and white coursers.
The Count of Sancerre,   5952
highly skilled at arms,
was there, and the chatelain of Issoudun .
I'm told there isn't a better knight
from here to Verdun,   5956
or one more fond of battle.
From Grand-Pré came Count Alain;
he, and all those I've named,

rode toward Châtillon-Coligny. 5960
Many a steed with flowing mane could be seen,
and many fine weapons. As for King Louis,
he was seated beneath a hornbeam tree,
surrounded by a great company of knights. 5964
Many of the young men were lined up
before him in double ranks.
You should have seen all the fine horses
and gleaming armor as they prepared for battle! 5968
At the start of the tournament,
a great number of newly made knights did battle.
Then, with a great cry,
Lisiart seized his shield and lance 5972
and galloped between the two ranks.
A herald shouted:
"Whoever wants to be the first
to joust with this man, 5976
present yourself at once!
But I doubt that anyone will dare!
I advise you all to pack up your lances
and your brand-new shields, 5980
for this man isn't the least bit afraid
to fight anyone here."
With that, the Count of Montfort
raised his shield to his chest. 5984
Lisiart will receive quite a blow,
if the count can get to him!
But Gerard knew how steal a march.
Gracefully and quickly, 5988
he adjusted his shield, lowered his lance,
and dug in his spurs.
He raced toward Lisiart with such abandon
that all other activity came to a halt. 5992
Gerard sped forward, overtaking the count.
Lisiart turned toward him and,
with a mighty blow,
smote his painted shield. 5996
So great was the shock,
that Lisiart's lance shattered,
right down to the grip.
Gerard was undeterred, and hit back 6000
high on his opponent's shield.
The entire span of his lance
ripped through it, passing under
Lisiart's chin and striking him 6004
in the throat with such force

that he was thrown to the ground.
Gerard rode past Lisiart in silence,
then shouted out in a strong, clear voice: 6008
"Sir knight, that was for my lady Euriaut!"
But it seemed to him that no one heard his cry.
The tournament started up again, each side gathering
under the appropriate banner.   6012
Many riders were struck down
and their horses then bolted, their reins torn.
All the knights fought valiantly, wielding their
swords and whatever remained of their lances.   6016
You could have seen many heraldic banners
lying trampled on the ground.
Amid the fiercest fighting was Gerard.
He didn't hold back, riding first   6020
in one direction, then another.
Wherever he saw the largest throng, he dove right in,
dealing powerful blows with his sword.
He struck with such ferocity that the men scattered,   6024
though he received his share of blows as well.
Nevertheless, he repeatedly plunged back into the melee,
bearing down on his opponents
and knocking many of them to the ground.   6028
Without realizing it,
he kept crying out: "Euriaut!"
King Louis watched him,
and to the knights who stood nearby, he said: 6032
"This knight will take the highest honors today.
If I'm any judge of prowess,
no man here is his equal.
No wonder people are talking about him;   6036
he's still wearing his helmet!
I see him, time and again,
and at great risk to himself,
join in the fight, rushing to support   6040
and defend his companions."
While the king was speaking,
Gerard looked to his right and saw
the Count of Auvergne and his men;   6044
they had wreaked havoc on several
of the companies that day.
The lord of Bar had distinguished himself,
as had the lord of Garland.   6048
Gerard dug in his spurs.
Everyone watched as he reentered the fight,
and it seemed to all who observed him

that his actions were effortless. 6052
Wherever Gerard attacked,
fighting elsewhere came to a halt.
Whoever wagered a thousand marcs
against him would have lost their bet![47] 6056
Some of his opponents fled in terror,
while others pursued him and did battle.
Many a fine horse met its death that day.
The fighting continued unabated 6060
until nightfall, and Gerard did indeed
take all the honors of the day.
He had captured seven of the best knights,
though not Lisiart, which infuriated him. 6064
He was almost dying of chagrin
for having failed in this.
The tournament ended,
and the king sent a message to Gerard, 6068
asking to see him before he left town.
Gerard didn't hesitate to accept
the king's invitation.
He went into town to find lodgings 6072
and, that evening, offered
such lavish hospitality
that all who heard of it were astounded.
You should have seen all the knights 6076
heading for his lodgings
to find out who he was!
Everyone wanted to make his acquaintance,
if he possibly could. They considered him 6080
to be so very distinguished
that anyone who became his friend,
became more worthy himself.
Those who hadn't seen him in a long time, 6084
and now recognized him, were overjoyed.
So many months had gone by!
They spent the evening celebrating,
and once they had rested, 6088
recovered quickly from the blows
they had received. At daybreak,
Gerard sent for his sweetheart.
He rose, as did the Duke of Metz 6092
and the others, who intended
to go together to court.
There, Gerard planned to accuse
Lisiart publicly of malfeasance, 6096
and thus, of holding his lands illegally.

(If Lisiart gets away with it,
Gerard must consider himself
no more capable than a child.)   6100
At that very moment,
Gerard turned around and saw
his beloved Euriaut approaching.
Unable to hold back,   6104
he rushed to meet and embrace her.
The gathered noblemen
were delighted to watch them!
The church bells rang   6108
and they all went to hear mass.
Afterwards, I believe, they left
the church together as a group.
You should have seen   6112
all the cloth of gold
they wore that day!
Gerard didn't delay;
he eagerly took his sweetheart   6116
by the hand and led her to the court.
His relatives followed,
with Gerard and Euriaut in the lead.
As young Gerard walked along,   6120
he sang this song.
The melody was very fine,
and he enunciated the words clearly,
for he wanted them to be heard: 6124
      I know two people—and yes, I'm one of them!—
      who have suffered greatly because of love.
The king, who had also heard mass,
knew nothing about Gerard's adventures.   6128
He had just left the chapel, and now
summoned his advisor, the lord of Roie.
"Who are those people
I see coming our way,   6132
so elegantly dressed
and in such high spirits?"
"Sire," he replied, "I do not know.
I don't believe I've ever seen them before.   6136
But wait! Unless I'm very much mistaken,
that's the young lord of Nevers,
whom Lisiart caused such grief last year
when won the wager concerning   6140
his beautiful lady friend, Euriaut."
Hearing this, the king raised his eyes
and took a closer look.

Recognizing Gerard, he exclaimed,   6144
"Upon my word, that *is* him!
And that's his lady, wearing clothes
that suit her most admirably.
I think—indeed I'm quite sure—   6148
we're about to hear some news
that Lisiart won't like!"
As Gerard entered the court,
everyone rushed to see him.   6152
He advanced, as was appropriate,
and greeted the king
and all his retinue most courteously.
The king embraced him   6156
and wished him joy.
He was eager to hear
what had happened to Gerard
since he had last seen him at court.   6160
Gerard told him everything:
about all the suffering he had endured
and how he had gone to Nevers
disguised as a minstrel and sung   6164
the four stanzas in the great hall,
where he heard the slanderer Lisiart
admit that he had never had
carnal relations with Euriaut,   6168
and how a wicked old woman
had told him about Euriaut's birthmark.
"I'm prepared to prove
everything I say, for I'm not lying.   6172
He holds my lands wrongfully,
and I'm asking you now for justice."
"I'll send a messenger right away
to summon him," said the king.   6176
"By heaven! He has been very foolish
if he has done such a thing."
The king sent two obliging noblemen
to summon Lisiart to court   6180
and tell him that he must not refuse
and must come immediately.
The men, quiet and competent,
quickly mounted their palfreys,   6184
one piebald, the other grey.
They arrived at Lisiart's lodgings
and announced that the king
was summoning him.   6188
Lisiart called immediately

for his own palfrey,
and hurriedly mounted.
Some sixty of his men did the same, 6192
for they were to accompany him.
All were lords with vast estates,
and every one of them was opulently attired.
They arrived at court, where the king 6196
was seated at the head of a great table.
He held Gerard's hand,
and next to him sat Euriaut.
Lisiart approached. 6200
When he saw Euriaut and Gerard,
he seethed with rage and fury.
However, to hide his feelings
so that no one would perceive 6204
or become aware of them,
he greeted the king,
then Gerard and all the others.
Gerard, who was neither arrogant nor spiteful, 6208
ill-bred nor malicious, leapt to his feet
as the assembled knights looked on.
Splendidly clothed, he turned
to face the king, knowing full well 6212
how to speak wisely and persuasively.
And so, with great eloquence
(for he was quite adept), he began:
"Sire, hear me now! 6216
You and all the noblemen
who are seated here are well aware
that Lisiart, whom I see over there,
challenged me to a wager, 6220
claiming he could seduce my beloved.
I didn't refuse, and even wagered
all my land against his.
He went to woo my lady, 6224
and when he returned,
claimed he'd had his way with her,
and enjoyed her favors.
By speaking of her birthmark, 6228
he won all my lands.
But an old crone named Gondrée,
greedy for gain,
helped him spy on my lady 6232
when she was in her bath.
Thus, the old woman showed him
the birthmark that he later used as evidence.

That is how he tricked me,   6236
injuring me and causing me great harm.
If the count wishes to deny it,
I'm ready to prove beyond any doubt,
in single combat with him,   6240
that he has wronged me in this way.
For I've been to Nevers,
and in the great hall
where I sang four songs, I listened,   6244
and heard the old woman reproach him,
saying that he only won the bet because of her.
The count admitted that it was true,
swearing on the bones of Saint Simon   6248
that he had never enjoyed Euriaut's favors."
Lisiart listened to this speech,
and nearly died of anger and wrath.
He addressed the king: 6252
"Noble Sire, don't believe it!
You know perfectly well that someone
who loses his love and his land
doesn't care at all if he loses his life!   6256
That, at least, is my view.
This knight would like to fight,
and take on anyone willing to respond.
He would do better to hide somewhere   6260
and conceal his shame!
He should never speak of this again."
So said Lisiart. But then,
there slipped from his lips   6264
a most injudicious statement,
foolish and harmful to himself.
(The devil made him do it!)
In the heat of anger, he said: 6268
"Gerard, Gerard! Shame on the king
if he doesn't burn or hang me—
and he has my oath on this—
should I not prove what a coward you are!"   6272
Gerard heard what he said.
He then bent over and folded
the border of his ermine cloak,
which he placed in the king's hands.   6276
Lisiart did not hesitate,
and hurriedly gave his own pledge as well.
The king acted forthwith.
He took hostages from each man   6280
to guarantee what they had undertaken

and made the men promise to produce
the two adversaries promptly on the appointed day.
Thus, they would fulfill their duty.   6284
The king then delivered the two men to them.
The battle was to take place at Pentecost,
a great and costly celebration.
Stout-hearted noblemen arrived without fail   6288
on the following Monday,
eager to watch the fight.
People came from far and wide,
knights and townsmen and magistrates,   6292
dukes and archbishops and counts,
provosts and inspectors and viscounts.
Those who stood surety for Gerard
arrived at court without delay.   6296
The others, who lived close by,
escorted Lisiart. Impressively armed,
the men promptly brought
the two adversaries before the king   6300
and promised him their faithful service.
After presenting offerings at church,
they accompanied the two men onto the field,
which was spacious, wide, and unencumbered.   6304
The king sat down beneath an elm tree,
surrounded by a large group of men.
They began to discuss whether
it might be possible to reconcile   6308
the two men and avoid the battle,
saying it would be fitting
for both to be questioned.[48]
"I can promise you that it will be   6312
no victory for the king if one of them
forces the other to submit.
But whoever is able to make peace
between them, and have this battle called off,   6316
would have found the best solution."
That's what the dauphin was saying.
"Good God," said the Count of Boulogne,
"that's just an evasion.   6320
There's no point in that!
Gerard has accused Lisiart of treachery,
and everyone heard him do so!
I swear I'll not remain in a place   6324
where treachery is covered up.
Neither love nor money
could persuade me to do so.

Where treachery exists 6328
it must be identified and exposed!
Scripture bears witness—
and clergy and monks confirm this—
that treachery is the greatest sin 6332
with which a man can be tainted.
Theology presents us with
yet another reason:
even if these two men are reconciled 6336
and Gerard's land returned to him,
the terrible reputation
that Euriaut has acquired
wouldn't be forgotten. 6340
There's no doubt about it.
It's well-known that once
a person is accused of treachery,
they'll be mistrusted forever after. 6344
Therefore, so help me God, I doubt
that any of them could live with honor,
even if they did make peace."
The king quickly rose and commanded 6348
that relics be brought; he didn't want to wait
any longer before seeing the two men
confront one another.
Both men swore an oath.[49] 6352
(Gerard went first, I believe, then Lisiart.)
Both were brave, and eager to fight,
and soon they were in the saddle.
May God in his holy goodness 6356
protect Gerard, for he is in the right!
The Duke of Metz,
riding alongside him,
led Gerard onto the battlefield. 6360
The people who were milling about
dispersed, and the mortal enemies,
armed to the teeth, faced off.
Each man rode a well-caparisoned steed 6364
and each one gripped his shield by the straps.
The despicable Lisiart called out to Gerard:
"Vassal! This is as far as you'll get!"
"By Saint Clement," replied Gerard, 6368
"a liar never speaks the truth!
When this battle is over,
it won't take long for *you*
to gather up your winnings, 6372
that I can promise you!

En garde! I challenge you!"
With that, they galloped toward each other,
each man aiming his spear straight ahead,   6376
just above his horse's neck.
They drew close, lowering their lances
and landing such fierce blows
that each man tore through the other's shield   6380
as though it were made of samite.
The steel ripped through their hauberks,
too, grazing the flanks of both men.
So violent was the impact when their bodies   6384
and horses collided, that both men
were knocked from the saddle,
and both horses went down.
The two knights were so dazed   6388
that they neither saw nor heard a thing.
The guards listened, trying to determine
whether they were still breathing.
The two men lay on the ground,   6392
moving neither hand nor foot.
It looked like the lances
had pierced their bodies,
but soon they recovered   6396
their senses and jumped up.
Each man reached for his sword
and both men were quick
to unsheathe their blades.   6400
Soon they clashed,
whacking each other
on the head and neck,
and landing such cruel blows   6404
to their shoulders and chests
that blood poured down their necks.
They injured each other grievously,
exchanging horrific blows   6408
and abandoning themselves so completely
to the fighting that their hauberks
and helmets were demolished.
The combat was savage and fierce.   6412
Seven times they clashed, and no one
could tell which man had the worst of it.
Lisiart, who was vicious and cruel,
swore by the Lord's death   6416
and by his own eyes
that Gerard would rue the day
he had challenged him at court.

Filled with fury, he rushed at Gerard   6420
and brought his sword down
on his head, cutting through
Gerard's helmet and white coif.
The blow landed in such a way   6424
that it grazed Gerard's face,
though it didn't actually harm him.
Gerard had slightly leaned away,
and that saved him, thank God!   6428
Lisiart paused for a moment,
then said: "Sir knight,
I'm about to serve you a dish
that will crush your insolence!   6432
I swear to God, you would have done better
to go wandering about the country
with your precious Euriaut,
travelling from town to town   6436
to see where you might sell her.
She would have fetched a pretty price!"
Gerard was silent; he spoke not a word.
Raising his shield,   6440
he rushed forward, took aim,
and hit Lisiart forcefully on the head.
Alas, demons intervened
and it was merely a glancing blow.   6444
But Gerard was vigorous and strong,
and he hurried to strike again.
This time, he tore from
Lisiart's thigh a great piece of flesh.   6448
He'll never spend another day
without pain, for as long as he lives.
Both men were strong and agile,
and they began to duel   6452
with their swords.
It seemed that neither man
feared the other at all.
Each one secretly hoped   6456
he'd soon have a funeral mass
sung for the other!
(That's what they both were thinking.)
They often feinted and thrust   6460
at one another, landing blows
to the head that cracked and split
their opponent's helmet.
But this didn't deter them!   6464
To the contrary, they sought each other out

and (trust me on this, for I believe it's true)
neither one of them had the advantage.
Lisiart thought he'd go mad   6468
when he saw Gerard waiting for him.
He raised his sword high in the air
and struck Gerard's helmet with such force
that he knocked him senseless.   6472
Unable to see or hear,
Gerard staggered about, not knowing
if it were day or night.
The spectators were unnerved   6476
to see him in this condition,
but he was a strong man,
and soon regained his equilibrium.
He ran towards Lisiart,   6480
who had shamed him before all these people,
and struck his silver-embossed shield
so fiercely that it was totally destroyed.
He struck his helmet too,   6484
slicing right through it,
so that his blade scraped the flesh
and eyebrows from Lisiart's forehead.
His eyes filled with the blood   6488
that ran down, and soon he was
completely covered with gore,
unable to see at all.
The despicable man now realized   6492
that to counterattack was pointless,
so he seized upon
a most treacherous scheme.
This will be the end of Gerard,   6496
unless God intervenes!
He called out to Gerard, most courteously:
"Gerard, in the name of God,
have mercy! Here is my sword.   6500
Take it! Bandage my head,
and then I'll tell the whole truth
about how I have wronged you.
If I delay, I'll no longer be able   6504
to speak. But come closer,
so that I can lean on you.
Then we'll call the king and I'll confess
how I accomplished the deed.   6508
I know I've been defeated."
He said all this to trick Gerard,
who believed that he spoke sincerely.

He approached Lisiart,   6512
tearing a large band of cloth
from his tunic, which was made
of fine Syrian silk.
Then he bent over his enemy,   6516
intending to bandage his wound.
Lisiart, meanwhile, had surreptitiously grasped
the handle of a sharp steel knife
which he had attached to an iron chain.   6520
A hundred devils from Hell
had put it just within reach!
Lisiart judged the distance,
and believed he could stab   6524
Gerard in the chest.
When Gerard caught sight
of the blade raised by Lisiart,
he pulled back as fast as he could.   6528
Nevertheless, Lisiart stabbed him
in the arm, piercing straight through it
and into his left side. Then he said:
"You would have done better   6532
to stay with your lady friend,
whom you hold so dear!" "Traitor!"
cried Gerard. "I'll make you pay dearly
for your deceit and treachery!"   6536
With that, he dealt a ferocious blow,
cutting off Lisiart's left shoulder
and arm. Then he asked:
"Do you want a priest?   6540
You need one, I think."
He spat in Lisiart's face,
and drove his sword
right through his neck.   6544
Then he knocked him
to the ground and held him
there on the hillside
until the wretch confessed his treachery,   6548
and told the whole story
about how the old woman
had shown him Euriaut's birthmark
when she was in her bath.   6552
In this way, the wicked woman
had betrayed Euriaut without her knowledge.
The young lady never suspected a thing.
After the king had listened   6556
to Lisiart's confession, he declared:

"I've never heard anything good said
about a traitor, and that's a fact.
Now I'll give you what you deserve."   6560
He immediately had him tied
to the tail of a strong packhorse
and dragged a long distance;
then they hanged him from a tree.   6564
Gerard wasted no time.
He sent men to Nevers to arrest Gondrée
and had a cauldron filled with metal filings
placed over a fire. The wicked old woman   6568
was put inside it and cooked
until she was completely burned up.
That's what happens to traitors!
That same week,   6572
Gerard married Euriaut.
The king and the highest aristocracy
attended the wedding festivities,
which went on for an entire week.   6576
No one has ever seen any grander!
No minstrel arrived on foot
who did not depart on horseback,
taking with him fur-lined clothes   6580
packed in a bag or pouch or trunk.
No one heard an uncivil word,
for joy, comfort and delight reigned.
Melodies, songs, and counterpoint   6584
were performed without ceasing,
and lively dancing
was not discouraged!
Never in Wales did King Arthur   6588
offer such splendid hospitality,
whether at Pentecost or Christmas.
At the end of the week,
the valiant knights took their leave,   6592
but first the king returned to Gerard
his entire inheritance,
including the counties
that had been so wrongfully seized.   6596
Gerard then took leave of his friends
and returned to Nevers with his wife.
Everyone there was overjoyed to see them!
Gerard often told his people   6600
about the hard times he had endured
since they had last seen him,
and everyone listened willingly,

thanking and praising God that Gerard   6604
had returned safe and sound.
Even if I went on all night,
I couldn't describe the great quantity
of money that the nobles of the two counties   6608
had spent to honor their lord!
No one has ever seen a greater celebration
than the one given in honor of Euriaut.
While sitting at table,   6612
Gerard began to sing
a delightful song.
He knew just how to deliver it:
    A true lover shouldn't be dismayed   6616
    by any hardship Love sends his way.
    A double boon is granted the one
    who endures heartache because of love.
    There's no genuine joy without it!   6620
When he had finished singing, he declaimed,
"Truly, my dear, sweet Euriaut,
Love tormented me so greatly
that I felt sure I'd been deceived.   6624
It is your fidelity and your loyalty
that has saved our love."
He often repeated these sentiments.
Neither of them opposed anything   6628
the other wanted to do,
so much were they of one mind.
The longer they lived together,
the greater was their affection.   6632
And that's as it should be, with true love.

And so Gerbert de Montreuil
brings to a close his story of the Violet.
He has no wish to go on,   6636
for he has rhymed his way to shore.
He has composed this work and put it
into rhyme for the best lady who lives.
All good qualities reside in her: 6640
benevolence, honor, and worth
all find their home in the heart
of Countess Marie de Ponthieu,
who experienced great suffering   6644
before she regained her lands.
She repeatedly applied for them,
and by dint of her fidelity and loyalty,
recovered her domain and inheritance.   6648

May God, who gives us every good gift,
grant us a place in Paradise
at the end of our days,
for our time in this world will be brief.   6652
Here Gerbert ends his book,
without further ado.[50]

Introduction to
Le Roman du Comte de Poitiers

Le Roman du Comte de Poitiers was composed in northern France by an unknown author, sometime during the late twelfth or early thirteenth century. It was originally identified as a principal source for Gerbert de Montreuil's *Roman de la Violette*, but further study suggests that the two authors used a common source. Both works are written in rhyming octosyllabic couplets and their story lines are closely similar: the wager is made publicly at court in the presence of the king; a beautiful and virtuous woman is described in lavish detail; a female servant betrays her mistress; the main characters confront similar physical and psychological challenges. But the two works differ in significant ways as well. Set in the time of Charlemagne's father, King Pepin the Short (714–768), the *Le Comte de Poitiers* presents a royal court governed by a fierce and famous warrior. Members of the court are presented only sketchily, unlike the lively aristocrats who sing and dance their way through the first portion of Gerbert's romance or figure in the various subplots of that much longer work. The story focuses single-mindedly on the matter at hand: the wager, misunderstandings, setbacks for the protagonists, resolution. The wager tale itself occupies the first, and much longer, portion of the work (ll. 1–1237). The second part (ll. 1238–1719), only tangentially related to the first, recounts the anachronistic (and highly fanciful) Roman emperor Constantine's quest for a bride. It is likely that the author attached this independent story to the preceding wager tale because it also features the theme of female chastity. Both segments illustrate, in very different ways, contemporary male anxiety about the legitimacy of heirs: only a chaste woman can guarantee the purity of a noble lineage.

The complete version of *Le Comte de Poitiers* has survived in a single manuscript, Paris, Bibliothèque de l'Arsenal 3527, a miscellany of chiefly pious works transcribed in Picardy in the early fourteenth century. The story has been edited three times: in 1831 by Francisque Michel; in 1937, by

V.-F. Koenig; and in 1940, by Bertil Malmberg, whose edition I have followed here. A fifteenth-century fragment of the work was discovered by Maurice Delbouille in 1944. The wager portion of the story was translated into modern French by Mireille Demaules in 1992. The work has never been translated into English.

The Count of Poitiers

Here begins the story of the Count of Poitiers.
For the sake of God, son of Mary,
listen to a very noble tale!
You've often heard songs
about the lineage of Aimeri,   4
and about powerful Charlemagne,
Olivier and Roland; Guillaume Fierebras, too,
and Rainourt with his club.
He's the one who singlehandedly   8
conquered ten kings.[1]
All these were surpassed by the dwarf Pepin,
who was only three and a half feet tall.
He vanquished the lion in Paris,   12
and was never unhorsed in battle.[2]
Between the gates of Pamplona
one night, by the light of the moon,
he killed four giants, brothers all.   16
To this very day there appear,
right next to the ravine,
the hoofprints of Taillefer,
the good horse given to him   20
by Graindor, his sister's son.
That steed could run a hundred leagues
in a single day.[3] During his reign,
Pepin conquered four kingdoms,   24
three duchies and six counties.
One day, he held court in Paris,
and from there to the far reaches of the sea,
no crowned king failed to come,   28
no duke, knight, or count;
they were all there.
A copious and elegant repast was prepared,
and Pepin and all the princes sat down to dine.   32
Never has a king been better served!

Then the bravest of them all,
and the liveliest, spoke.
This was the handsome Count of Poitiers,   36
who wore garments worth five hundred marks.
The name of this fine-looking man was Gerard.
"King, you rank higher than Archedeclin,[4]
for the whole world bows down before you!   40
You've accomplished more than anyone.
But I lie naked whenever I like
with the most beautiful woman in the world!
She's constantly beseeching me,   44
day in and day out,
morning and night, to have her.
I swear to God, who sees all,
that anyone who searched the world over,   48
whether in pagan lands or Christian,
would not find another such beauty.
No rose, however new,
can surpass her beauty.   52
She's my wife and I'm her lord!
Her skin, whiter than snow,
glows beneath her chemise of Syrian silk.
She would never allow another man   56
to delight in the body that brings me
such pleasure,[5] not for a thousand times
her weight in pure gold!
She's lovelier than a fairy, noble, wise,   60
and learned. To see her is to love her.
And she's not slow to serve God!
It will never be so bitterly cold in January
that she doesn't go barefoot to church.   64
King Pepin, her beauty is worth more
than your entire kingdom!
I'm therefore richer than you are,
and not the least bit envious."   68
The Duke of Normandy then spoke up:
"My lord count, this is all nonsense.
A blow on water leaves no mark![6]
To prove you're exaggerating,   72
I'll stake Normandy against Poitou that,
within a month, I'll have my way
with your wife just like you,
and I do mean carnally.   76
But first you must swear an oath
not to tell her in advance."
"Agreed!" the count replied.

Both men then delivered hostages.[7]   80
Delighted with this plan, the duke mounted
and set off, accompanied by fifty of his knights.
He travelled until he came to Poitiers,
where he donned fine garments   84
worth a good hundred marks.
How handsome and dashing he looked
with a circlet of gold around his head!
How imposing, astride his sorrel steed!   88
Through the grey marble gates,
he rode into Poitiers,
and there he found the countess sitting under a tree
on a cloth of bright red cendal silk.   92
She had just returned from mass.
The duke dismounted with alacrity,
as did his fifty knights.
The lady had with her a hundred maidens,   96
all dressed in newly made garments,
and thirty courtly young men, all of whom
wore bliauts banded with golden embroidery.
No woman was ever fairer of face: 100
her brown eyebrows and laughing eyes,
bright red mouth and gleaming teeth,
her neck white as crystal,
all made her look like a heavenly angel.   104
(If I described how beautiful she was,
it would take far too long!)
Her clothes were worth a hundred gold marks.
Hector's friend Joiouse,   108
who was so beautiful and gracious,
wasn't worth two besants next to her.[8]
When the duke saw how gorgeous she was,
his heart skipped a beat.   112
He bowed deeply and greeted her courteously.
"May God bless you," she replied.
"Now tell me, and conceal nothing:
why are you travelling   116
with such a company?"
"I'm returning from Spain, dear lady,
and am on my way to Normandy,
but first I wished to visit with you.   120
In truth, the count is very fond of me,
so I thought to stay here tonight."
The lady didn't refuse his request
and kindly replied   124
she wouldn't have it any other way.

"You'll have plenty to eat," she assured him.
"There will be fowl and venison,
good, aged wine and fortified claret.   128
For love of my husband,
may God protect him from dishonor,
you'll be well cared for
by my household and my people."   132
She then had a bell rung,
the signal for everyone to wash their hands.
They all sat down at the dinner table[9]
and, out of courtesy,   136
the shapely countess
sat next to the duke,
as she did with her husband.
She did this to honor him, for it seemed   140
to her the appropriate thing to do.
And so, the two of them dined together.
The duke watched her but remained silent.
The lady bit into a wing,   144
then put it down.
The duke grabbed it immediately
and sank his teeth into the very spot
touched by the lady's teeth.   148
She could hardly take a piece of bread
without him putting his hand over hers.
He tried to play footsy
and pinched her hips,   152
bruising her delicate flesh.
The countess grew pale;[10]
she didn't know what to do or say;
she merely bowed her head and sighed.   156
After dinner, all the knights stood up
and left, except for the duke,
who was seated next to the countess.
He leaned over her snowy bosom   160
and placed his right hand on her hip.
The countess recoiled and exclaimed,
"Sir, I swear by Saint Peter,
if you don't remove your hands,   164
I'll punch you in the mouth!"
"Ah, my lady," said the duke, "be kind!
You've conquered me, I swear it,
and placed me in chains and shackles!   168
Henceforth, I'm yours to command.
My love for you gnaws at me
and pierces me. I'm struggling,

like a bird caught in a net,   172
and will surely die
if I don't satisfy my desire.
Your beauty speaks for itself.
No other woman in the world   176
is as beautiful as you are.
Neither queen nor chatelaine,
not even Helen of Troy,
could possibly rival you.   180
Grant me your love, my lady!
I want you so much
that I'll surely die
if I don't possess your fine body   184
and satisfy my desire!"
The countess angrily replied:
"Stop this mad talk at once!
I'd sooner be dead and buried,   188
or thrown headfirst into a cauldron
full of boiling lead,
drowned in the ocean,
burned and scattered to the wind,   192
than dishonor my husband,
who holds me in such high esteem!
He honored me so greatly
the day he put this ring on my finger,   196
that it's only right—indeed, it's his due—
that I remain forever faithful to him,
without any malice or misbehavior.
If the count were now a leper,   200
I swear he'd still be a finer
and handsomer man than you!
May God punish you, sir,
for wishing to betray my lord   204
who has honored me so greatly.
He's honest and kind to everyone,
and a better knight than you are.
When he's mounted on Saigremor,   208
you couldn't get near him,
not for a hundred gold marks.
He'd run you through with his lance!
There's not another knight to equal him   212
in all of France, save King Pepin himself.
That's what all the palatine princes say.[11]
You must leave immediately!
If the count comes back and I tell him   216
what you've said, my lord duke,

you'll be strung up by your neck.
You'll never have me in bed!"
When he saw that he had failed,   220
the duke turned away and left.
He leaned against a window and wept,
his face contorted with grief,
for he feared he had lost his land.   224
The countess also left the hall
and sought refuge elsewhere.
She related the whole story
to the woman who had reared her.   228
(May God punish her, body and soul,
for she betrayed the faithful lady.)
This woman went straight to the duke,
who still stood at the window,   232
despairing, and said to him:
"My handsome lord duke,
you are certainly pensive
and you seem quite upset.   236
Tell me what's wrong,
and I promise I'll help you
if I possibly can. That way,
I can earn a handsome reward."   240
The duke listened to her,
and her words cheered him up.
"Dear lady," he replied,
"I swear by my body and soul   244
to tell you everything,
for my heart is truly heavy."
And so, he told her the whole story
from beginning to end,   248
without omitting a single detail.
When this hard-hearted woman
had heard his account,
she said to him at once: 252
"You needn't worry!
The problem will soon be resolved.
But first you must do something for me.
or at least promise to do so: 256
give me either jewels or money,
as much as I desire."
"You'll certainly have them,"
replied the duke, who by now   260
was feeling desperate.
"As Saint Nicaise is my witness,
you'll have an abundance

of jewels, money, and other riches.   264
But how are you going to do it?"
"Don't worry about that.
I believe I can arrange matters
so that you'll have her wedding ring   268
before suppertime.
She never takes it off.
You'll have more than that, too.[12]
You needn't be concerned!"   272
She left him there
and went back to her lady,
who was exceedingly distressed
about what the duke had done.   276
Straightaway the nurse said:
"My lady, for heaven's sake,
forget about all that now!
Let's return to your room   280
and have a nice rest.
And let's be quiet about all this,
lest the whole household finds out.
They wouldn't tolerate it."   284
Off they went, hand in hand,
to the lady's chambers.
To deceive her mistress more easily,
the servant closed the door;   288
that way, no one could see what she did.
Why belabor the point?
The woman, may God bring her
shame and woe, slipped the ring   292
from her mistress's finger
when she wasn't paying attention.
This was the very ring with which
the handsome, noble count had married her.   296
From her gold comb, she extracted
ten strands of hair and tucked them away.
They shone more brightly than gold on a shield.[13]
And from the fine samite the countess   300
had been wearing, she snipped
a bit of cloth from the lap of the skirt.
You could cover the hole with a small coin.[14]
These three items she then delivered to the duke,   304
who gave her four hundred marks for them.
"My lord," she said, "you can now return
to Paris, whence you have come."
(Alotru was the name of the crone,   308
and a more deceitful woman has never lived.[15])

"Before Pepin, you'll announce to the count,
who will be distraught and ashamed,
that you have lain with his wife and enjoyed   312
her fine body at least three or four times.
Then show the evidence,
so that you will be believed."
"My profound thanks," replied the duke.   316
He mounted his Hungarian horse,
and his knights also mounted.
They didn't rest or tarry along the way
and on the fifth day arrived in Paris.   320
The duke strode into the great hall
to meet with Pepin. Many a palatine prince
was there, as was the count himself.
The duke wasted no time   324
and haughtily cried out:
"Noble Count of Poitiers, hear me now!
I swear by Saint James, that I've never seen
a more beautiful woman   328
than your wife, the countess.
But she thinks you're a coward,
and loves me a thousand times more than you!
I swear that you've been cuckolded,   332
for I lay naked in her arms
and took great joy and pleasure
in holding her and feeling her
and in kissing her sweet face.   336
I declare before Pepin
that I had her three times that night,
and may Jesus send me shame and death
if I've uttered one false word!   340
Noble count, you're wrong to doubt me,
for I have proof of what I say.
Look! Here are ten strands of her golden hair;
they shine more brightly than pure gold.   344
And look at this—it's the ring you gave her
on your wedding day!
And here's some silk
taken from the garment of royal samite   348
that your wife was wearing.
I've won and you have lost!
My holdings are now vast, for both
Poitou and Normandy are mine!"   352
When the count heard this speech,
he grew redder than a hot coal.
In pain and grief,

he struck the duke with his right fist,	356
breaking two of his front teeth	
and knocking him flat.	
The duke began to lose consciousness	
and soon passed out.	360
Pepin leapt to his feet in rebuke:	
"My lord Count of Poitiers,	
why did you strike my duke?	
All the hostages you gave	364
will now hang from the gallows!	
It's a foolish man	
who sows his seed on stone;	
Solomon himself was dishonored by his wife.[16]	368
Send for the countess but show no anger.	
Let her come to Paris and defend herself.	
Before she leaves the court,	
the strands of golden hair, the piece of cloth,	372
and the gold ring will prove whether or not	
the duke had his way with her."	
"I agree to everything," replied the count.	
He then summoned Duke Jeffrey.	376
"My dear nephew," said the count, "go get her."	
"Most willingly," the young man replied.	
He took his leave, set out, and soon returned	
with the lady, who was accompanied	380
by a hundred worthy knights	
and twenty comely maidens.	
She arrived at the splendid palace,	
where four counts helped her to dismount.	384
King Pepin told everyone	
how the wager had been made,	
and then showed the evidence	
that the thief had brought.	388
First, he showed her the ring.	
"My lady," said the Count of Poitiers,	
"as God is my witness,	
it was with this ring that I wed you."	392
From his alms purse Pepin drew	
the strands of hair that the old witch	
had stolen from the dignified countess	
when she led the lady to her bath.	396
From end to end,	
they shone brighter than gold.	
Pepin held them next to her head	
and everyone agreed it was a close match.	400
They all said: "Dear God, how sad!	

The count will now lose his land.
He was crazy to boast about her!"
Then they went to measure   404
the piece of cloth.
The count himself compared the length
and width of the piece to the garment itself,
and found it an exact match,   408
as fresh and new as the cotte itself.
(Here is wrong defeating right!)
Shamed, the lady's face grew somber.
"Have mercy, noble count!" she pleaded,   412
"You mustn't believe that I bore
any love for this traitor!
Before you married me
he asked my father for my hand.   416
I was only thirteen years old
and wouldn't have him for all of Milan!
You've been so good to me.
Let my body be consumed by flames   420
and my ashes scattered by the wind
if I've ever been touched
in a carnal way by any man but you.
I call upon Our Lady as my witness,   424
for I'm her faithful servant.
To prove my innocence, I'll submit
to a most painful and horrible ordeal,
in a cauldron of boiling lead."[17]   428
Pepin replied: "By Saint Denis,
there will be no judicial ordeal.
The Franks are saying among themselves
that the evidence has proven your guilt,   432
so there's no point in asking.
I held you very dear,
for you were my uncle's daughter,[18]
but I'd sooner let a nail be torn   436
from my middle finger
than deny the duke his due.
He deceived you through lust,
and so will have both Poitou and Normandy.   440
As for you, you will have poverty and shame."
"Vassal," said Pepin to the count,
"you're a fine knight.
Go seek your fortune in some other land.   444
I shall convey Poitou to the duke
and hereby affirm,
with my Franks as witnesses,

that I side with him against you."   448
The count didn't dare to argue.
He made the countess mount
a chestnut riding mule
equipped with an ivory saddle,   452
then took leave of his family.
Dear God, how sad and angry they were!
They all wanted to leave the country,
renouncing their own lands and fiefs   456
to follow him, but the count said:
"As God is my witness, no one will go
with me save the lady who betrayed me,
for I will avenge myself on her."   460
You should have seen how the twenty maidens
tore their hair and scratched their cheeks!
Each and every one of them fainted
when the countess kissed her goodbye.   464
Having bid them all farewell,
she rapidly rode off, with the count following
close behind. Her heart and body trembling,
she implored God the Creator   468
and protested most pitifully,
her tears streaming down
and wetting her lovely face and bosom.
When she recalled the shame   472
brought upon her by the accusation,
she yanked her beautiful hair and tore it out.
She was more frightened of her husband,
the count, than of a wild bear or a lion.   476
When she imagined the suffering
to come, her heart sank. She fainted,
and would have fallen to the ground
were it not for the gilded cantle of the saddle.   480
For two whole days and nights they rode,
never stopping to eat or drink.
On the third day, they entered a wood
where mighty oaks loomed.   484
The forest, with its dense foliage,
was forbidding and vast,
extending more than fifteen leagues.
It was after sunrise when they rode into   488
a bleak and gloomy valley,
though they soon came upon a pleasant meadow,
in the middle of which stood an olive tree.
There was also a stream,   492
issuing from a gentle fountain,

its water clear and pure.
The count rode over to the fountain
and dismounted next to it.   496
He put his arms around his wife's waist
and sat her down on a dark-grey marble stone,
situated at the base of the tree. Her beauty
was more dazzling than a precious jewel.   500
"My lady," he said, "what a pity
I ever saw you! Because of you,
I've been so utterly disgraced
that I can never be happy again.   504
By loving you, I've lost my fine
and prosperous city, Poitiers,
twenty castles and thirty towers.[19]
Countess, how could you be so shameless,   508
giving yourself to the duke?
Was I a prisoner or dead?
Couldn't you have waited for me?
They should burn you to ashes   512
as they burn a thief who lurks in a ditch.
What if you're carrying his child?
It could be true!
My lady, your lovely face,   516
more radiant than a damask rose,
makes your reckless behavior
even more painful to me,
for I loved you in good faith.   520
I loved to gaze into your eyes,
but can't bear to look at them now.
I'm sure what people are saying about you
is true, and the knowledge is killing me.   524
I used to call you 'sweetheart,'
but we're enemies now.
You'll remain here in this wood,
with no love from me.   528
You've shamed me, your faithful lover,
and by Saint Amant, you'll pay for it!
I adored you! But today we'll part forever.
Let's not prolong the agony."   532
With that, he drew his sword
with the hilt of pure gold;
the blade shimmered in the sunlight.
The countess blanched.   536
Hands clasped, she fell at his feet
and covered them with kisses.
"Noble lord, I beg you!" she pleaded,

"have mercy on this miserable creature   540
who has never known any man
but you! I am your wife
and your humble servant.
Mother of God, Virgin maid,   544
today I place my honor, my body,
my soul and my life in your care!
As you love chastity,
protect me from my husband,   548
who holds his bared sword.
Don't let me be cut to pieces!"
The count responded: "I've already waited
too long to cut off your head!   552
You've covered me with shame."
Grabbing hold of her blond tresses,
he raised the sword with its sharp blade.
But just then a lion appeared,   556
racing through the woods,
its jaws opened wide! Its tail was thick
and strong, its claws powerful,
and sharper than a swift falcon's.   560
With its teeth, keener than daggers,
this lion had killed many a leopard.
The countess saw it first. "Look out,
my lord!" she cried. "Here comes a wild beast!   564
I swear it by Saint Peter!
I fear it will harm you.
It looks very fierce!"
Then the count saw the lion rushing   568
toward him, its maw agape.
He moved away from his wife
and raised his sword,
where the holy names of God   572
had been placed.[20] The lion moved fast.
It leapt at the count's chest and knocked him flat!
He jumped up, seized his sword
with both hands and bravely attacked,   576
bringing the blade down on the lion's head.
His courage grew, for the lion now lay
on the fresh grass, jaws agape, teeth bared.
But the beast's strength quickly returned.   580
It moved toward the count and sprang,
intending to seize his head
between its front paws.
The count moved quickly to defend himself.   584
He raised his sable-lined cloak,

but the lion ripped through it,
tearing his bliaut of richly patterned silk,
his chemise, hacqueton, and the tender flesh 588
beneath, right down to the bone.
"My God'," said the count,
"if this mighty devil kills me,[21]
my friends will never see me again! 592
I must retaliate for my wound.
I won't give up, and I won't let it get away."
He held the sword in his right hand
and bounded forward a full seven feet. 596
In a rage, he lunged at the lion
and cut off its front paws.
He then struck its neck with such force
that he sliced through the throat. 600
With a roar, the lion fell to the ground
and breathed its last.
The count wiped his sword on the grass
and then looked at his wife. 604
"My lady," he said, "you are so beautiful.
Let me tell you something.
I give thanks to the Creator,
who just granted me a great honor: 608
though wearing no armor, I've killed a lion.[22]
I'll go now. I will spare you,
but leave you here in the forest.
May God watch over you and protect you." 612
He slid the steel blade into the scabbard,
mounted his sleek charger
and galloped off,
leaving his wife all alone and in tears. 616
Thrice she called herself wretched,
the fourth time she fell in a faint,
hitting the grey marble and bloodying her face.
"Dear God," she said, "bring shame today 620
to the man who turned the count against me!"
Just then, the chatelain Harpin appeared.[23]
This noble knight was a nephew
of the count and was now returning 624
from Compostela with some thirty men,
all worthy knights who lived nearby.
As they approached,
they heard the countess 628
bitterly lamenting her fate.
Harpin rode toward her and saw,
sitting by the fountain, a woman

more beautiful than Helen of Troy.　　　　　　632
He greeted her courteously, saying:
"Lovely lady, where are you from?
Have you a husband or lord?"
Then he saw the lion that had been wounded　　636
and slain by the count. "Beautiful one,
who killed the demon that lies here,
next to the sycamore tree?
He was braver than Hector,　　　　　　　　640
slain by Achilles before the walls of Troy."
The countess remained silent,
though at last, with a sigh, she replied:
"My lord, a great misfortune has befallen me.　644
Even if I took all day, it wouldn't suffice
to recount half my woes.
I'm dedicating myself to the Lord
and will become his handmaiden.　　　　　648
I swear to God, born of the uncorrupted Virgin,
that I'll never be the sweetheart or lover
of any man save the one
who just vanquished this lion.　　　　　　652
And if any man tries to force himself on me,
may the devil take my soul
if I don't stab myself,
as soon as I find a sharp knife!　　　　　656
I swear I'll not live beyond three days
if I dishonor my good lord."
"I believe you," Count Harpin replied,
"but you'll come with me now　　　　　　660
to my lands. I promise not to harm you.
You must come. You have no choice."
He took hold of her silk cloak
and pulled her along,　　　　　　　　　664
then had her helped onto a riding mule.
So great was the lady's lament
that the whole wood rang with it.
But now we'll leave them there　　　　　668
and return to the Count of Poitiers,
that proud and arrogant man.
Off he went, galloping through the woods.
Dear Lord, how sad and mournful he was,　　672
having lost his land and even worse, his wife,
the countess, whom he had left behind.
He hadn't gone very far
when he encountered a dragon,　　　　　676
huge and heavily spiked.

It was a good fourteen feet long
and its coiled tail
was full of venom.[24]   680
From its mouth issued forth so much smoke
that a whole field of reeds was scorched!
The beast had done great harm in this land,
killing more than a hundred men.   684
When the dragon saw the count approaching,
it sped toward him, thinking
it could easily strangle him.
The count saw it coming   688
and was filled with dread.
It was so enormous, so savage!
The powerful beast charged him
and darted its stinger.   692
Fearing for his life, the count
twisted the remains of his cloak
over his chest,
though this did little good.   696
The dragon struck with such force
that its stinger pierced
the folds of his cloak, his cotte
and ermine-lined pelisse,   700
then grazed his linen chemise,
nearly frightening him to death.
Had it touched his flesh, the count
would have been silenced forever!   704
With its enormous tail,
the dragon then struck such a blow
to his ribs that it knocked him
backwards onto the ground.   708
After the creature had struck him down,
it moved to choke him between its jaws.
But the count, enraged,
defended himself and his horse.   712
Drawing his gleaming sword,
he called on God, the son of Mary,
to protect him from this demon.
He delivered great blows with his steel blade,   716
landing a heavy and direct hit
on its large, wide head.
But the blade bounced off
and flew high into the air!   720
The dragon's head was so hard
that it wasn't hurt at all.
Full of fury, it emitted a great cry.

Belching flame, it rushed toward the count. 724
(Trust me, he wasn't happy about this!)
He was terrified when he saw
the gaping maw of the dragon
as it sped towards him. 728
In his right hand he gripped the sword
upon which the holy names were inscribed,
then made the sign of the Cross
and blessed himself in God's name 732
and the Virgin's. With the sharp
and shining blade he once again
hit the dragon's hard head,
exactly where he had struck before. 736
This didn't bother the beast one bit.[25]
It was so ferocious
that weapons didn't faze it at all.
When the count realized this, 740
it's little wonder he was afraid,
for his life hung in the balance.
The dragon was by now exceedingly angry,
for no man, however strong, 744
had ever been able to defend himself
from its attack, so great was its might.
Closer and closer it came, fangs bared.
The count was in a terrible state, 748
certain he was about to die.
The dragon's jaws opened wide.
But hear how God came to the rescue!
The count thrust the steel blade 752
into the dragon's maw, bearing down
with such force that the blade
went straight to its heart. With a roar,
the dragon fell. The count then rode off, 756
leaving the dragon where it lay.
Before long, he encountered a peasant
and asked the man to exchange clothes
with him. The peasant, however, refused. 760
"Peasant," said the count,
"you're a dolt and a coward
to refuse fine clothes of silk!
It's clear you come from base stock."[26] 764
The count turned away and left him there.
(A fool will never become a worthy man!)
At the entrance to a well-worn path,
he next encountered a pilgrim, 768
an elderly man of eighty years,

his beard and moustache white.
The count, who was both noble and kind,
inquired, "Friend, whence do you come?"   772
"Greetings, my lord," the pilgrim replied.
"You appear to me most unhappy."
With a sigh, the count told him
the whole story. Then he said,   776
"For the love of Saint Thomas,
please loan me your clothes,
including your hat and staff.
Your hooded cape too, if you please.   780
I want to go to Poitiers."[27]
"Willingly, my lord," the pilgrim replied.
"I won't budge from this place
until you return."   784
He undressed without further delay,
and the noble count took everything.
Under the cape he hid his sword
with its hilt of pure gold.   788
He longed to chop off the duke's head
because he had dishonored his wife.
Now listen to what the pilgrim did next!
He drew from his alms purse an herb   792
that Caïfas, a pagan born in Baghdad,
had given to him and he blackened
the count's face so that
it was darker than boiled ink.   796
No one would recognize him
until the time was right!
Thus disguised, the count set off,
and soon entered the tower at Poitiers,   800
where the duke was seated at dinner.
As soon as he saw the pilgrim
the duke had a bowl brought to him
and a goblet filled with claret.   804
The count took them without hesitation,
for he didn't dare refuse hospitality. To himself
he said, "My lord duke, if I killed you today,
it would be an act of gravest treachery."   808
He then sat down by the fire with its hot coals.
Now hear what the high-born duke did next!
He embraced his mistress,
who had betrayed the countess.   812
"My lady," he said, "I swear by Saint Simon,
that I'm giving you this house.
You're my sweetheart,

for you betrayed your young lady for me!　　　816
You snipped her cotte and gave me
the bit of cloth, along with her ring.
That's why she lost her honor
and the love of her lord.　　　820
As almighty God is my witness,
I never had any commerce with her!
My words didn't please her one bit.
She loathed me more than a leper!　　　824
The mother of God, whom she used to serve
so faithfully, has given her a poor return,
for the count has cut off her head
and his fief now belongs to me!"　　　828
When the count heard these words,
he was overjoyed! He swore he wouldn't rest
until he found his wife, whom he had left
in a swoon in the forest.　　　832
"Then I'll gather my friends
and take my wife to Paris.
In the court of Pepin the Brave,
I'll make the duke pay for this!　　　836
Ah, noble, loyal lady,
it is I who have failed *you*!
You are a most excellent and faithful wife,
and I'm a coward and a traitor.　　　840
How greatly I have wronged you!
Even if you were now a fallen woman,
I'd take you back
and bow down at your feet!　　　844
My lady, you who are so lovely,
have lions devoured you,
bears or leopards eaten you?
Noble, high-born lady,　　　848
here's what I'll do: I'll find you
or die in the attempt!
If I don't get you back again, my sweet love,
I'll never take another wife or lover."　　　852
With that, he rode into the forest,
retrieved his good clothes and put them back on.
When he washed the dark juice from his face
he was handsomer than Narcissus.　　　856
He mounted his swift horse,
and gave the pilgrim a ring;
the stone alone was worth a castle.
Then he rode off into a meadow　　　860
and there began to pray most fervently

that God would return his wife to him.
My lords, we sincerely believe
that no earthly treason,   864
however horrible or secret,
has ever remained hidden from God.
The countess has been shamed,
but the Lord will right this wrong.   868
The count wandered through
the vast and wild forest,
weeping over his misfortune,
so harsh and cruel,   872
asking everyone he met
for news of his wife.
He was so persistent that I feel sure
he'll soon discover the truth: 876
she had remained a lady, loyal and fine.
With hope in his heart, he quit the forest
and headed to the residence
of the chatelain Harpin, his aunt's son,   880
arriving there on Saint Martin's eve.[28]
Encircled by walls of grey marble,
Harpin's town was a delightful place
and widely admired.   884
Outside the walls were cultivated fields,
and within there was a fine fleet of ships.
It was, in short, a charming burg.
The great tower, built of grey stone,   888
sat atop the fortified castle. There was no need
to fear mangonels or stones![29]
The count paused next to a laurel tree.
Within the walls he heard a great commotion: 892
the sound of harps and fiddles,
and of maidens singing little songs;
of jousting and fencing, and bells clanging.
He was utterly astonished,   896
and prayed most fervently
for God's protection.
The count rode up to the gate,
where he saw a squire transporting   900
a dead boar on the croup of a horse.
"Friend," he said, "kindly speak with me.
Why on earth is the town
in such an uproar?   904
I'm amazed by all the noise I'm hearing."
"My good man," he replied, "I'll tell you.
The chatelain is taking a wife today.

From here to Montpellier, there's none finer,   908
none so wise or so gracious.
That's why there's such a commotion inside.
The palatines are all quite upset about it,
for they believe the lady is of low estate,   912
but Harpin won't renounce the marriage,
no matter what people say about her.
She's been taken to the church of Saint Peter
and that's where they're to marry."   916
The count replied: "That may be so,
but I think that the priest
who would bless such a union is a fool."
With that the noble count rode on,   920
clutching the golden hilt of his sword.
Inside the church were other counts,
all fine men, though the Count of Poitiers
stood a head taller than any of them.   924
Passing in front of these worthy lords,
he approached the crucifix.
He had covered his head with his hood,
and was waiting until he saw   928
the right moment to speak
and reveal his identity.
The chatelain was dressed in silk,
embroidered with beaten gold.   932
Rose, the Countess of Poitiers,[30]
was beautifully attired in a chemise
more finely spun than a spider's web;
it had been made in Spain.   936
Under her ermine-lined pelisse
she wore red samite, beautiful
and most becoming. A hundred birds
embroidered in pure gold thread   940
adorned the garment, which suited her perfectly.
It had a silk belt, and the buckle
was set with a costly gem
that shone brighter than a hot coal at night.   944
I truly believe there's none finer
in all the world.
Her beautifully made cloak
was lined with sable,   948
and the clasp at her neck
was worth fourteen gold besants.
Her shiny blond hair fell to her feet in waves
and gleamed more brightly   952
than gold on a shield.

On her head she wore a circlet of beaten gold.
Her forehead was whiter than snow,
her eyebrows brown and delicate.   956
Her ears were finely made,
and her mouth was sweet, with red lips.
She had a straight nose and a dimpled chin
and her complexion was just the right hue.   960
Her breasts gave no hint
that she had ever been touched by a man.[31]
Her hands were lovely and her arms slender,
her figure shapely and fine.   964
Her white skin was smooth and voluptuous,
surpassing that of all other women.
No one who saw her failed to proclaim
that she was the most beautiful woman alive.   968
When the count saw how beautiful she was,
his heart leapt within his breast.
He'd sooner be torn limb from limb
than see another man marry her!   972
The abbot, wearing his vestments,
arrived and softly intoned "Sanctus,"
to which more than thirty monks responded:
"Alleluia!" Then the abbot said: 976
"Let us turn to other matters.
Bring me that missal."
Harpin stood to the right of the abbot,
who took him by the right hand.   980
"My lord," he said, "do you want this lady?"
"By Saint James, I do!" replied Harpin.
"My lady, do you want to take him as your lord?"
"I'd sooner be hanged!   984
I'd rather be dragged by a horse
than become his wife!
I'll never marry or have a lover
now that I've lost my dear husband.   988
You're mad, Abbot Gautier, to marry someone
who is already the wife of another!"
Infuriated by her words,
Harpin struck her with his gloves,   992
hitting her nose. Blood trickled down,
reddening her mouth and chin.
When the Count of Poitiers saw this,
he almost went mad with rage.   996
No longer able to hold back,
he lunged at Harpin
and in front of all his people,

punched him in the mouth, 1000
breaking two of his teeth.
He grabbed the chatelain
and threw him to the ground,
then lifted his cloak and drew his sword. 1004
"Son of a whore!" he shouted,
"even though you're the child
of my aunt and Huon of Pierelee!
My mother's sister bore you, 1008
and I myself dubbed you a knight.
By Saint Marcel, the Gascons
would have taken this city
had I not defended it for you. 1012
And now you want to marry my wife?
I call this high treason!"
The count then told everyone
how he had wandered far and wide 1016
ever since he had abandoned his wife
in the forest after she had fainted.
He told the whole story about the countess
and how God had protected her. 1020
But the lady was especially pleased
when he said that he had seen the duke
in the court of Poitiers,
when he went there disguised as a pilgrim 1024
and had learned that the duke
had never touched her fine body.
The lady felt it had been far too long
since she had spoken to her beloved husband. 1028
She threw off her cloak and ran to him,
collapsing in a swoon at his feet.
Her head hit the paving stone,
bloodying her chin. 1032
The count took her in his arms
and very gently raised her up,
covering her face with kisses.
I feel sure he wouldn't exchange 1036
his wife for any other,
even if someone offered him
Chartres and Blois, Laon
and Reims and Paris! 1040
When the count was reunited
with his wife, everyone sighed and wept,
moved by pity. Then Harpin said,
"For God's sake, noble count, 1044
have mercy! I never slept with her!

As God is my witness,
I never once touched my lady.
I'd have lost all honor   1048
had I done so before marrying her."
"I believe you," the count replied.
"Now help us!
Come with me to Paris,   1052
where I intend to kill the duke."
After mass had been sung, they returned
to the great house in high spirits.
The countess appealed to the count: 1056
"My lord, avenge the shame that the duke
so wrongfully made me suffer.
He should certainly die because of it!
And may holy Mary help me,   1060
until you prove his guilt,
you'll never lie with me again,
not for as long as I live."
The count smiled at this and said: 1064
"My lady, I promise to do my best."
They then washed their hands and went in to dine.
Afterwards, they sent for the forester,
who came with his fourteen sons.³²   1068
The count was braver than Alexander
and not at all reluctant to fight.
He sent word to his brother, the Count of Flanders,
to come with his barons, and so he did: 1072
a thousand Flemish noblemen,
all held in high esteem and well-armed,
their helmets laced for battle.
Once they were assembled,   1076
they headed for Paris,
where they found the emperor Pepin
holding high court.
The Duke of Normandy was there,   1080
and the old woman, may God curse her.
(She had been betrothed to a viscount,
but will have a very different kind of wedding!)
The count, who was more valiant than Alexander,   1084
his brother, the Count of Flanders,
Harpin and the forester were all there,
along with the Duke of Normandy,³³
his nephews and other relatives.   1088
They all went into the great hall and approached Pepin.
The Count of Poitiers' men were ready for battle;
had they wanted to cause trouble,

the duke would have been killed right there, 1092
despite the presence of the king.[34]
They refrained, for their hearts were loyal and proud.
Then the Count of Poitiers spoke.
He told the whole story, then concluded: 1096
"I accuse the duke of treason, punishable by death!
If he denies it, I'll prove he's a liar."
He went forward and extended his pledge,
which Pepin received without hesitation. 1100
The duke then offered his own.
He dared not refuse,
though he was trembling all over.
The countess cried out: "Duke! 1104
May you be hanged today,
for you were never my lover!
May you be strangled by the rope,
for you never slept with me! 1108
I'll see you ruined,
for you never lay with me.
May God restore my honor to me today,
and may your body hang from the gallows!" 1112
Eager to fight, the vassals armed themselves.
They took up their hauberks and shields,
laced up their pointed helmets
and mounted their swift horses. 1116
Tarrying no longer, they gathered up
all the lances with their sharp metal points;
none were left behind.
Those who monitored the battlefield 1120
led them from the city.
Pepin had holy relics brought onto the field
and placed on a cloth of golden silk
which shone brightly in the sun. 1124
Upon these relics the men would swear their oaths.
Both men dismounted. The Duke of Normandy
came forward first; he didn't delay.
He swore, asking God to help him 1128
and deliver him safely from this battle,
for he had truly lain with the countess
and taken his pleasure with her. The count,
who was deeply pained to hear these words, 1132
knelt before the relics and said:
"My lord duke, I swear
by the saints here present,[35]
that you are lying! You never lay with her, 1136
nor took your pleasure with her,

and I'll prove it.
Before it is time for vespers,
I'll make you confess   1140
that you've lied about everything."
Neither man hesitated after that.
They strode to their horses, mounted,
and dug in their spurs.   1144
They smote each other so hard
with their stout lances
that both of their shields were broken
and the lances splintered,   1148
the fragments flying high into the air.
Again they clashed, horses,
men, and shields crashing together.
The two men fell to the ground   1152
with such force (this is the truth)
that they were very nearly killed.
But as soon as they could, they stood up
and slung their shields around their necks.   1156
They now planned to attack each other
with their steel swords, if they were able.
The Duke of Normandy was fierce.
He struck the count first,   1160
hitting him directly on his shield.
You can be sure he wasn't holding back!
He split the shield, which broke into pieces,
But the count, who was very strong,   1164
did not stagger or fall.
He gripped the good sharp sword
with which he had killed the lion,
and dealt the duke a vigorous blow   1168
on his helmet of beaten gold.
He sliced and split the helmet,
scattering gems and crushing flowers.[36]
The sword came down hard,   1172
for he was wild with rage.
The duke's hood of mail wasn't worth two straws;
the count would have split him right down
to the chest, but the steel blade missed its mark.   1176
and sliced along the side of the duke's head,
severing his right ear. The count then
hit the duke with such ferocity
that he knocked him flat.   1180
Mortified, the duke got up.
He tightly gripped his sword
and returned the blow,

hitting the count's golden helmet 1184
and shattering its gems and flowers.
The blow landed with such force that,
had God not wished to protect the count,
the duke would have split him in two. 1188
The sword came down hard,
and then the duke said:
"If God spares me, Count,
you'll hang today. 1192
You're fighting for one who has,
without any doubt, dishonored you."
"Duke," replied the count, "you lie,
and God willing, you'll pay for it." 1196
Then, fiercer than a lion or a leopard,
the duke attacked him
with his steel sword,
smiting him repeatedly. 1200
But things will go badly for the duke,
for the false oath he swore that day
had stripped him of all honor.
The two men attacked each other vigorously, 1204
and exchanged great blows.
They were well matched,
and both suffered grievous harm.
The duke would have pressed on, 1208
but he lacked the strength.
The blood from his head wound
obscured his vision and he could endure
no longer. The count, however, kept on; 1212
he vanquished the duke right there on the field.
No need to elaborate: the duke lay in the dirt
at Pepin's feet, and the noble count
made him confess his crime. 1216
With everyone looking on,
he swore on his hope of salvation
that the countess was a faithful wife.
The duke was hanged on the spot, 1220
then dragged by horses, and the old woman
had her nose cut off and both her ears;
her eyes were also gouged out.
To atone for her wicked life, 1224
she was consigned to a convent.
The countess was filled with joy
for she was now the Duchess of Normandy.
Pepin accorded her this rank 1228
as all the princes and noblemen looked on.

The knights all left the court,
and the count returned to Poitiers
accompanied by the countess, his wife.   1232

They spent the night together
in his chamber paved with stone
and I do believe that the best knight
ever born was engendered then and there.   1236
My lords, this was the good count Guy
who, after he had turned thirteen,
left land and inheritance,
father and mother, and went to Rome   1240
in search of adventure.
The Roman emperor soon retained him;
he loved Guy and held him dear.
He became King Constantine's bailiff   1244
and held this position for many years.[37]
Now hear how the noble Guy
gained Constantinople
through a lady he loved.   1248
(The Count of Poitiers travelled there
with his wife, the countess,
when their son became emperor.)
One Ascension Day,[38]   1252
Constantine was in Noiron's Field
where, before the church of Saint Peter,
his mother had boldly come.[39]
Following the law of vassalage,   1256
Constantine said to Guy, his seneschal:
"Master,[40] I'd be much obliged if you
would have these letters of mine sealed.
Then bring me some good riding mules,   1260
and thirty valiant messengers.
We'll search the land,
as far as the frozen sea,
so that not a single knight remains,   1264
no king or prince, count or duke
who doesn't come to Rome
within two weeks, accompanied by
a large retinue. As a courtesy to me,   1268
let each man bring with him
his sister or his sweetheart.
Let no married ladies
or non-virgins be brought.   1272
No lady, however beautiful, is to come,
unless she's a virgin maiden.

The one I like best, provided she is of noble birth,
will become my wife and I her lord. 1276
She'll be empress of Rome!
I'll be so happy to know for certain
that she will bear my child!
I'll then summon all my subjects, 1280
and travel beyond the sea of Greece,
not stopping for any reason
until I reach Babylon.
If the emir doesn't release my uncle, 1284
Noiron, whom he holds prisoner,
I'll destroy every marble tower
from there to Dry-Tree.[41]
If the pagans don't accept God and Saint Peter, 1288
I'll remain there in my bier."
"Sire," said Guy, his seneschal,
"how devout you are!
May God on high grant you the strength 1292
to achieve your goals!"
The thirty messengers mounted the mules,
which had reins of pure gold,
and carried the letters throughout the land 1296
to kings, counts, and marquesses.
Whether grudgingly or joyfully,
they all obeyed the emperor's command.
Gerard, the old count of Milan, 1300
brought his worthy daughters,
(the written source says he had seven),
all of them dressed in striped cendal silk.
One hundred knights accompanied them, 1304
each one wearing a padded hauberk.
Count Richard rode towards Rome
with six hundred and ten knights.
He brought with him his five daughters, 1308
dressed in ermine and silks embroidered in gold.
This count held Verceil and Ivrée,
and he was a great lord.
With three hundred knights 1312
(there's no doubt about this),
came the Duke of Plaisance,
bringing with him his four beautiful daughters,
all dressed in newly made clothes. 1316
Guillaume, who was lord of Genoa,
brought three daughters,
along with four hundred knights,
their horses draped all the way to their hooves. 1320

Renaud, who governed Pavia, brought his sister
and his sweetheart, and the prince of the Germans
brought a girl who was fifteen years old.
The king of Apulia had ten daughters;   1324
he brought four of them, and left six at home.
Aigline, who was much admired, came;
she was the daughter of the Duke of Sicily.
Parise, who was very noble, came;   1328
she held Constantinople. And Lorette,
more beautiful than any of them, came.
Having lost both her father and mother,
she was now Lady of Fat Bologna.[42]   1332
Guy, one of her handsome brothers,
brought her. She had blue-black hair
and was regally attired in a cloak
banded with gold embroidery,   1336
its buttons of Spanish gold.
Each of the maidens was a virgin
and a beauty, and each felt it was only right
that she be chosen as empress.   1340
The story makes it clear that the barons, kings,
and counts were all aware of the situation.
Because of young Constantine's letter,
so many people descended on Rome   1344
that it became difficult to traverse
the tapestry-hung streets.
The men and the young ladies
all admired the great towers;   1348
grand and beautiful,
they were draped in heavy green silk,
their floors strewn with reeds.
From the high windows,   1352
the knights hung their gilded shields.
Their mules and chargers
were covered with fine Greek cloths,
embroidered and lined with miniver.   1356
The greyhounds had silver collars,
and the falcons, goshawks, gerfalcons,
and merlins sat on perches.
Some men practiced fencing,   1360
aiming at their opponent's head.
The palatine counts played backgammon
and the elders played chess.
The sweet sound of fiddles   1364
accompanied the happy voices of the maidens.
After jousting, the young noblemen

gave their fine clothing
to ragamuffins and rhymesters,   1368
vagabonds and jongleurs.[43]
Every imaginable kind of wild game
could be found for sale on the bridge,
where one could also find fowl   1372
and freshly caught fish.
In the cellars were clarets and spiced drinks
laced with honey and hyssop.
The palace was ablaze   1376
with the light of many candles
and the worthies of the town
all wore their best clothes, made of silk.
There was never such joy in Rome   1380
as when the young ladies arrived!
In all the world, you couldn't find
thirty women more beautiful than these,
not from Saint Jacques to Otranto.   1384
Into the main tower, built by Julius Caesar,
they were all obliged to go.
When all thirty were inside,
King Constantine entered   1388
and shut tight
all three of the gilded brass doors.
No other man was then allowed to enter.
Inside the fortified tower,   1392
each of the maidens will be made to strip
and stand as naked as the day she was born.
Then the emperor will choose the one
he likes best, with the loveliest body,   1396
and that lady will become queen
of all Constantinople and Rome.
(Before the day is over,
every one of these ladies   1400
will grow ghastly pale.)
Constantine said: "By the Cross
upon which our Lord suffered death,
nothing shameful will occur.   1404
You need not remove your chemise
and stand completely naked.
God help me if I do not speak the truth.
I will still see your white breasts,   1408
your arms, your flanks, and your hips.
Your companions will all do likewise.
I can then observe the signs
each of you has on her body,   1412

and determine whether you are worthy
of a high-born husband.
I'll then choose the one I like best.[44]
This is a command, not a request.   1416
As Saint Peter is my witness,
my sword will remove the head
of the first one who refuses."
When the maidens heard   1420
Constantine's command that,
one way or another,
he would examine their bare bodies,
Parise of Constantinople,   1424
who was exceedingly refined, spoke up:
"Ladies, I can see that some of you
are shivering and others are trembling.
Many a woman has been married who was first   1428
the mistress of another and then believed
she could pass herself off as a virgin.[45]
Such deceit deepens her shame!
A counterfeiter who tries to sell fake coins   1432
should be hanged high on the gallows.
Disrobe with confidence!
I'll go first.
It must be done sooner or later,   1436
and as for me, I do so willingly."
All the maidens then murmured,
"We'll do as you say. It's only right."
And so, they removed their belts   1440
of beaten gold, tearing the silk laces
with which they had fastened their sleeves.
You could see them all trembling
as they removed the clasps at their necks.   1444
Many of these,
worth one hundred marks or more,
were broken or damaged.
They then removed their bliauts   1448
and other garments of patterned silk and cendal.
When they had stripped to their chemises,
they were so dazed and overcome
that you could have travelled two leagues   1452
before they allowed those garments to fall to the ground.
When they had all undressed,
you may be sure they were miserable.
The king looked them over, then approached   1456
each one and kissed her on the mouth.
He didn't want to insult any of them,

for he knew it would cause them anguish.
The courtly Lorette spoke: 1460
"My lord, if it doesn't displease you,
and if you will agree to it,
allow us to get dressed again,
for by God in heaven,   1464
it is shameful to look upon a naked woman.
When you see us clothed once again,
you may then, at sunrise, choose the one
among us who pleases you best."   1468
"My lady, that is you!
And yet, by Saint Denis,
I love and cherish every woman here.
I'd willingly keep you all   1472
if I could, each one of you
as my lady and beloved.
But that cannot be,
for the law forbids it.   1476
It is fitting that I take you, Lorette,
for you are both courtly and wise,
and you have a most attractive figure, too."
With that (so I'm told),   1480
the doors were unlocked
and the maidens returned
to their lodgings.
The king granted them all safe conduct.   1484
Constantine's chosen lady was at his side
and she was, indeed,
wise and learned.
The nobles who attended   1488
the forthcoming festivities
were treated to a grand celebration.
After two weeks had gone by,
they prepared to return to their own lands.   1492
They were leaving in great numbers
when Samson the Strong arrived at court,
leading a great company of a hundred men.
He brought with him his sister,   1496
in whom he had great confidence,
for there wasn't another woman as beautiful
in all the world, not as far as the sky stretches.
He was sure the emperor would marry her   1500
because she was so very beautiful.
When the king heard the news of his arrival,
believe me, he was absolutely delighted.
He dispatched twenty knights   1504

to bring back all the nobles
who had already left.
These knights, as commanded by the king,
set off, and soon they returned   1508
with the departing barons.
Without any urging,
King Constantine left his palace,
accompanied by his men and his friends.   1512
He showed great honor
to Samson the Strong
and heartily embraced his sister.
He had to admit   1516
that her beauty outshone
that of all the other women
who had come to court
and he wanted to make her his wife.   1520
But this young woman declared
that she wouldn't even consider it,
nor would he ever wed her,
as long as he had another sweetheart: 1524
"I do not seek to wrong the other lady.
If I take the king away from her,
I'll have brought shame to one who loves him deeply.
I've heard it said—in fact, it's well known—   1528
that a lady's heart is broken
when her sweetheart's love turns to another.
All her joy then turns into pain.
I therefore do not seek to take him from her."   1532
Lorette replied: "I cannot gainsay my lord.
May he do as he wishes,
with no anger on my part.
I can honestly say that in terms of beauty,   1536
I cannot compete with you.
So I agree, and willingly declare
that you should be the sovereign lady of Rome
and of the empire, even though   1540
it may be displeasing to some."
The king was overjoyed when he heard
Lorette's speech and called out
to Samson the Strong: "My lord,   1544
let me tell you what I'm thinking.
I'll take your sister for my wife
and make her the sovereign lady of Rome,
Jerusalem and all the empire.   1548
And you shall marry Lorette,
who is beautiful and wise, and no less worthy.

There isn't a nobler woman
from here to Carthage.   1552
With her, I want you to have
my cities of Sour and Rome.
I give them to you most willingly.
Together with you, I love her more than life itself."   1556
When Samson the Strong heard this,
he went to kneel at the emperor's feet.
The king raised him up;
he was filled with happiness and joy.   1560
In the great church of Saint Peter,
both women were wed,
and joy reigned.
At the emperor's wedding,   1564
everyone made merry,
and it was the same for Samson the Strong,
who experienced great joy and delight.
The wedding festivities lasted for many days,   1568
and when, at last, it came time
for the assembled nobles to depart,
the king made a speech.
He announced that he intended to persevere   1572
until he once again ruled Babylon,
Jerusalem, and Tiberias,
Constantinople and Persia.
Each of the men solemnly swore   1576
to help him and to send reinforcements.
They would return home,
assemble their troops,
and then accompany the emperor to Babylon,   1580
where they would dethrone the emir.
They left without further ado.
Samson the Strong took with him his wife,
whom he deeply loved, and the men   1584
all returned to their own lands
to have their troops provisioned;
they would then move quickly
to aid the emperor. When they were equipped   1588
and all was ready, they returned to Rome.
The king was overjoyed
when he saw them arriving.
They soon left Rome,   1592
and set out for Constantinople,
where they intended to prevail.
When they arrived in Babylon,
the emir saw them coming,   1596

but he underestimated their strength.
They had all gathered there to defeat him.
The emir, along with twenty thousand armed knights,
rode out onto the plain.   1600
Count Guy, who was bearing the standard,
hastily said to his lord:
"Sire, this is serious;
See how the emir is advancing to fight."   1604
The emperor's knights took up arms
and brooking no delay,
went to do battle
with the king of Babylon's men.   1608
In the clash that ensued,
one could see many hauberks
and shields pierced.
Those who fell did not rise again,   1612
for the emir's men fought hard,
causing many of the emperor's knights
to fall to the ground, where they lay dead
on the field. As the saying goes,   1616
"scythes continually mow the field."[46]
The Romans were heavily attacked,
for the emir's men didn't fear them,
but in the end, they cut off the emir's head,   1620
entered the city,
and freed Noiron from prison.
They brought him (so I'm told)
to his nephew Constantine,   1624
who honored his uncle
whom he loved devotedly.
Noiron left Babylon and went to Jerusalem,
intending to lay siege.   1628
But the inhabitants
simply brought him the keys to the city,
and he accepted them all as his subjects.
Twenty brave sons of Jerusalem   1632
were delivered as hostages.
The emperor was pleased;
joy shone on his handsome face.
He subsequently left standing no castle,   1636
city, or marble tower,
from there to Dry-Tree,
unless the people swore allegiance to him.
When the king had achieved his purpose   1640
and conquered the kingdom,
he left his bailiff there and assigned

each man his proper place.
From that day forward,   1644
the whole country was obedient to Constantine,
and for many years,
Jerusalem paid tribute to Rome.
Constantine, who had a noble heart,   1648
returned to Constantinople.
The inhabitants didn't oppose him,
but instead, opened wide their gates.
I find in the written record   1652
that they had no lord at that time.
The emperor had died, and Parise,
his beautiful daughter, was his heir.
A nobler woman couldn't be found.   1656
She went forth to honor the king,
and showed him every courtesy.
This lady, who was so beautiful and noble,
governed Constantinople.   1660
She wished to honor the emperor,
and so invited him to her palace.
The bell was rung for everyone to wash their hands,
and the barons did so gladly.   1664
The seneschal, Guy, served wine
for his lord Constantine.
Parise stared at Guy and her heart
was overcome by love.   1668
When everyone had finished eating,
they all washed their hands
and the servants removed the tablecloths.
Guy, who was brave and loyal,   1672
courtly and valiant, was attracted to Parise.
He saw how beautiful she was,
and he too felt the stirrings of love.
The two spoke together for a long time   1676
and their feelings for each other were clear.
Parise delayed no longer
and said to the emperor:
"My lord, as a sign of your favor,   1680
I ask you to give me as husband
one of your most valued barons."
"Willingly, my lady," replied the king.
"I'll give you the first man   1684
you ask for. He'll be yours!"
Then lady leaned forward
and said: "My lord king,
I ask for your seneschal Guy.   1688

He'll be crowned
as soon as he marries me."
And so, the king granted her request.
Parise wanted to proceed immediately,   1692
but Guy wouldn't comply unless
his father, the Count of Poitiers,
and his mother were present.
The king said that he would see to it,   1696
and that he himself would wait until they arrived.
For this, Guy thanked him profusely.
The king made his messengers prepare
and then sent them to Poitiers.   1700
The count came most willingly,
and his wife, still more beautiful than a jewel,
came with him.
They travelled without ceasing   1704
until they arrived in Constantinople
where Count Guy kissed them both
and showed them great honor.
The next day, having wed his lovely wife,   1708
he was made emperor. For two full weeks
they celebrated most joyfully,
and then they all returned home.
Constantine left for Rome,   1712
and with him his barons and all his men.
The count left for Poitiers,
taking his lovely,
noble wife with him.   1716
Guy remained in Constantinople.
Of them I can tell you no more,
for this is all I have heard.

Introduction to
Li Contes dou roi Flore et de la bielle Jehane

Of unknown authorship, this tale was probably composed in the mid-thirteenth century in northern France. Written in prose, it is often cited as a source both for Boccaccio's "Tale of Bernabò" (*Decameron* II.9) and Shakespeare's play, "Cymbeline." Despite its influence on these well-known works, *Flore et Jehane* has rarely been studied independently. This relative neglect may be due to the comparatively short length of the story and its existence in a single manuscript, BnF fr. 24430, an anthology of works transcribed in the mid-fourteenth century in or around Tournai (Belgium). The text has been edited twice: by Francisque Michel in 1838 and again in 1856 by Louis Moland and Charles d'Héricault, whose edition is followed here.

The story offers a vivid portrait of the prevailing social hierarchy, in which wealthy male aristocrats exercise unquestioned control over both their families and their entourage. At the same time, it presents an alternate vision of authority by showcasing the intelligence and courage of an unjustly accused woman who goes to extreme measures to achieve justice.

The Tale of
King Flore and the Fair Joan

Here the story tells of a king named Flore of Ausai, a fine knight and a nobleman of high birth.[1] This king took to wife the daughter of the prince of Brabant, a noble lady from a great family. She was a beautiful young woman, lovely both in appearance and manners, and when they wed, she was only fifteen years old and King Flore seventeen. The two lived happily, as young people in love are wont to do, but they were unable to have a child, which deeply saddened them both. This beautiful lady loved God and holy Church and was so very generous and charitable that she fed and clothed the poor and kissed their feet and hands. She kept close company with both male and female lepers and served them with devotion. It was evident that the Holy Spirit dwelled within her. As for her lord, King Flore, when he wasn't at war, he attended tournaments in Germany and France and many other countries. Whenever he heard that a tournament was to be held, he made sure to be there, always spending lavishly and gaining much honor.[2]

The story now turns to a knight who lived on the border between Flanders and Hainaut. He was a worthy, brave, and most self-assured man with a beautiful wife and a lovely twelve-year old daughter named Joan. There was much talk about this young girl, for there was not another in the entire country as beautiful as she was. Her mother often said to her husband that he should arrange a marriage for her, but he was so intent on attending tournaments that he gave scarcely any thought to it. His wife repeatedly admonished him about this whenever he returned from his travels.

This knight had a squire named Robin, the most valiant fellow imaginable. In fact, it was through Robin's heroic deeds and thanks to his merit that his lord often won the tournaments. So admirable was this young man that his lord's wife confided in him:

"Robin, my lord is so intent on these tournaments that I don't know what to do. I'm at my wits' end! I want him to spend some time and effort arranging my daughter's marriage and he keeps delaying. I'm therefore asking you, as a friend, to speak to him about this when you find the opportunity. Tell him he's behaving badly and is at fault for not arranging his lovely daughter's marriage, for there isn't a knight in the land, however rich, who wouldn't be delighted to marry her."

"My lady," said Robin, "what you say is true. I'll explain it to him, for he believes me about many things, and I think he'll believe me about this, too."

"Please do, Robin," she replied, "and I'll reward you well!"

"I'm at your service, my lady," said Robin. "Rest assured that I'll do my best."

"That's all I ask," she replied.

Scarcely any time had elapsed before the knight began preparations for a tournament in a distant land. When he arrived there, he was soon selected for one of the teams, along with the knights who had accompanied him, and his banner was carried to his leader's lodgings.[3] The tournament began and, thanks to Robin's valiant efforts, the knight did so well that he won great praise and honor, whether he was attacking or on the defensive. On the second day, as the knight got ready to return to his own lands, Robin took him to task, blaming him for not seeing to his lovely daughter's marriage. He was so persistent that his lord finally said:

"Robin, you and your lady won't leave me in peace about this, but I haven't yet found anyone in my country to give her to."

"Ah, my lord!" said Robin, "there isn't a knight in your lands who wouldn't marry her most willingly."

"My dear friend, they're not worthy of her! I won't give her to one of them. I don't know anyone right now to whom I'd give her, except for one man who isn't even a knight."

"Tell me who it is, my lord," said Robin, "and I'll talk to him, or else have someone else speak with him and arrange the marriage."

"Judging by the way you're behaving, Robin, you must be eager for my daughter to wed!"

"That's true, my lord, for it's high time."

"Well," said the knight, "since you're so eager for her to be married, she soon will be, if you agree."

"Of course, my lord! I agree most willingly."

"Do you solemnly swear it?" said the knight.

"Yes, my lord," Robin replied.

"Robin, you've served me well and I've found you to be both brave and loyal. You've made me what I am, for thanks to you I've gained five hundred acres of land.[4] Not long ago I had only five hundred and now I have a thousand. So, I'll follow your advice and give my beautiful daughter to you, if you wish to have her."

"For heaven's sake, my lord! What are you saying? I'm far too poor to have such a highborn lady, and one so rich and beautiful! I'm not worthy of her. There isn't a knight in this land, no matter how noble, who wouldn't be delighted to marry her."

"Robin, be advised that a knight from my land will never have her, but I'll give her to you, if you wish, and with her four hundred acres of my land."

"You must be making fun of me, my lord!"

"Robin," replied the knight, "rest assured that I'm not joking."

"My lord, your lady wife and her noble family would never agree to it."

"I'm not doing this for them, Robin. Here's my glove. I hereby invest you with four hundred acres of land and guarantee that it is all yours."[5]

"I can hardly refuse, my lord! This is a wonderful gift, for I see that it is genuine."

"You've earned it, Robin."

And so, the knight gave him his glove, along with the land and his beautiful daughter.

The knight rode for a number of days until he arrived back home. When he got there, his lovely wife welcomed him joyfully, and said:

"My lord, for goodness' sake! Please give some thought now to your daughter's marriage."

"My lady," he replied, "you've talked about it so much that I've made the engagement."[6]

"To whom, my lord?"

"To a man who will never fail to act worthily. I've given her to Robin, my squire."

"Robin? Oh, no! Robin has nothing, and there isn't a brave knight in the entire country who wouldn't be thrilled to have her. Robin never will!"

"Ah, but he will, my lady, for I've already made the gift. Along with my daughter, I've given him four hundred acres of land. All this I must, and will, grant him."

When the lady heard this, she became very sad and said to her husband that Robin would never have her.

"My lady," said the lord, "he will indeed have her, whether you want him to or not. I've made a promise and I intend to keep it."

When the lady heard what her husband had done, she went to her chambers and began to weep and lament. Afterwards, she sent for her brothers and nephews and cousins and told them what her lord wanted to do. They replied:

"My lady, what do you want us to do about it? We have no desire to oppose your husband, for he's a brave, worthy, and powerful knight. Besides, he can do whatever he likes with his daughter and with the land he has acquired. We'll never take up arms against him."

"No? Alas!" says the lady. "I'll never be happy again if I lose my beautiful daughter like this. I ask you, noble lords, at least to show him that if he behaves this way it's dishonorable."

"My lady," they replied, "that much we will do most willingly."

They went to the knight and tried to reason with him, and he answered them very courteously:

"Dear friends, I'll tell you what I'll do. If you like, I'll renounce the marriage in the following way. You're all quite rich and have a great deal of land and you are good friends to my lovely daughter, whom I cherish. If you want to give her four hundred acres of land, I'll have the marriage cancelled and she'll be married according to your advice."

"Good heavens!" they replied. "We wouldn't go that far!"

"Well then," said the knight, "since you don't agree to this proposal, allow me do what I like with my daughter."

"Yes, of course, my lord," they replied.

The knight sent for his chaplain, brought his daughter to him, and had her engaged to Robin. They then set the date for the wedding. Three days later, Robin asked his lord to make him a knight, for it was unsuitable for him to marry such a highborn and beautiful woman before he had been knighted. His lord was delighted to do so, and Robin was knighted the following day. On the third day, amidst great rejoicing, he was wed to the lovely maiden.

Once Robert had been knighted, he said to his lord:[7]

"You've made me a knight, my lord, and now I must tell you the truth. I swore on pain of death that, on the day following my knighthood, I would travel to the shrine of Saint Jacques of Compostela.[8] I ask you to be patient, for tomorrow morning I must be off, as soon as I've married your beautiful daughter. I cannot break my vow."

"Well, Sir Robert, if you go off like this and leave my daughter, you'll be greatly to blame."

"My lord," he replied, "I'll be back soon, God willing, but this is something I absolutely must do."

One of the knights of the lord's court heard this exchange and vehemently condemned Sir Robert for leaving his wife at this time. But Robert said that he had to do it.

"Certainly," said the knight, whose name was Raoul, "if you go off like this to Saint Jacques without even touching your beautiful wife, I'll make a cuckold of you before you return. And when you get back, I'll give you proof I've had her. I'll even wager my land against the land you received from my lord, for I have four hundred acres of land just like you do."

Robert replied: "My wife would never betray me! She's not from that kind of lineage, and I would never believe her capable of doing such a thing.[9] Naturally, I'll make the bet."

"Well then," said Raoul, "do you swear it?"

"I do," replied Robert. "And you?"

"I do. Now let's go to my lord and record our bargain."

"Agreed," said Sir Robert.

And so, they went to their lord and had their agreement recorded, and they swore to abide by it.

The next morning, Sir Robert married the lovely girl and afterwards, when mass had been said, he left the great hall and the wedding celebrations and set off for Compostela.

Now the story turns to Sir Raoul, who was pondering how he could bed the beautiful lady and win the bet. The story relates that the lady behaved quite modestly while her husband was away, attending church regularly and praying for God to bring him back to her.

Raoul, on the other hand, focused on finding a way to win the bet, for he was very much afraid of losing his land. He spoke to the old woman who served the young lady and told her that if she could arrange things so that he could speak to the lady Joan privately and thereby have his way with her, he would give her so much money, she'd be a rich woman for the rest of her days.

"Of course, my lord," said the old woman. "You're such a handsome knight, and so fine and courtly, that my lady should certainly fall in love with you. I'll do everything I can."

The knight pulled out forty sous and gave them to her to buy some clothes. The old woman took the money gladly and put it in a safe place, promising that she would talk to her lady. The knight then departed. When her mistress returned from church, the old woman began to reason with her:

"My lady, for heaven's sake, tell me the truth. When my lord left for Compostela, had he ever lain with you?"

"Why do you ask, lady Hersent?"[10]

"Well, my lady, it's because I think you might still be a virgin."

"But of course I am, lady Hersent! How could it be otherwise? I've never heard such nonsense."

"That's a great pity, my lady," said Hersent. If you knew how much joy women have when they're with men they love, you'd say there was none greater! That's why I'm surprised you haven't loved the way other women do. But if you'd like to try it, you're in luck, for I know a handsome, valiant and fine knight who would willingly love you. He's a very rich man and handsomer than the craven coward who abandoned you. If you dare to love him, you'll have everything you could ask for, and greater joy than any other woman."

The old woman talked on like this to such an extent that the spurs of Nature began to prick Joan. Out of curiosity, she asked who the knight was.

"His name, my lady? By God, one *should* name him. It's the handsome, worthy and brave Sir Raoul. He's a member of your father's household and he has the courtliest heart imaginable."

"Lady Hersent," said the lady, "you'd do well to forget about this, for I don't intend to dishonor myself. I'm not from that kind of family."

"I was afraid of that, my lady," replied the old woman, "You'll never know the piercing joy that comes when a woman lies with a man."

And so, things remained at an impasse. Sir Raoul came back to the old woman, and she told him how she had spoken to her lady, and what Joan had replied.

"Lady Hersent," said the knight, "that's just what a good woman is obliged to say. You must speak to her again, since one never succeeds on the first try. And here: take twenty sous to buy yourself a lining for your surcoat."

The old woman took the money and spoke repeatedly to the lady, but to no avail. The time passed so quickly that they soon heard that Sir Robert was returning from Saint Jacques and was already close to Paris. The news spread rapidly and Sir Raoul, who was afraid of losing his land, went back to the old woman and spoke with her again. She told him that she couldn't carry out her task, but that, for love of him, and so that he would compensate her, she would arrange for him to be alone in the house with her lady. He could then have his way with her, either with her consent or by force. He told her that was all he asked.

Then the old woman said: "My Sir Robert will come back within the week. Before he arrives, I'll have my lady bathe in her chamber and send the servants away. Then you can come bathe with her and do what you will, whether she likes it or not."

"A good plan," he replied.

And so things remained until Sir Robert sent word that he was on his way and would arrive home on Sunday. The old woman arranged for the lady to bathe on the preceding Thursday. The bathtub was placed in her chamber and she climbed into it. The old woman then sent for Sir Raoul, who hurried to get there. Afterwards the old woman sent everyone in the house away.

Raoul entered the lady's chamber and greeted her, but she did not return his greeting. Instead she said:

"Sir Raoul, you are most discourteous. Do you really think I'm glad to see you? For shame!"

"My lady, for God's sake, take pity on me! I'm dying, because of you."

"Sir Raoul, she said, " I will never, out of pity, become your mistress! If you don't leave me in peace, I'll tell my father about the 'honor' you're asking of me. I'm not that kind of girl."

"Say it isn't true, my lady!"

"It most certainly is," she replied.

With that, Raoul approached the bath and clasped her tightly in his strong arms. He dragged her from the bath, completely naked, and carried her toward her bed. As soon as he had pulled her from the bath, he saw a black mark on the right side of her groin, quite near her private parts. He immediately realized that this knowledge would be powerful proof that he had lain with her. However, as he carried her to her bed, his spurs got caught in the covers near the foot of it, and he and the lady fell, with him below and Joan on top. She quickly scrambled up, seized a stick of kindling, and struck Raoul in the face, inflicting a large, deep wound that spattered the ground with blood. When Raoul realized how badly he had been hurt, all desire for Joan left him; instead, he got up and hastily left the room. He made it to his lodgings which were more than a league away, and once there had his wound attended to. As for the good lady, she got back into her bath, and called Hersent, to whom she related her encounter with the knight.

The father of the fair Joan made elaborate preparations for Robert's impending return, summoning folk from all around and inviting his knight, Sir Raoul, to come. But Raoul sent word that he was ill and therefore couldn't make it. On Sunday, Sir Robert arrived and was eagerly welcomed. Joan's father went looking for Raoul and, finding that he had been wounded, told him that he should not, on that account, stay away from the festivities. Raoul did the best he could to cover up the wound on his face and went to the celebration, where there was plenty to drink and eat and the dancing and singing went on all day.

When night fell, Sir Robert and his wife retired to their bed, and she welcomed him most joyfully, as a good lady should do for her husband. They had delight and joy for the greater part of the night.

In the morning, the festivities continued; food was prepared and everyone ate. Later, after they had all dined, Raoul began to speak to Robert and told him that he had won his land, for he had known Robert's wife carnally. He could prove it by a black mark she had on her right thigh and a mole near her "jewel."

"I know nothing about it," replied Robert. "I haven't looked that closely."

"Then I'm telling you," said Raoul. "By the oath you've sworn to me, you must take a look and fulfill your obligation to me."

"I most certainly will," said Robert.

When night came, Sir Robert lay with his wife and saw with his own eyes the black mark on her right groin and the mole close to her beautiful jewel. When he discovered this, he was deeply saddened. The next day he went to Raoul and declared before his lord that he had lost the wager. All day long he grieved and when night fell, he went to the stable, saddled his palfrey and left the house. Taking with him what he could in the way of silver, he set out for Paris. Once there, he stayed for three days.

Now the story leaves off speaking of him and turns to his wife, who was deeply saddened and distressed when she learned that her husband had left her again. She couldn't understand why this had happened and she wept and grieved so much that her father came to her and announced that he would have preferred for her to remain single, for she had brought shame to him and all those of his lineage. Then he told her about the wager. She was extremely upset when she heard this, and denied everything, but to no avail. It's well known that a woman's reputation is such that, even if she burned herself alive, she would never be believed when accused of such a misdeed.

That night, when everyone had fallen asleep, the lady rose and took all the money she had in her strongboxes. She then selected a coffer and a packhorse and departed, having first cut off all her beautiful hair and dressed herself as a squire.[11] Thus disguised, she rode until she came to Paris, thinking to find her husband there, and swearing she would never give up until she had found him. Having no luck, she set off one morning for Orléans. Before long she came to the tomb of Ysoré,[12] and there she found her husband, Sir Robert. She was overjoyed to see him and went immediately to greet him. He returned her greeting, and then said to her:

"Good friend, may God give you joy!"

"Sir," he replied, "where are you from?"

"I'm from Hainaut, my friend."

"And where are you going, sir?"

"Well, my friend, I don't really know where I'm going, nor where I'll stay. It suits me to go wherever fortune leads, even though it has been unkind to me. I've lost the one person I loved most in this life and she has therefore lost me. And I've lost my land, which was extensive and beautiful. But what is your name and where is God taking you?"

"Well, sir," replied John,[13] "I believe I'll go in the direction of Marseille, by the sea, where there is, I hope, some fighting. There, God willing, I'll serve some worthy man in whose company I'll learn about weapons, for I am so dishonored in my own land that I'll never find peace there. Sir, you seem to me to be a knight, and I'll serve you most willingly, if you like. You won't suffer from my company!"

"My friend," replied Robert, "I am indeed a knight, and I would willingly go where there is fighting. But first tell me what your name is."

"My name is John, my lord."

"May this be a good omen," said the knight.

"And what is your name, sir?"

"My name is Robert," he replied.

"Sir Robert, please take me as your squire and I'll serve you to the best of my ability."

"I'd do so gladly, John, but I have so little money that, before three days are up, I'll be obliged to sell my horse. I don't know how I can retain you."

"Don't worry about it, my lord, for God will help you, if he wishes to. Tell me where you'd like to dine."

"Dinner won't take long, since I'm down to my last three sous."

"Don't worry, sir. I have almost ten pounds, which will be entirely at your disposal for whatever you need."[14]

"My good John, many thanks!"

Then they made the long journey to Montlehéry, where John persuaded his lord to eat. When they had dined, the knight went to sleep in a bed, and John slept at his feet. After they had rested, John saddled the horses and they set off, riding for many days until they arrived in Marseille, by the sea. They were disappointed to find no fighting there. But here the story stops speaking about the two of them and returns to Sir Raoul, who had won my lord Robert's land through treachery.

The story now relates that Raoul held Robert's land unjustly for seven years. He then became gravely ill, and was so severely afflicted he was on the verge of dying. He was deeply afraid because of the sin he had committed toward the lovely lady, the daughter of his lord, and her husband, who had both vanished because of his wickedness. His sin caused him grievous suffering, made all the greater because he dared not make confession. One day, he was so oppressed by his illness that he finally sent for his chaplain, whom he held very dear, for he had found him to be worthy and loyal. He said to him:

"Sir, you who are my father through God, I believe I'll die from this malady. I'm begging you for advice, for I sorely need it. I have committed a sin so ugly and dark that I need pardon for this misdeed."

The chaplain encouraged him to speak up, advising him as best he could, so that Raoul finally told him the whole story, just as you have heard it. He begged the chaplain to tell him what to do, for he wanted to be pardoned for this great sin.

"Sir," he said, "don't worry. If you carry out the penance I enjoin upon you, I will, in the meantime, take your sin upon myself and my own soul, so that you will be free of it."

"Tell me," said the knight.

"Sir," he replied, "you must take up the Cross and go to the Holy Land and you must promise to make the trip sometime within the year in which you've been cured. You must swear an oath to God that you will do this, and that whenever and wherever you are asked the reason for your pilgrimage, you'll tell the truth to whoever asks."

"All this I will certainly do," said the knight.

"Sir, you must now make a pledge."

"Most willingly," replied the knight. "You yourself will be my surety, and I swear to you, on my honor as a knight, that I'll make good on my promise."

"Sir," said the chaplain, "as God wills it. I stand surety for you."

The knight recovered completely, but the year passed without him going overseas. The chaplain often reminded him that he was behaving as though his promise were a joke. Finally, the chaplain told him that, if he didn't acquit himself before God on the pledge for which the chaplain himself stood surety, he would tell Joan's father that he had lost her because of Raoul. When the knight heard this, he swore to the chaplain that he would join the March passage and sail within the next six months.[15] But now the story leaves the knight and turns once again to King Flore of Ausai, about whom it has long been silent.

Here the story tells that King Flore of Ausai and his wife led a very worthy life, for they were young and very much in love. But they were sad and deeply distressed because they were unable to have a child. The lady often prayed about it, and had masses sung, but since it wasn't God's will, it was not to be. One day a worthy holy man who had his humble abode in a remote part of the great forest of Ausai came to the home of King Flore. When the queen heard that he had come, she went to him and welcomed him warmly. Because he was a worthy man, the lady made her confession to him and told him all about her grief and how distressed she was because she had no child by her lord.

"Ah, my lady," said the worthy man, since it is not God's will, you must bear it. When it *is* his will, you'll soon have two or three children."

"Indeed, sir," said the lady, "I would wish it so, for my lord holds me in less esteem, as do the noblemen of this land. I understand they've told my lord he should leave me and take another."

"Truly, my lady," said the worthy man, "he would be wrong to do so, for it would be contrary to God and Holy Church."

"Ah, sir! I beg you to pray to God for me that I might have a child by my lord, for I'm very much afraid he will leave me."

"My lady," replied the worthy man, "my prayer will carry little weight if it is not God's will. Nevertheless, I'll gladly pray about it."

The worthy man left the lady, and the noblemen of the land and of all the country came to King Flore and told him to repudiate his wife and take another, since he could not have a child by her. They added that, if he did not follow their advice, they would go elsewhere to live, for they couldn't accept for the kingdom to remain without an heir.

King Flore feared his nobles and believed what they said, so he promised to repudiate his wife and seek another, and that is exactly what happened. When the lady was told, her heart was heavy, but she dared not object. She knew her lord would leave her. She summoned the hermit who was her confessor and told him all about the noblemen who sought another wife for her lord.

"And so I beg you, holy father, help me and tell me what I should do."

"My lady," said the worthy man, "if it is as you say, you must accept their decision, for you cannot coerce your lord or his nobles."

"Sir," said the good lady, "you're right. But if it pleases God, I'd like to become a nun and live near you. That way I can serve God for the rest of my days and be comforted by you."

"This would be inappropriate, my lady, for you are a young woman and beautiful. But I'll tell you what to do. Near my hermitage there is an abbey of white nuns who are very good women, and it is there that I advise you to go. They will be overjoyed to receive so good and noble a lady as you."[16]

"Sir," she replied, "you've advised me well. That's what I'll do, since you have recommended it."

The next day King Flore spoke to his wife and said to her that "it is necessary for us to part, for you are unable to bear me a child. But know that I'm grieved by our separation, for I will never love another woman as I have loved you."

Then King Flore broke down and wept, and so did the lady.

"My lord," she replied, "have pity, for God's sake! Where will I go and what shall I do?"

"My lady, God willing, all will be well. I'll send you back with riches and in state to your own country and your friends there."

"That will never be, my lord. I know of an abbey of nuns and, if you will agree to it, I'll go there and serve God for the rest of my life. For if I must lose your company, I'll never live with another man."

Then King Flore and the lady wept again. Three days later, the queen went to the abbey, and the new queen arrived. To celebrate, there was great feasting and joy among the king's friends. King Flore lived with her for three years, but was never able to have children by her. And now the story is silent about King Flore, and returns to my lord Robert and John, who had arrived in Marseille.

In this part the story it says that, when they arrived in Marseille, Sir Robert was most unhappy to learn that there was no unrest in the area. He said to John:

"What shall we do? You've loaned me your money, for which I am most grateful. I'll pay you back when I sell my horse and then you'll have what I owe you."

"My lord," replied John, "please trust me when I tell you what we should do. I still have a hundred sous. If you agree, I'll sell our two horses and get some more money. I'm the best baker you've ever seen. I make French bread and I'm quite sure I can make back my investment." "John," said Sir Robert, "I agree to do whatever you want."

The very next day John sold the two horses for ten pounds and bought wheat and baskets. He then began to make such good French bread that he sold more than the two best bakers in town. He did so well that in two years' time he had one hundred pounds in savings.

Then John said to his lord, "I advise that we lease a very large house. I'll buy wine and lodge worthy folk there." "John," said Robert, "do whatever you want. I'll agree to it. I have complete confidence in you." And so, John leased a large, handsome house and rented out rooms to respectable folk, thereby earning a great deal of money. He clothed his lord in beautiful and expensive clothes and Robert had a palfrey and went to eat and drink with the most prominent residents of the town. John served such good wine and food that his companions all marveled. He earned so much that within four years he earned more than three hundred pounds in cash, not counting other property which was worth fifty pounds. But here the story falls silent about John and Sir Robert, and returns to speak of Raoul.

According to the story, the chaplain repeatedly urged Sir Raoul to travel overseas and release him from the pledge he had made to assume Raoul's guilt; he greatly feared that Raoul would fail to follow through. Raoul, finally seeing that he would have to comply, prepared for the trip, provisioning himself lavishly, for he was now very rich. Accompanied by three squires, he set off. The men travelled for many days until they reached Marseille, by the sea, and there they took lodging at the French Inn run by Sir Robert and John. As soon as John saw Raoul, she recognized him both by the scar she had given him and because she had seen him many times.[17] The knight remained in town for two weeks and booked passage on a ship. While he was staying at the inn, John took him aside and asked him why he was going overseas. Raoul, not recognizing her, told the whole story, just as it was recounted above. John listened but said nothing. Soon Sir Raoul had his baggage stowed and went on board, though the ship didn't sail for a week. On the ninth day, they went to the Holy Sepulcher and there Raoul accomplished his pilgrimage and confessed as best he could. As penance, his confessor required him to return to its rightful owners the land he was holding unjustly. Raoul told his confessor that, when he returned to his own country, he would act as his heart directed him. He left Jerusalem and went to Acre, where he arranged passage, for he was eager to return home. They set sail and, travelling night and day, arrived at the port of Aigues Mortes in less than three months.

Raoul left the port and went straight to Marseille, where he stayed for a week at the inn of Sir Robert and John, known as the French Inn. Sir Robert never recognized Raoul, for he no longer thought about what had happened in the past. At the end of the eight days, Raoul and his squire left Marseille and journeyed home. There he was welcomed with great joy, for he was a knight of substance and much property. Soon his chaplain made him tell what had happened and asked him whether anyone had asked the reason for his trip. He replied that yes, they had, in three different places: Marseille, Acre, and Jerusalem.

"And the one who advised me said I should return the land to Sir Robert when I hear news of him, or to his wife or heirs."

"He gave you very good advice," said the chaplain.

Thus, my lord Raoul remained in his own country for a long time, peacefully and at ease. But here the story leaves off speaking of him and returns to Sir Robert and John.

Here the story relates that after Sir Robert and John had spent six years in Marseille, John had earned the sum of six hundred pounds. They were already into their seventh year and John was still earning as much as he wished. He was so easy-going and charming that he endeared himself to all his neighbors. In addition to this, he was extremely happy and supported his lord so nobly and in such abundance that it was a wonder to behold. When the seventh year was drawing to a close, John spoke to Robert, and this is what he said:

"My lord, we have been in this region for quite some time and have succeeded so well that we have around six hundred pounds worth of property, either in cash or silver dishes."

"John, these things certainly do not belong to me, but to you, for you have earned them."

"My lord," replied John, "saving your grace, they aren't mine; they belong to you. For you are my rightful lord and, God willing, I'll never exchange you for another."

"I give you my deepest thanks, John. I think of you not as a servant, but as a companion and friend."

"My lord," said John, I've always been your faithful servant and will continue to be so."

"By heaven," replied Robert, "I'll do whatever you like. But I don't know what to say about returning to my own land. I've suffered such loss that the harm can never be remedied."

"Do not distress yourself about that, my lord. If it pleases God, you'll have good news as soon as you're back home. Don't worry about anything, for wherever we go, God willing, I'll earn enough for us both."

"I'll do whatever you like, John, and go wherever you wish."

"Then I'll sell our holdings, my lord, and prepare for our trip. We'll leave within the next two weeks."

"As God wills it, John," said Sir Robert.

John sold all his fine belongings and bought three horses: a palfrey for his lord and one for himself, and a packhorse. They then took leave of their neighbors and the worthies of the town who were very sad indeed to see them depart.

Sir Robert and John rode so quickly that within three weeks they arrived in their own land. Robert sent word to his lord, whose daughter he had wed, that he was coming. The lord was delighted, for he believed that his daughter must be with him. And so she was, but disguised as a squire!

Sir Robert was graciously received by his lord, whose daughter he had married so long ago. When his lord realized that there was no news of his daughter, he was deeply saddened. Nevertheless, he gave Robert a very warm welcome, ordering his knights and his neighbors to come for the celebration. Sir Raoul, who wrongfully held Robert's land, was among them. Great was the joy that day and the next, and Sir Robert finally told John about the bet and that Raoul wrongfully held his land.

"My lord," said John, "call him out for his treachery and I'll fight him for you."

"No, John, you will not."

And so things stood until the following day, when John went to Sir Robert and told him he wished to speak with his father-in-law. Here's what he said:

"My lord, you are the overlord of my lord Robert, who married your daughter long ago. A wager was made between him and Sir Raoul, who said that he would cuckold him before he returned from Compostela. But Sir Raoul lied about this, for he never had relations with your fair daughter and instead engaged in a wicked betrayal. All this I'm ready to prove in single combat with him."

Then Sir Robert came up to him and said: "John, dear friend, no one will do battle, or hang a shield around his neck, unless I do so myself."

With that, Sir Robert held out his pledge to his lord. Sir Raoul was very sorry to see this, but was obliged to defend himself, lest he be called a coward. And so, he gingerly offered his own pledge, as well. Thus, the pledges were given and the day of the combat, two weeks hence, was announced.

Now listen to an account of the wondrous thing John did! John, whose name was really Joan, had a first cousin who was residing in her father's house; she was a beautiful maiden and twenty-five years old. John went to her and told her the truth, recounting the whole affair from beginning to end without omitting a thing and asked her to please conceal the truth until the time was right and she made everything known to her father. Her cousin, who easily recognized her, said she'd keep it a secret and that no one would find out about it from her. Then Joan dressed in her cousin's chamber. During the two weeks prior to the combat, she took warm baths and rested as much as she could, for she had great need of it. She had four outfits made to her measurements, of red, green, and shimmering dark blue silk.[18] Joan rested to such good effect that her great beauty returned, and she was lovelier than ever. When the fifteen days had come to an end, Sir Robert was very upset because his squire, John, had disappeared without a trace. But he did not for that reason neglect to prepare for battle, for he was both brave and strong.

The next day, when the combat was scheduled to take place, both knights arrived, already armed. They distanced themselves from one another and then, with the iron of their lances lowered, raced at each other with such speed that both men were knocked to the ground, their horses still beneath him. Sir Raoul was slightly wounded in the left flank. Sir Robert was the first to rise to his feet. He ran towards Raoul and struck a great blow to his helmet, crushing the flat top.[19] The blade tore through it to the iron coif beneath and cut through that. But the coif was made of strong steel and Raoul wasn't hurt at all. The blow, however, was so powerful that he staggered and was obliged to grab the pommel of his saddle. If he had not, he would have fallen to the ground. Raoul, who was a valiant knight, then landed such a hard blow on Robert's helmet that he was stunned. The blow came down on his shoulder and tore the mail of his hauberk, but he escaped injury. Robert struck back with all his strength, but Raoul defended himself with his shield, a quarter of which was destroyed. When Raoul felt these great blows, he became terribly afraid, and wished he were overseas, so that he would be free of this fight and Robert could once again have the land he was holding. Nevertheless, he put all his strength and skill into the fight and came back harshly on Robert, striking such a powerful blow to his shield that he clove it right down to the grip. Robert struck back, hitting Raoul's helmet. He raised his shield to ward off the blow, but Robert split it down the middle. The sword struck the neck of Raoul's horse and cut right through it, striking down man and horse together. But Raoul soon jumped up; he was well-accustomed to battle. Robert dismounted, for his opponent was on foot, and he wouldn't fight with an unfair advantage.

Then the two knights got down to business, each one tearing apart the other's shield and helmet until they were severely damaged. With their sharp blades, they drew each other's blood. Had they been striking blows as great as these when the battle began, they would soon have slain one another. Now so little was left of their shields they could barely cover their fists. Both men feared dying or living in shame, and the great valor they both possessed led them to finish the fight. Robert took his sword in both hands. With all his strength, he struck Raoul on his iron helmet, splitting it. Half of it fell onto his shoulders and he was badly wounded in the head. Raoul was so stunned by the blow that he fell to his knees, though he soon rose. He was distressed to find that his head was bare and was now terrified that he would die. He approached Robert and struck with all his strength on what remained of his shield. The blow cut through Robert's helmet, cleaving the width of three fingers. The blow to the sturdy iron caused the sword to break apart. When Raoul saw that his sword was broken and his head bare, he was sure he would die. He bent down and, with both hands, grabbed a great stone. With all his strength, he threw it at Robert. But Robert saw it coming and dodged. He then ran towards Raoul, who began to flee through the field of battle. Sir Robert called to him, saying that if he didn't admit his treachery, he would kill him. To this, Sir Raoul called back:

"Have mercy, noble knight! Here's my sword, such as it is. I surrender it to you and place myself at your disposal. I beg you to take pity on me, and I beg your lord and mine to take pity as well, and that you both will spare my life. I give you your land and my own, for I have held yours unlawfully, without any right to it, since I wrongfully defamed your beautiful, good lady."

When Sir Robert heard this, he said to himself that he was satisfied. He begged his lord to such good effect that he agreed to pardon Raoul for his misdeed. The other knights urged him to forgive Raoul, if he would go overseas and never return.

Thus, my lord Robert won back his land and also gained the land of Sir Raoul. But he remained sad and heavy of heart because of the good and beautiful lady he had lost. For this reason, he could find no comfort. He was, in addition, utterly miserable about his squire John, whom he had also lost. His lord was no less upset about his beautiful daughter whom he had lost and about whom no one had heard a word.

Lady Joan, who had been relaxing in her cousin's chambers these past two weeks, was absolutely delighted to learn that her lord had won the battle. She selected the most elegant of her four new dresses and put it on; it was made of silk and trimmed with embroidered bands stitched with fine Arabian gold thread. She was so beautiful, both in form and face, and so gracious, that one couldn't find a more beautiful creature in the whole world. Even her cousin was dazzled by her great beauty. She had been taking baths and caring for herself, relaxing completely for two weeks, and all her astonishing beauty had returned.[20]

Lady Joan looked lovely and was quite suitably attired in her gown of silk with its golden bands. She called for her cousin and said to her:

"How do I look?"

"Ah, my lady!" said her cousin, "you're the most beautiful woman in the world!"

"My dear cousin, here's what I need you to do. First of all, go tell my father that he shouldn't grieve, but should instead be joyful, for you are bringing him good news about his daughter, who is safe and sound. Tell him to come with you and you'll prove it to him. Bring him here. He'll be glad to see me, I think."

Her cousin said she would gladly deliver the message. She went to Joan's father and told him what his daughter had said. When the lord heard this, he thought it a great wonder. He went with his niece and found his daughter in her chambers. He recognized her immediately and put his arms around her neck. Weeping from joy and relief, he was so overcome that he could hardly speak. At last he asked where she had been all this time.

"Dear father," said the lady, "you'll hear all about it in due course. But please send for my mother, for I'm very eager to see her."

The lord sent for his wife, and when she came into the room and saw her daughter, she fainted from joy and couldn't utter a single word for quite some time. When she came to, the great happiness she showed on finding her daughter was indescribable. While she was thus immersed in joy, the father of the beautiful young woman went looking for Robert, and here's what he said to him:

"Robert, my dear son, I have news that will make you as joyful as it has made me."

"Truly," said Robert, "I could use some joy, though no one, without God's help, can bring it to me. I've lost your beautiful daughter, and my heart is heavy because of it. And then I lost the young man who did more for me than anyone in the world: my squire, the good John."

"Sir Robert," said the lord, "don't worry about that. You'll find another squire easily enough! But I have some good news for you concerning my lovely daughter. I've seen her just now and I can assure you that she is still the most beautiful lady in the world."

When Robert heard this, he began to shake for sheer joy and replied: "Ah, my lord! For heaven's sake, if this is true, please take me to her!"

"Gladly," he replied. "Come with me."

The lord led the way and soon they were in the chamber where the mother was still making a great fuss over her daughter, each of them crying on the other's shoulder. When they saw their rightful lords, they rose. As soon as Sir Robert recognized his wife, he ran to her with his arms outstretched. They embraced and kissed each other sweetly and wept for joy and relief. They remained clasped together for as long as it would take to traverse ten acres of land, before anyone could pull them apart. The lord ordered that tables be set up for supper and they all dined and had a wonderful time.

After supper, and the great celebration that accompanied it, they all went to bed. That night Sir Robert lay with the lady Joan his wife, and each gave the other great joy. They spoke together about many things, and Sir Robert asked her where she had been for so long. She replied:

"My lord, there's much to tell. You'll hear all about it before long. But tell me what you've been doing and where *you* have been all this time."

"My lady," said Robert, "I'll be happy to tell you."

He began to tell her everything that she already knew perfectly well: about his squire, John, who had done so much for him. He told her how distressed he was at having lost him—so much so that he would never stop searching until he found him, and that he planned to leave in the morning.

"My lord," said the lady, "that would be madness. What on earth are you thinking? Do you want to leave me?"

"My lady," he replied, "I certainly must do it, for no man has ever done more for another than he did for me."

"My lord," she replied, "if he did things for you, he did so wisely. It's what he should have done."

"To hear you speak, my lady, it sounds like you know him."

"But of course!" said the lady. "I ought to know him, for he never did a single thing I didn't know about."

"My lady, your words astonish me!"

"You shouldn't be the least bit surprised, my lord. If I tell you something that is absolutely true, will you believe me?"

"Yes, of course, my lady."

"Then take my word on it," she said. "I am that John you wish to go searching for and I'll now tell you how that came to be. When I learned that you had left because of the great grief you had, believing I had misbehaved and that you had lost your land forever, and when I learned the circumstances of the wager and the way my lord Raoul had cheated you, I was angrier than any woman has ever been. So much so that I had my hair cut off and filled my trunks with money—some ten pounds, and I dressed as a squire and followed you to Paris. I found you close by at Ysoré's tomb and joined company with you. We went together to Marseille and stayed there together for seven years, where I served you, my rightful lord, to the best of my abilities. And I consider all those years of service time well spent. You may rest assured that I'm pure and innocent of all that the wicked knight accused me of. It's only right that he was vanquished in battle and admitted his dishonesty."

Then lady Joan embraced Sir Robert, her husband, and gently kissed his mouth. When Robert heard that it was she who had served him so well, his joy was greater than anyone could imagine or tell. He marveled greatly that she had been able to think of doing this thing from which such great good had come, and he would love her even more for it for the rest of his life.

These two good people were thus brought together and went to care for their lands, which were extensive and fine. They led a good life as young people do who are deeply in love. Sir Robert often went to tournaments with his lord, from whom he held his land, and gained much honor. He achieved considerable renown and won great rewards, acquiring even more land than he already had. When Joan's parents, their lord and lady, died they inherited all of their land, too. Robert did so well thanks to his great skill that he was made a double banneret and had four thousand pounds worth of land.[21] But he was never able to have a child by his wife, and this made him very sad. He lived with her for more than ten years after having won the battle against Sir Raoul.

At the end of the ten years, it was the will of God, to whom we all submit, that he fall mortally ill. He died bravely, receiving the special prayers for the dead, and was buried with pomp and ceremony. His beautiful wife was so grief-stricken that everyone who saw her, pitied her greatly. After a time, the grief began to subside and she was somewhat, if only slightly, comforted.

During her widowhood she behaved as a good lady should, strong in her faith, for she deeply loved God and holy church. She acted with great humility, loving the poor and doing much for them. She was such a fine lady that no one could reproach her for anything, or say anything but good about her. Above and beyond all this, she was still so fair that everyone proclaimed her the epitome of feminine beauty and goodness.[22] But now the story falls silent for a while about her, and returns to King Flore, about whom we have heard nothing for quite some time.

The story now relates that King Flore of Ausai resided in his lands most unhappily, after the departure of his first wife. The next one was brought to him and she was also beautiful and noble, but he couldn't love her as dearly as the first one. They lived together for four years, but he was never able to have a child by her. At the end of this time, the lady fell ill, died, and was buried, which greatly pained her husband. Services were conducted as befitted a queen.

King Flore remained a widower for more than two years, but he was still a young man, not more than forty-five years old, and so his noblemen told him he should marry again.

"Truly," said King Flore, "I'm not eager to do so, for I've had two wives and never been able to have a child. In addition, the first one I had was so beautiful, and I loved her so deeply for the great goodness that dwelled in her, that I'm unable to forget her. I tell you that I'll never take a wife if I can't find one as beautiful and as good as she was. And may God have mercy on her soul, for she has now passed away in the abbey where she was living. That's what I've been told."

"Ah, my lord!" said a knight who was a member of his privy council. "There are many good ladies in the land—you don't know them all! And I know about one whose beauty and goodness is unsurpassed in all the world. If you knew about her goodness, and saw her great beauty, you would surely say that the king who could possess such a lady was indeed a happy man! You may rest assured that she's a noble lady, worthy, wealthy, and possessed of much land. I'd like to describe her qualities further if you'll agree."

The king replied that he would be glad to hear more about her. The knight began to tell how she had gone to look for her lord, found him, and then led him to Marseille. Then he described all the great kindnesses and services she had done for him, just as we have heard it told. King Flore was quite amazed by this account. He told this knight, who was one of his advisors, that he would willingly take such a wife.

"My lord," said the knight, who came from the lady's lands, "I'll go to her, if you wish, and, if I am able, speak with her to such good effect that a marriage between the two of you will be arranged."

"Agreed," said King Flore. "I want you to go, and ask you to devote yourself to the task."

With that the knight took his leave and travelled so speedily that he soon arrived in the land of the lady whom the story calls Lady Joan. He found her staying in one of her chateaux and she gave him a most warm welcome, for she knew him well. The knight spoke privately with her and told her that King Flore of Ausai had sent him to her because he would gladly take her as his wife. When the lady heard the knight say this, she began to smile, which was very becoming, and replied:

"Your king is neither as wise nor as courteous as I imagined if he sends word to me like this, asking me to come to him so he can make me his wife. I'm not some hired soldier he can order about! Tell your king that he may come to *me* if he values and loves me so much and would like for me to accept him as my husband and spouse. For men should seek out women, not the other way around."[23]

"My lady," said the knight, "all that you've told me I'll gladly convey to him. But I fear he will consider it pride on your part."

"Sir knight," said the lady, "he'll think what he pleases, but in that which I've said to you, there's nothing but courtesy and good sense."

"My lady," said the knight, "may it be as God wills. I take my leave of you now and will return to my lord the king, and tell him what you've said to me. If you want to add anything else, please tell me."

"Yes, I do," replied they lady. "Tell him that I send him my greetings and that I am most grateful to him for the honor of the proposal he has sent."

The knight was soon on his way and four days later had arrived in King Flore's lands. He found him in his chambers, where he spoke privately with his privy council. The knight greeted the king, who returned his greetings and had him sit next to him. He then asked him for news of the beautiful lady. The knight relayed the messages she had sent back: that she would not come to him, for she was not a hired soldier at his beck and call; men were supposed to court ladies in person. That was the message she had sent, with her greetings and her thanks for the honor of his proposal. When King Flore heard these words, he began to ponder and didn't say a word for quite a while.

"Sire," said the knight who was his chief counsellor, "what are you thinking about so intently? Certainly, all such words are befitting a good and wise lady and, as God is my witness, she is both wise and worthy. I advise you in good faith to find a day when you're able to travel there. Send word to her that you'll arrive there on such and such a day, to do her honor and ask for her hand in marriage."

"Well, then," said King Flore, "I'll send word to her that I'll be with her in the month of Easter and ask her to get ready to receive me."

Then King Flore said to the knight who had visited the lady that he should be ready to leave in three days' time to convey this news to the lady.

On the third day, the knight left and hurried along until he arrived at his destination. He told the lady that the king sent word that he would come to her in the month of Easter. She replied that it was in God's hands, and that she would speak of it with her friends. She would be ready to do as he wished because her honor as a noblewoman required it.

After he had delivered this message, the knight left and went back to his lord, King Flore. He told the king what the beautiful lady had said, just as you've heard it. King Flore gathered all that was required for travel and left with a large entourage of nobles. When he arrived in the lady's lands, he took her to wife and married her, and there was great joy and celebration. He took her back to his own country where everyone welcomed her with great joy. King Flore loved her very much for her great beauty and for the wisdom and valor she possessed.

Within the year after they married, she was with child, as was befitting. She carried the fruit in her womb until she delivered first a daughter, and then a son immediately after. The boy's name was Florent and the girl's, Floris. Florent was very handsome and when he became a knight, he was the best fighter anyone had ever seen. He was a most brave man, who fought many battles against the Saracens, causing them considerable grief. Eventually, he was chosen to be emperor of Constantinople. The daughter became queen of her father's lands and married the son of the king of Hungary. She was therefore queen of both realms. God granted these great honors to the fair lady because of her goodness and her steadfastness.

King Flore lived with his beautiful wife for many years and when it pleased God for his end to come, he made such a good confession that he went to God as a pure soul. After he died, the lady lived but six more months. She left the world as a good and faithful person, and had a good end and a good reward.

Here ends the tale of King Flore and the Fair Joan.

Appendix I:
The Songs of
The Romance of the Violet

The following is a list of the (translated) first lines of the songs cited in the *Roman de la Violette*, followed by the text as it appears in Douglas Buffum's edition. Most of the songs are anonymous; authors, when known, are indicated, along with other pertinent information about the song, such as the genre. These identifications follow Buffum's descriptions of the songs in the introduction to his edition (pp. LXXXII–XCI). For additional information, see his earlier study, "The Songs of the *Roman de la Violette*," published in 1911. Maureen Boulton's discussion of the songs in *The Song in the Story*, published in 1993, offers suggestive interpretations of the function of the songs within the given narrative context.

1. Go gently, for I am pained by love!
   (Alés bielement que d'amer me duel.) l. 104
Refrain.

2. Go sweetly and serenely
   (Alés cointement et seri,
   Se vous m'amés.) ll. 110–111
Refrain.

3. Never will I marry, though
   (Je ne mi marïerai,
   Mais par amors amerai.) ll. 119–120
Refrain.

4. If I love with a true heart,
   (Se j'ainc par amors,
   Joie en ai plus grant:
   Mal gré en aient li mesdisant. (ll. 126–128)
A refrain attributed by K. Bartsch to the late-12th-century trouvère

Pierre de Corbie. (*Romances et pastourelles françaises du XIIe et XIIIe siècles.* See Buffum, p. LXXXIV)

    5. All alone, I go to my lover's side,
        (Seulete vois a mon ami;
        S'ai grant paor.) ll. 134–135
Refrain.

    6. A good husband learn to be,
        (Aprendés a valoir maris,
        Ou vous m'avés perdue.) ll. 141–142

    7. Whatever my husband may think
        (Ja ne lairai pour mon mari ne die
        Que mes amis n'ait un resgart de moi.) ll. 152–153

    8. Since a lovely lady (Love her very self) asks me,
        (Quant biele dame et fine amors me prie,
        Encor ferai chanchon cointe et jolie,
        Ne ja ne quier k'envïeus mot en die,
            Car onques nes amai,
            Ne ja nes amerai;
            Et kis aimme, bien sai
            K'il fait cruël folie,
        K'envïeus sont molt plain de felonnie.) ll. 191–198

Attributed to the trouvère Gace Brulé (ca. 1159–1212). A member of the lower nobility of Champagne, he was among the most admired trouvères of his time; some seventy of his songs have survived.

    9. I have a love tailor-made for me,
        (J'ai amours fait a mon gré,
        Miels en vaurra ma vie.) ll. 204–205

    10. Have I not the right to stand tall,
        (Dont n'ai jou droit que m'envoise,
        Quant la plus biele amie ai?) ll. 237–238

A refrain that concludes a pastourelle by Guillaume le Vinier, active in Arras ca. 1220–1245.

    11. There's no harm or sin,
        [Non es enugs ni fallimens
        Ni vilanïa, so m'es vis,
        Mas d'ome can se fa devis
        D'autrui amor, ni conoixens.
            Enuios, e queus enanza,
            Sim faitz enug ni pesanza?

Cascus se vol de so mester formir:
Mi confondetz, e vos non vei iausir.) ll. 324–331

A "poitevin," or Occitan song. The manuscripts offer widely varying versions of it. Ms. A, Buffum's base text, gives a French translation of a song by Bernard de Ventadour. Buffum has substituted for it the original, as published by L. Gauchat (*Les Poésies provençales conservées par des chansonniers français*).

12. Love makes me joyful and makes me sing!
    (Amors mi font renvoisier et canter,
    Et me semont que plus jolie soie,
    Et me donne talent de miels amer
    C'onkes ne fis pour cest fol ki m'en prie;
    Que j'ai ami, a nul fuer ne volroie
    De son gent cors partir ne desevrer;
    Ains l'amerai, que j'en sui bien amee.
    Laissié me ester, ne m'en proiés ja mais;
    Sachiés de voir, c'est parole gastee.) ll. 441–449

The first stanza of a "chanson de mal mariée" (unhappily married woman's song) by the Artesian trouvère, Moniot d'Arras, who wrote ca. 1213–1239. As Buffum notes, Gerbert seems to have altered the typical refrain found in this type of song to reflect the context in which it is being sung.

13. "There goes one who loves well!"
    (Ensi va ki bien aimme, ensi va.) l. 719

A "carole," or song for dancing. Attribution is uncertain.

14. One who would love a lady like this
    (Ki ameroit tel dame a chi,
    Il n'aroit mie mescoisi.) ll. 935–936

Unique example of this refrain.

15. He who counsels me on love
    (Cil qui d'amours me conselle
    Que de li doie partir
    Ne set pas qui me resvelle
    Ne quel sont mi grief souspir.
    Petit a sens et voisdie
    Cil qui me velt castoier,
    N'onques n'ama en sa vie;
    Cil fait trop niche folie
    Qui s'entremet del mestier
    Dont il ne se set aidier.) ll. 1266–1275

First stanza of a song by Gace Brulé.

16. Dear God! What folly
(Par Diu! je tienc a folie
D'essaier ne d'esprouver
Ne sa femme ne s'amie,
Tant com on le velt amer;
Si s'en doit on bien garder
D'enquerre par jalousie
Chou c'on n'i volroit trouver.) ll. 1315–1321

Attribution uncertain; perhaps by Gace Brulé or the Champenois poet Aubouin de Sézanne (d. sometime beween 1221 and 1229).

17. Great was the gathering at the court of Laon;
(Grans fu la cours en la sale a Loon;
Molt ot as tables oisiaus et venison.
Ki ke mangast le car ne le poisson,
Onques Guillaumes n'en passa le menton,
Ains manga tourte et but aige a fuison;
Quant ont mangié li chevalier baron,
Les tables ostent sergant et escanchon.
Li quens Guillaumes mist le roi a raison:
"C'as empensé, dist il, li fils Carlon?
Secorras moi vers la gieste Mahon?
Ja deüst estre li os a Carlïon."
Et dist li rois: "Nous en consilleron,
Et le matin savoir le vous feron
Ma volenté, se jou irai ou non."
Guillaumes l'ot, si taint comme carbon.
"Comment dyable, dist il, s'en plaideron.
Chou est la fable dou tor et dou mouton.
Il s'abaissa, si a pris un baston,
Puis dist au roi: "Vostre fief vous rendon,
N'en tenrai mais vaillant un espouron,
Ne vos amis ne serai ne vos hom,
Et si venrés, ou vous voelliés ou non.") ll. 1407–1428

Gerard, who performs these decasyllabic epic verses, states that they are from *Guillaume au court nes*, the epic "Cycle of William of Orange." More specifically, they are from the chanson de geste *Aliscans* (second half of the twelfth century), Laisse LXXII, ll. 3416–3440 (*Aliscans*, ed. Claude Régnier (Paris: Champion [CFMA], 1990), vol. 1.

18. I've desired true love for so long
(Tant arai bonne amour quise
C'or l'arai a ma devise.) ll. 2050–2051

Attribution uncertain; also cited in the *Roman de la Poire* (mid-thirteenth century), by "Thibaut."

19. Beautiful Euriaut sits all alone, shut away
     (Siet soi biele Eurïaus, seule est enclose;
     Ne boit ne ne manguë ne ne repose;
     Souvent se claimme lasse, souvent se cose
     C'a son ami Renaut parler nen ose;
         Souvent s'escrie en halt:
         "Ha! Dex! verrai jou ja
         Mon douc ami Renaut!") ll. 2303–2309

Unique example of this text.

21. Love, when will this fierce pain end
     (Amors, quant m'iert ceste painne achievee
     Qui si me fait a grant dolour languir?
     Souvent mi fait mainte dure escaufee,
     Souvent rougir et maintes fois palir,
     Fremir, trambler, tressuër, tressaillir.
     Souventes fois n'est a joie tornee,
     Et aussi tost sor le point de morir.) ll. 2339–2345

22. I swear to God, love's sweet pain
     (En non Diu, c'est la rage
     Li dous maus d'amer,
     S'il ne m'asouage.) ll. 3123–3125

Refrain

23. You sing, and I die of love.
     (Vous cantés et je muir d'amer:
     Ne vous est gaires de mes maus?) ll. 3141–3142

From an anonymous pastourelle.

24. Anguished, brooding, in dread I sing
     (Destrois, pensis, en esmai,
     Cant de bonne amor souspris,
     Et faic semblant cointe et gai
     La ou sui plus d'ire espris.
     Ma douche dame ou j'ai pris
     Les maus dont ja ne garrai,
         Ains en trai
     Les painnes come fins amis.) ll. 3236–3243

First stanza of a song by Audefroi le Bâtard, a trouvère under the protection of Jean II de Nesle and Michel III de Harnes. He wrote during the first half of the thirteenth century in Arras.

25. I do not see here the one
(Je ne le voi mie chi
Cheli dont j'atenc ma joie.) ll. 3331–3332

26. May the one who knows how to cure love's pain
(Ki set garir des maus d'amer,
Si viegne a moi, que je me muir.) ll. 3450–3451
Refrain.

27. With one kiss alone, from a willing heart
(Par un seul baisier de cuer a loisir
Poroit longhement mes maus adoucir;
Mais de desirier me fera morir.
     S'encor n'en ai joie,
     Bonne est la dolours
     Dont naist la douchours
     Et solas et joie.) ll. 3641–3647

28. You can guess who it is that I love
(Adeviner porés cui j'aimme,
Par moi ne le sarés vous ja.) ll. 3665–3666
Refrain.

29. I await my joy from her
(J'atenc de li ma joie;
Diex! arai le jou ja?) ll. 4172–4173

30. When I see the lark joyfully lift
(Quant voi la loëte moder
De joi ses eles contrel rai,
Qui s'oblide et laisse cader
Per la douçor qu'al cor li vai,
Diex! tant grant envide mi fai
De li quant vi la jausion!
Mirabillas son cant de se
Lou cor de desier ne fon.) ll. 4187–4194

The first stanza of an Occitan *canso* by Bernard de Ventadour. (The text provided by Buffum follows a reconstruction by Gaston Paris.) The canso was particularly identified with the "code" of courtly love. Gerard sings this song for Aiglente and not Euriaut, thereby demonstrating his lack of fidelity to his long-lost partner. (See Boulton, p. 42 and Zingesser, pp. 121–137.)

31. Dear God, my heart will break!
(Dex! li cuers me faurra ja;

Trop le desir a veoir.) ll. 4344–4345
Refrain from an anonymous pastourelle.

32. You who go, for God's sake let him know
(Vous qui la irés, pour Diu, dites lui
C'a la mort m'a trait, s'il nen a merchi.) ll. 4409–4410)
Refrain from an anonymous pastourelle.

33. How glad I'd be if I could see
(Volentiers verroie
Cui je sui amis;
Diex m'i maint a joie!) ll. 4478–4480
Anonymous refrain.

34. Oh God! Oh Love! It's so hard to forgo
(Par Diu! amours, grief m'est a consirer
Dou douch solas et de la compaignie,
Et des biaus mos dont sot a moi parler
Cele ki m'ert dame, compaigne, amie,
Et quant recort sa simple cortoisie
Et son douc vis et son vïaire cler,
Comment me puet li cuers el cors durer?
Que ne s'en part? certes, trop est malvais.) ll. 4624–4631

A stanza of a song by the Châtelain de Coucy, a trouvère from Picardy
who participated in the third and fourth Crusades. The historian Geoffroy
de Villehardouin relates that he died during the crossing of the Aegean
Sea in 1202. Approximately thirty songs are attributed to him; probably
only half of these are authentic. His work is considered among the most
remarkable of the period.

35. Alas, however shall I survive?
(Lasse! comment porrai durer?
Or ne sai mais que devenir,
Quant cil que je voloie amer
Ne m'a daigné ne velt oïr.
Si ne me puis recomforter,
Ains m'estuet le mal endurer;
Ki me destraint et lasse et fait fremir;
Ne de nule autre amour ne quier joïr.) ll. 5051–5058
Refrain.

36. I would have had some fun with love,
(Or aroie amouretes,
Se voloie demourer.) ll. 5068–5069

37. I have regained my joy by loving well!
(J'ai recouvré ma joie par bien amer.) l. 5701
Refrain.

38. No one should have a sweetheart,
(Nus ne doit amie avoir
N'amer par droit, ki miex n'en doie valoir.) ll. 5719–5720
Refrain.

39. I have no need to sing about
(Ne mi sont pas ochoison de canter
Pres ne vergiés, plaseïs ne buisson;
Quant ma dame mi plaist a commander,
N'i puis trouver plus loial ochoison
Et molt m'est bon que sa valour retraie,
Sa grant biauté et sa coulour veraie,
Dont Dex li volt si grant plenté donner
Que les autres m'en couvient oublïer.) ll. 5790–5797
A stanza of a song by Gace Brulé.

40. I know two people—and yes, I'm one of them!
(J'en sai deus, li uns en sui,
Cui amours ont fait grant anui.) ll. 6125–6126
Refrain.

41. A true lover shouldn't be dismayed
(Qui bien aimme ne se doit esmaier
Pour grevanche c'amors sache envoier;
Que a chelui donne double loier
Ki pour lui trait plus de painne et essaie;
Ne sans amour n'a nus joie veraie.) ll. 6616–6620
Refrain.

Appendix II:
Clothing, Textiles and Armor in the Thirteenth Century

Self-presentation played an important role in thirteenth-century French aristocratic life and it is a central feature in all three of the works translated here. The *Roman de la Violette* (*RV*), in particular, presents multiple descriptions of aristocratic behavior and extravagant attire. The heroine Euriaut's first appearance at court sets the tone for the rest of the narrative: wearing a violet *bliaut* lavishly embroidered with gold crosses, a bejeweled brooch, and a gold circlet on her head, along with a gem-encrusted silk belt and an ermine-lined cloak with tiny silver bells attached, Euriaut is the very portrait of a wealthy thirteenth-century noblewoman. Later in the story, when she tries to conceal her identity, Euriaut's fine clothes betray her high station in life. As the story moves toward its conclusion, the king himself takes note of her clothes, observing that they suit her admirably. The clothing worn by her lover Gerard is also described in considerable detail: at various times he wears silk bliauts; a pleated *chemise* embroidered with gold thread along with a short ermine-lined cloak made of silk; ragged garments that serve to disguise his identity; all-white clothing and accoutrements that allow him to fight incognito. He and his numerous male relatives arrive at court "smartly dressed," their heads bedecked with garlands of roses.

The clothing worn by minor characters in the *RV* is also frequently referenced. Advisors to the Duke of Metz are all "elegantly attired" and knights attend church swathed in cloth of gold. In contrast to such displays of wealth, a chatelaine whose lands are under attack appears in a worn tunic, its seams unravelling; her belt is a length of cloth with a buckle of brass or copper. The noblemen who defend her wear battered, rusty armor and threadbare clothes. In a later episode, Gerard does battle with an evil giant who wears a somewhat startling, form-fitting leather garment made of dragon skin (whether smooth or scaly, we are not told).

In *Flore et Jehane* (*FJ*) a change of clothing allows Joan to change her gender identity as well. To reestablish her reputation as a chaste woman, she slips easily into the role of a squire and continues thus for several years. When she reassumes female clothing at the conclusion of the work, her garments are presented in colorful detail: red, green, and variegated dark blue (*piers*) indicate the rich dyes of the elegant silk cottes and sur-coats that have been tailored to her measurements.

The *Comte de Poitiers* (*CP*) presents Rose's clothing as part of her allure: her beautiful skin glows under her silk chemise; a detailed physical portrait of her includes a description of her elegant clothes made of red samite embroidered with golden birds, her pelisse lined with ermine. The author focusses throughout on the costliness of his characters' clothes and their monetary value is often specified.

The expensive fabrics and textiles used to make the garments described in these works is often noted: they include *syre* (Syrian silk); *escarlate*, a fine silk or woolen fabric, originally bright red (whence the modern term "scarlet"), but eventually dyed in other colors, as well; *paile*, a generic term for silk, often gold in color; *samis* (samite), a heavy silk, similar to satin, with gold thread in the weave; *cendal*, a lightweight, taffeta-like silk; and *siglaton*, a patterned silk. *Cainsil* was a finely woven, soft fabric, probably linen. It was typically used for undergarments (but for other garments as well) and was often dyed with saffron, which yielded a light yellow or cream color and an enticing fragrance. *Toile* refers generically to linen. Aristocratic clothing was often decorated with embroidery or brocade, which was sometimes encrusted with gems. *Orfrois* refers to embroidery in gold thread, usually appearing as decorative bands on a silk garment. Many kinds of fur were used to trim or line garments, including ermine, squirrel (*vair*), and miniver (*gris*), all mentioned in *RV*, and *sebelin* (sable), mentioned in the *Comte de Poitiers*.

Fine clothing was valuable and prized as a gift. Certain items, such as the brooch given to Euriaut by her aunt, the Queen of Hungary, carry a quasi-heraldic significance, signaling the owner's status within an illustrious family. Euriaut also owns a gem-studded belt, reportedly the very one that the epic hero Roland (of *Song of Roland* fame) gave to his betrothed, Aude. This item situates Euriaut within an illustrious literary lineage, as well. Expensive clothing was frequently bestowed in reward for services rendered. When minstrels leave a grand celebration at the end of *RV*, for example, they are given both horses and fur-lined clothes as rewards for their performances. Fine clothes were also frequently bequeathed in wills.

Historians of costume sometimes refer to the thirteenth century as a turning point in the development of fashion. During this period, and more significantly in the fourteenth century, women's and men's clothing began to diverge in significant ways. Toward the end of the twelfth century, women began to tweak the *bliaut* or *cote* (basic unisex tunics) in various ways, often using laces or stitching to create a tighter fit in the bodice and sleeves. Men's clothing also began to evolve, with tight sleeves and elongated shoes, among other features. As Sarah-Grace Heller has discussed, the terms "new" and "fresh" began to appear in literary descriptions of clothing, indicating both the superior value and novel style of the garment. Although the clothes and armor featured in the *RV* remain closer to the styles of the late twelfth century, they are on several occasions referred to by these adjectives.

One additional social function of clothing is depicted in the *RV* and merits explanation. On two occasions, garments serve as pledges of good faith. When Aigline hands a glove to Gerard, she signals acceptance of his offer to fight for her; a reciprocal favor is understood. Later in the story, Gerard swears an oath before the king; to formalize his vow, he folds the material of his "ermine cloak" and places it in the king's hands.

The following glossary of clothing terms is restricted to those found in the three works translated here. For further information about clothes and textiles in this period, consult the works listed below.

FURTHER READING

A concise description of early thirteenth-century clothing is included in *The Romance of the Rose or Guillaume de Dole, Jean Renart*, Patricia Terry and Nancy Vine Durling, trans. Philadelphia, University of Pennsylvania Press, 1993. Appendix I.
For more detailed descriptions of clothing and textiles in this period, see:

Burns, E. Jane. *Courtly Love Undressed: Reading Through Clothes in Medieval French Culture*. Philadelphia: University of Pennsylvania Press, 2002.
Evans, Joan. *Dress in Medieval France*. Oxford: Clarendon Press, 1952. Evans devotes a chapter to fashions of the late twelfth to early fourteenth centuries.
Goddard, Eunice Rathbone. *Women's Costume in French Texts of the Eleventh and Twelfth Centuries*. Baltimore: John Hopkins Press, 1927. (Much of late twelfth-century dress carried over into the early thirteenth and is relevant to the three works presented here.)
Heller, Sarah-Grace. *Fashion in Medieval France*. Cambridge: D.S. Brewer, 2007.
_____, ed. *A Cultural History of Dress and Fashion in the Medieval Age*. London: Bloomsbury Academic, 2017 (pbk., 2021). An excellent resource with extensive bibliography.
Houston, Mary G. *Medieval Costume in England and France: The 13th, 14th, and 15th Centuries*. London: Adam & Charles Black, 1939; Dover pbk, 1996. With color illustrations.
Koslin, Désirée G., and Janet E. Snyder. *Encountering Medieval Textiles and Dress: Objects, Texts, Images*. New York: Palgrave Macmillan, 2002.
Lundquist, Eva Rodhe. *La Mode et son Vocabulaire*. Göteborg: Wettergren & Kerber, 1950.
Michel, Francisque. *Recherches sur le commerce, la fabrication et l'usage des étoffes de soie, d'or et d'argent et autres tissues précieux en Occident, principalement en France, pendant le Moyen Âge*. 2 vols. Paris: Crapelet, 1852–56. (Rpt. London: Forgotten Books, 2018).
Pipponier, Françoise, and Perrine Mane. Trans. by Caroline Beamish. *Dress in the Middle Ages*. New Haven: Yale UP, 1997.

Scott, Margaret. *Medieval Dress and Fashion*. London: British Library, 2007. Ch. II "The Start of Fashion, c. 1100-ca. 1300."

Smith, Nicole D. *Sartorial Strategies: Outfitting Aristocrats and Fashioning Conduct in Late Medieval Literature*. Notre Dame: University of Notre Dame Press, 2012.

Clothing terminology

When no English equivalent is available, the Old French term (in italics) has been retained. English translations, when possible, are given in brackets. Spelling was fluid in this period, in part due to dialectical differences. The most prevalent spelling in the text is given here.

Afiche [brooch/clasp]: A brooch or pin, usually used to close the neck of a surcoat or cloak.

Amit [amice]: A liturgical vestment worn next to the skin, around the neck and shoulders. It is designed to protect the more lavish material of liturgical overgarments. Women are often depicted in literary texts embroidering such vestments for the Church.

Atour [clothing]: A term that refers to apparel in general.

Ausmoniere (alms purse): In addition to alms, this small pouch, worn by both men and women, might be used to carry other essentials, such as jewelry, or even needles and thread. It was worn suspended from a belt or cord at the waist.

Baston [staff]: Used in the *RV* as a symbol of authority.

Bliaut: An elegant dress or tunic worn by noble men and women in the twelfth and thirteenth centuries. For women, the bliaut was floor-length and sometimes extended into a train; the men's version was shorter. As worn by the aristocracy, bliauts were made of high-quality fabrics such as silk, taffeta, or velvet; winter versions were lined or trimmed with fur. Bliauts were often elaborately decorated with bands of brocade or embroidery at the wrists and neck. Sleeve length varied; some were quite long, even extending to the hem. A cord belt was usually worn at the waist, to which an ausmoniere was attached. The men's version of the bliaut was usually cut in one piece and could be long or short; it was occasionally dagged at the hem. For court wear, it was made of fine, often brightly colored fabric; as worn under armor, it was made of a less expensive material, such as cotton. The men's version was generally slashed at the sides for ease of movement. Bliauts were eventually replaced by the *cote* (see below). The two garments appear interchangeably in the *RV*, perhaps reflecting the transition.

Bouclete [little buckle]: Buckle of a belt; the metal tip was called a *morgant*.

Braieul [garters]: Worn over *braies* (men's "breeches," or underpants). Garters were attached to stockings and held them up.

Cainse [tunic]: A simple, lightweight version of the bliaut. It was often white or cream-colored.

Capuchon [hood]: Hoods were made of soft material and were often attached to a surcoat.

Caucemente [shoe]: Shoes in this period were similar for men and women. They were usually made of leather and had a pointed toe.

Ceinture [belt]: Belts were made of silk or other textiles, and occasionally of leather. In the early thirteenth century, these were usually slender, light-weight cords, worn by both men and women over the *cote*.

Chapiel [circlet/garland (depending on context)]: A circlet, usually of gold, worn atop the head, or a garland of roses or other flowers. Worn, sometimes simultaneously by both men and women.

Chausses [leggings]: Sturdy stockings made of linen or silk and held up by garters. These could be knee-high or extend to mid-thigh.

Chemise: An essential undergarment made of a soft fine fabric, usually long-sleeved and calf-length. Worn by both men and women.

Cote [cotte]:A tunic (or dress) with sleeves, worn by both men and women. (Cf. *bliaut*, above.)

Dras [linens/skirt]: Refers to the aggregate fabric of a garment.

Esclavine [hooded cloak]: Probably refers to a Slavic cloak; may also refer to a rough velour fabric.

Estole [stole]: An ecclesiastical garment, often heavily embroidered. (Cf. *amit*, above.)

Garnement [clothes/gear]. A generic term for an entire ensemble of clothing or armor.

Gimple [wimple]: A cloth head covering always worn by married women and sometimes by young unmarried women, as well. According to Evans, it was made of soft cloth and covered the neck and chin; it was attached to the hair at the sides and worn under a veil.

Linge [undergarments]: The chemise, for both men and women, along with britches for men.

Mantiel [cloak]: Worn by both men and women, cloaks were sometimes lined or trimmed with fur and were worn in all seasons. Fastened at the neck by a brooch or a silk cord, a cloak may or may not have a hood. The *mantelet* (*RV*, l. 3462) was a shorter version of the cloak, popular in the early thirteenth century.

Pliçon (or *pelisson*) [pelisse]: A fur-lined overgarment worn in cold weather.

Robe [attire]: A complete ensemble of clothing.

Sidoine [probably a "cloak"]: In other contexts, this term refers to a "suaire," or winding cloth.

Sorcot [surcoat]: A loose garment worn over the cote. According to Goddard, the sorcot was usually sleeveless (or with wide half sleeves) and of a different color than the cote, allowing a pleasing contrast of colors. It was typically open at the (rounded) neck and fastened together by a pin, brooch, or cord. Worn unbelted, it was of varying length.

Trechoir [ribbon]: A ribbon or ornamental band worn either around the head or as a trim on clothing.

Armor and Weaponry

Multiple battles and tournaments are portrayed in the *RV*, and armor and weapons are described in considerable detail. At one point, Gerard asks to borrow armor, noting that it didn't have to be elegant, just sturdy and well made; at another, he purposely wears armor that allows him to fight incognito (see n. 45, *RV*). Enemy Saxons appear brandishing battle axes and iron mallets instead of lances and swords; a giant wields a lethal club. The perfidy of one character is revealed (in a "tale-within-the-tale") when he has expensive-looking, but shabbily constructed armor made for a relative he hates. Gerbert makes frequent mention of heraldic banners and highly decorated shields and his references to armor and weapons are specific and often detailed. In *FJ*, we are told that Flore's (heraldic) banner was subsumed into the group identity of the tournament team on which he fought. The battle that concludes the wager portion of *CP* highlights the shattering of the jewels and flowers that adorn the golden helmets of the noble combatants.

FURTHER READING

For additional information about armor and heraldry in this period, see:

Brault, Gerard J. *Early Blazon: Heraldic Terminology in the Twelfth and Thirteenth Centuries with Special Reference to Arthurian Heraldry.* Woodbridge: Boydell Press, 1972; rpt. 1997.
Crane, Susan. *The Performance of Self: Ritual, Clothing, and Identity During the Hundred Years War.* Philadelphia: University of Pennsylvania Press, 2002. Ch. 4.
Ffoulkes, Charles. *Armour & Weapons.* Oxford, Clarendon Press, 1909.
Gaier, Claude. "The Lost Shield of Baldwin of Flanders and Hainault." *A Companion to Medieval Arms and Armour,* edited by David Nicolle, 91–96. Woodbridge, Suffolk: The Boydell Press, 2002.
Girbea, Catalina, ed. *Armes et jeux militaires dans l'imaginaire, XIIe-XVe siècles.* Paris: Classiques Garnier, 2016.
Pastoureau, Michel. *Heraldry: An Introduction to a Noble Tradition.* New York: Harry N. Abrams, 1977.

Armor and Weapons

Appareil [gear]: A knight's armor and equipment.

Armes [armor/weapons]: Refers to either the armor or, more specifically, the weapons carried into battle.

Atour [equipment]: Generic term for the aggregate equipment of a knight.

Baniere [banner]: Banners were usually made of cloth and were either painted or embroidered with the arms of the knight, allowing spectators to identify him. They were typically attached to the lance.

Bouclier [buckler]. A small round shield, usually made of metal and held by a handle located behind the boss. It was lightweight and used in hand-to-hand combat.

Branc [blade]: A term often used interchangeably with *epee*.

Broche [spear]: Cf. *espie*.

Cane [pike/staff]: Carried as a sign of authority.

Caperon [hood]: Soft head covering worn under the helmet to protect the skin.

Chantel [corner arms]: A shield "en chantel" has heraldic arms painted on the canton (i.e., in one corner of the shield).

Chausses de fier [mail leggings]: These were attached to the lining of the hauberk.

Coiffe [coif]: A closefitting, padded hood. The "coiffe de maille" was a hood of mail, designed to protect the head, neck, and shoulders. It was part of the hauberk and had to be laced around the head to stay in place during battle.

Colière [breastplate]: Armor to protect the front of the horse.

Confanon [gonfalon]: A banner or streamer, attached to the lance.

Cote a armer [battle tunic]: A tunic, often made of leather and usually sleeveless and belted, on which iron mail has been sewn.

Couvreture [saddlecloth]: These were sometimes made of rich materials and color-coordinated with the knight's gear. Cf. *housse*.

Crois [guard]: The cross-shaped bar between the blade (*branc*) and the grip (*puing*) of a sword.

Cuirie [cuirass]; A leather piece worn over armor for extra protection.

Enarmes de l'escu [straps]: Sturdy leather straps by which a large shield was held.

Enseigne [banner]: These were made of cloth, often bore heraldic markings, and were attached to the lance.

Epee [sword]: In the early thirteenth century, the knight's sword was made of steel and was quite long (typically 30"–35"), with a heavy pommel above the hilt. It was relatively light-weight, double-edged and used both to cut and thrust.

Escu [shield]: A knight's shield was made of a wooden frame typically covered with animal skin or heavy fabric. By the start of the thirteenth century, the surface was usually painted (or even embroidered) with the family coat of arms of its owner. In descriptions of combat in the *Roman de la Violette*, opponents are sometimes said to slash through each other's shields as though they were made of silk, an indication of the knight's prowess and strength. The escu was broad enough to protect the entire upper body; a large strap on the inner top side of the shield was passed over the knight's head, allowing him to carry the shield on his back when it was not in use. In battle, it was held by crossed straps attached to the inner side. Most evidence about shields in the thirteenth century comes from historical or literary sources, rather than archeological ones. A rare example of an actual early thirteenth-century shield (now lost) is discussed by Gaier. This shield, which was acquired by Baldwin of Flanders in the Holy Land ca. 1204, and eventually brought back to France, measured approximately 35" × 23"; it was U-shaped and elaborately decorated on the surface with gold and gems. The interior was "padded in red satin"; a single green leather strap had also survived.

Espauliere [shoulder protectors]: Part of body armor designed to protect the upper part of the arms and shoulders.

Esperons [spurs]: Early thirteenth-century spurs were usually of the fixed prick variety (i.e., not rotary). They were a prized part of a knight's armor and were often made of gold or silver.

Espie [spear]: A long wooden shaft with a sharp pointed metal head.

Fuere [scabbard]: A sheath for a sword or long-blade dagger, usually made of leather or metal. In *RV*, the single scabbard referred to is made of cloth of gold.

Hache [battle axe]: A heavy axe used in combat.

Haqueton [hacqueton]: A padded or quilted jacket with sleeves worn underneath a hauberk and/or under mail.

Harnois [gear]: Refers to the aggregate equipment of a knight, including the gear for his horse.

Hauberc [hauberk]: A coat of mail usually extending to mid-calf. A *hauberc doublier* (referred to in *CP*, l. 1305) seems to refer to a coat of mail lined with a quilted material.

Heu [hilt]: The hilt (or haft) of a sword is the lower part of the guard, joining it to the blade. It is usually cruciform in shape.

Housse de feutre [felt saddlecloth]: cf. *couverture*.

Ielme: A thirteenth-century knight's helmet was made of metal and consisted of three parts: a basic flat-top cylinder that protected the head; an œillère (eyeholes or visor); and an aventail. It was tied on with laces (see *las*, below) just before actual fighting began. A variant was the pointed-top helmet, a style better suited to deflecting head blows. It is referred to in *CP*.

Lance: Lances were made of iron and wood (oak and applewood are both mentioned in *RV*). Banners (often heraldic) were attached to them so that combatants could be more easily identified.

Las [laces]: Used to tie on the knight's helmet. They could be made of leather or cloth, such as silk. The cloth version was sometimes woven with gold thread or decoratively embroidered.

Lumiere [œillère]: A horizontal band of eyeholes (or a horizontal slit) in a helmet, allowing the knight to see. May also refer to a visor, depending on the type of helmet.

Mache [mace]: A heavy club with a blunt head.

Mail: Usually made of iron links and worn over (or attached to) a hacqueton.

Maillet [mallet]: A blunt-force club.

Pignon [pennant]: A streamer-like banner.

Porpoint [padded vest] A padded and fitted vest, usually worn under the hauberk; it helped hold the body erect. A precursor of the doublet.

Puing [grip]: Handle of a sword.

Saiete [arrow]: Bows and arrows were considered inferior to a knight's other weapons.

Targe: A round shield similar to the buckler, but slightly larger. Held by leather straps in the back.

Tibel [club]: A heavy mace or bludgeon.

Ventaille [aventail]: A curtain of mail that protects the throat and lower part of the face; typically, part of the mail coif.

Notes

Preface

1. A classic study of the genre is Northrop Frye, *The Secular Scripture: A Study of the Structure of Romance* (Cambridge: Harvard University Press, 1976). There were, of course, many permutations of this basic structure. For an overview of the medieval French tradition, see Matilda Tomaryn Bruckner, "The shape of romance in medieval France," in *The Cambridge Companion to Medieval Romance*, edited by Roberta L. Krueger (Cambridge: Cambridge University Press, 2000), 13–28, and Simon Gaunt, "Romance and other genres," idem: 45–59. For in-depth analysis, see Isabelle Arseneau, *Parodie et merveilleux dans le roman dit réaliste au XIIIe siècle* (Paris: Classiques Garnier, 2012); Francis Gingras, *Le Bâtard conquérant, Essor et expansion du genre romanesque au Moyen Âge* (Paris: H. Champion, 2011); and Lydie Louison, *De Jean Renart à Jean Maillart: Les romans de style gothique* (Paris: Champion, 2004).

2. Stith Thompson devotes considerable attention to "Wagers on wives, husbands, or servants," as a folktale category. Among the variants, the "Chastity wager" (N15) stands out, both for the number of sources listed and for the widespread geographical diffusion of the tales. (*Motif-Index of Folk Literature: A Classification of Narrative Elements in Folk-Tales, Ballads, Myths, Mediaeval Romances, Exempla, Fabliaux, Jest-Books, and Local Legends*, rev. and enl. edition, 6 vols. Copenhagen: Rosenkilde and Bagger, 1955–58.)

3. "Le cycle de la gageure," *Romania* 32 (1903), 481–551. V.-Frédéric Koenig proposes a somewhat different typology of the tales in "A New Perspective on the Wager Cycle," *Modern Philology* 44.2 (1946), 76–83.

4. The most recent edition is by Y.J.N. Monmerqué and Francisque Michel, in *Théatre français au Moyen Âge* (Paris: Firmin-Didot, 1929), 431–80.

5. For an edition, see Maria Colombo Timelli, "Le manuscript BAR Reg. lat. 1716: un recueil de Nouvelles? Quelques remarques sur le manuscript des *Nouvelles* dites *de Sens*," in *Le recueil au Moyen Age. La Fin du Moyen Age*, edited by Tania Van Hemelryck, et al. (Turnhout: Brepols [Texte, codex et contexte, 9], 2010), 79–100.

6. A transcription was published by Koenig in "Guillaume de Dole and Guillaume de Nevers," *Modern Philology* 45.3 (1948), 145–51.

7. *Histoire de Gérard de Nevers, Mise en prose du Roman de la Violette de Gerbert de Montreuil*, Édition critique de Matthieu Marchal (Villeneuve d'Ascq: Presses Universitaires du Septentrion, 2013).

8. Jean Renart's romance has been translated into English twice. For a version in prose, see *The Romance of the Rose or Guillaume de Dole: Jean Renart*, translated by Patricia Terry and Nancy Vine Durling (Philadelphia: University of Pennsylvania Press, 1993). For a bilingual edition, see Regina Psaki, *Jean Renart: The Romance of the Rose or of Guillaume de Dole* (New York: Garland, 1995). Eugene Mason's translation of *Flore et Jehane*, originally published in 1910, is not entirely faithful to the original ("The Story of King Florus and of the Fair Jehane," in *Aucassin and Nicolette and other Mediaeval Romances and Legends* [London: J.M. Dent & Sons, 1910; rpt. New York: E.P. Dutton & Co., 1958], 99–

139). The *Roman de la Violette* and the wager portion of *Le Comte de Poitiers* have been translated into French prose by Mireille Demaules, *Le Roman de la Violette, XIIIe siècle* (Stock/Moyen Age, 1992) and Friedrich Wolfzettel has translated *Flore et Jehane* into German (*Französische "Schickalsnovellen" des 13. Jahrhunderts* [Munich: Fink, 1986]).

Introduction to *Le Roman de la Violette*

1. Selections from Chrétien's romance and from the medieval continuations of it are included in *The Finding of the Grail: Retold from Old French Sources*, Patricia Terry and Nancy Vine Durling (Gainesville: University Press of Florida, 2000). The various texts in their entirety are included in *The Legend of the Grail*, Nigel Bryant, trsl. (Woodbridge, Suffolk: D.S. Brewer, 2015). For a translation of Jean Renart's romance, see *The Romance of the Rose or Guillaume de Dole* by Jean Renart, trans. Patricia Terry and Nancy Vine Durling (Philadelphia: University of Pennsylvania Press, 1993).

2. John W. Baldwin discusses the dispute in detail in *Aristocratic Life in Medieval France* (Baltimore: Johns Hopkins University Press, 2000), 58–67. It is worth noting that Marie's daughter Jeanne, who became Queen of Castile (m. Ferdinand III of Castile in 1237), ruled Ponthieu after Marie. Jeanne's daughter Eleanor of Castile eventually ruled the county after her mother and became Queen of England upon her marriage to Edward I in 1254. Kara Doyle has argued that Marie's story is, in effect, "narratized" in Gerbert's work ("'Narratizing' Marie of Ponthieu," *Historical Reflections/Réflexions Historiques* 30.1 (2004): 29–54). While parallels are certainly discernible, the story also alludes to contemporary events occurring within the houses of Nevers and Forez (see below, n. 6). The role of female patrons and audiences is examined in detail by Roberta L. Krueger in *Women Readers and the Ideology of Gender in Old French Verse Romance* (Cambridge: Cambridge University Press, 1993); she discusses the *Violette* at 137–140. See also the useful collection of essays concerning female patronage published

by June Hall McCash, ed., *The Cultural Patronage of Medieval Women* (Athens: University of Georgia Press, 1996).

3. "This Romance of the Rose ... is something quite new. It is so different from other works, being embroidered here and there with beautiful songs, that an uncouth person could never understand it... No one will ever tire of hearing it, because it can be both sung and read.... Everyone will imagine that the author of this romance also wrote the words of the songs, so well do they go with those of the story" (*The Romance of the Rose*, trans. Terry and Durling, 20). Romances were generally read aloud in the thirteenth century. One should, however, keep in mind that Jean Renart may have been overstating his claim. As Hendrik van der Werf has observed, there are many references to singing in the early Tristan texts, and even though "Thomas includes neither the text nor the melody of the lai ... [the prose versions of the Tristan story] have seemingly complete texts of lais sung by either protagonist; two have music for at least some of them" ("Jean Renart and Medieval Song," in *Jean Renart and the Art of Romance*, ed. Nancy Vine Durling (Gainesville: University Press of Florida, 1997), 164.

4. The "rules" governing "courtly love" were codified by Andreas Capellanus, a clerk in the employ of the Countess Marie de Champagne (daughter of Eleanor of Aquitaine), the patroness of Chrétien de Troyes and an important figure in the dissemination of vernacular romance in the late twelfth century. According to Andreas, "When love is revealed, it does not help the lover's worth, but brands his reputation with evil rumors and often causes him grief" (*The Art of Courtly Love*, trans. John Jay Parry [New York: Columbia University Press, 1990], 34).

5. The other thirteenth-century manuscript gives her age as twenty. It should be noted, however, that the younger age would have been entirely plausible to Gerbert's noble audience, among whom eligible young girls were often married at the age of eleven or twelve.

6. One of the "inside jokes" of this romance is the choice of Nevers and Forez as the counties belonging to the two men who bet on Euriaut's fidelity. Historically,

Nevers had passed to the female line in 1181. In the period in which Gerbert was writing the *Violette*, Mathilde, countess of Nevers, remarried (in 1226); her new husband was Gui IV, Count of Forez. How Gerbert's contemporaries would have reacted to his sense of humor is difficult to assess. The historical characters in the work are identified by Buffum, ed., lv–lxiii and discussed in detail by Baldwin, *Aristocratic Life* (see n. 2, above). Eliza Zingesser provides additional information in *Stolen Song: How the Troubadours Became French* (Ithaca: Cornell University Press, 2020). Her discussion of geographic detail is particularly useful.

7. Michel Zink, for example, has discussed in some detail the difference between Jean Renart's and Gerbert's use of songs. He argues that the fragmentary quotations of songs in the *Violette* serve as "a useful system of abbreviations" and that the rest of the song would have been supplied in performance. Zink further argues that, unlike Gerbert, Jean Renart intended for the fragments to remain fragmentary and not invite a performance of the entire song. I would suggest that both authors use the fragmentation effect in ways that reflect their individual fascination with hiding information. See Zink, "Suspension and Fall: The Fragmentation and Linkage of Lyric Insertions in Le Roman de la Rose (Guillaume de Dole) and Le Roman de la Violette," in Nancy Vine Durling, ed., *Jean Renart and the Art of Romance* (Tallahassee: University Press of Florida, 1997), 105–122. Given the importance of song in the work, it is worth noting that the *Roman de la Violette* inspired an opera. *Euryanthe* (1823), a German Romantic-era work composed by Carl Maria von Weber with a libretto (in German) by Helmina von Chezy, is loosely based on Gerbert's romance. Chezy claimed to have translated the work prior to writing the libretto, although, according to Michael C. Tusa, she specified that she "based her translation on an early printed prose version that she found in the Bibliothèque royale in Paris" (*Euryanthe and Carl Maria von Weber's Dramaturgy of German Opera* [Oxford: Clarendon Press, 1991], 84, n. 11). As Tusa observes: "Two sixteenth-century prints … come into question as the possible source for her translation: see Fran-

cisque Michel's preface to *Roman de la Violette* (Paris, 1834), xxv-xxxiii." The opera follows the essential wager tale scenario and keeps several of the names of key figures (Lysiart, Euryanthe, and Eglantine), but Chezy has radically reformulated the "secret" that discredits the heroine in the eyes of the public. According to Tusa, the reason for altering the work was due to the stringent censorship authority in Vienna at the time (86). He notes that "Weber never explained his reasons for selecting the *Euryanthe* text as the source for his new opera, although in a letter written in 1824 to his friend Gottfried Weber, he defended the choice of subject on musical grounds: 'Of course I myself chose the libretto of *Euryanthe*; I make nothing according to an ordered mould. If *you* don't recognize the musicality of the situation and so forth, then who should?'" (Tusa, 84). The medieval songs quoted in *Le Roman de la Violette* do not, however, figure in the opera.

8. Most of the songs would have been well-known to the audience and any alterations to them would have been noticed. Boulton provides an excellent discussion of the function of the songs of the *Violette* in *The Song in the Story: Lyric Insertions in French Narrative Fiction, 1200–1400* (Philadelphia: University of Pennsylvania Press, 1993), 35–42, 124, n. 9, and 170.

9. The narrative "I" intervenes some seventy times in the *Violette,* and even if half of these interventions are essentially "fillers," with no particular narrative function, half of them do serve a specific purpose, "[reassuring] the audience of the truth of the story," for example, or providing commentary about the organization and presentation of the material. See Christopher Callahan's incisive study, quoted here, "A l'ombre du jongleur disparu. La grammaire de la performance dans deux romans lyrico-narratifs dérimés," *Revue des langues romanes* 101.2 (1997), 211–33; at 223.

10. Romances were, of course enjoyed by both men and women. It is, however, noteworthy that "romances comprise the second largest genre owned and/or transmitted by women" (Roberta L. Krueger, "Questions of gender in Old French Romance," in *The Cambridge Companion to Medieval Romance*, edited by Roberta

L. Krueger [Cambridge: Cambridge University Press, 2000], 132–149). Krueger describes an event that suggests the popularity of Gerbert de Montreuil: "After her castle was sacked, Mahaut d'Artois demanded restitution from Parliament in 1316 of a list of books that included three Tristan romances and the *Roman de la Violette*, among other secular works" (135). Mahaut was a great-granddaughter of King Louis VIII, with whom Marie de Ponthieu (cousin to the king) struggled to regain control of her hereditary lands.

11. Derhyming verse romance became popular in the late thirteenth century; a renewal of interest in prose versions occurred in the fifteenth century. For discussion, see Callahan, op. cit.

12. Douglas Labaree Buffum, *Le Roman de la Violette ou de Gerart de Nevers par Gerbert de Montreuil* (Paris: H. Champion, 1928).

The Romance of the Violet

1. On the identity of the Countess of Ponthieu, see the Introduction, 5–6.

2. Most birds "molt" (i.e., replace their feathers) in the late summer or early fall. Raptors generally do not assume their definitive feather patterning until they have undergone three or four molts. This is therefore a young bird.

3. Ruddiness of complexion was considered a particularly attractive attribute in a man. The locus classicus is the description of the beloved in the Song of Songs 5.10: "My beloved is white and ruddy, chosen out of thousands" *The Holy Bible*, Douay-Rheims Version (Rockford, IL: Tan Books, 1989).

4. Ganelon was the treacherous stepfather of Roland in the *Song of Roland*. His name has become a synonym for "traitor."

5. It was legally required for disputants to offer a "pledge," or surety of some kind guaranteeing the seriousness of their intent. The king himself is here agreeing to ensure the appearance of both men at court, to ascertain the outcome of the wager.

6. Saint Giles was a Benedictine monastery near Nîmes, built in the eleventh century at the site of Saint Giles's tomb. He is evoked here primarily for the sake of

rhyme in the French couplet. The wordplay on the name *Giles* and *guile* is reminiscent of *Guillaume de Dole*, in which the character Guillaume is repeatedly associated with acts of guile. See Patricia Terry, "On the Untranslatable Surface of *Guillaume de Dole*," in Durling, ed., *Jean Renart and the Art of Romance*, 143.

7. Tables were generally set up just before the meal was served. They consisted of trestles on which planks were placed; these were then covered with tablecloths.

8. The Beguines were an unofficial religious lay order for women, established in the late twelfth century. Because the order was unregulated, it was subject to severe criticism from clerics who often accused the women of lax morals. See Tanya Stabler Miller, *The Beguines of Medieval Paris: Gender, Patronage and Spiritual Authority* (Philadelphia: University of Pennsylvania Press, 2014). The idea that wicked qualities (especially treachery) were inherited was a commonplace in the Middle Ages. The troubadour Bernart de Ventadorn (active ca. 1145–1175) refers to this idea in a famous song, "La dousa votz ai auzida" [I've heard the sweet voice],

> Una fausa deschauzida
> traïritz de mal linhatge
> m'a traït et estraïda…
> [a false, decadent
> traitress of a base lineage
> has betrayed me]

Traitors are often said to belong to "Ganelon's line" (see n. 4 above). The image of bad fruit from bad trees derives from the New Testament: A good tree cannot bring forth evil fruit, neither can an evil tree bring forth good fruit. / … / Wherefore by their fruits you shall know them (Matthew 7. 18–20; *The Holy Bible*, Douay-Rheims Version).

9. Probably a reference to the Benedictine priory of Charité-sur-Loire in Nièvre (Burgundy).

10. Thessala is Fénice's clever nurse in Chrétien de Troyes' romance *Cligès*. She helps Fénice deceive her husband and become the lover of his nephew, Cligès. Brangien, Iseut's attendant, unwittingly serves a love potion to her mistress and Tristan. In these stories, the servant becomes an accomplice of her mistress; neither woman is portrayed as intentionally malicious.

11. The Old French reads *ensaignes*, literally "signs."

12. A little later (at l. 895), we are told that Euriaut is only fifteen years old, which seems at odds with Gondrée's statement here (following BnF fr. 1374). The other thirteenth-century manuscript states that Euriaut is twenty years old. On the question of Euriaut's age, see Introduction, note 5.

13. The reference to a source book in which the author presumably found the original of the story was a commonplace in vernacular literature. Written information was thought to carry authority. The comment underscores the reliability of the account.

14. The illicit viewing of a woman in her bath has several important literary analogues. Among the most significant are the Old Testament tales of David and Bathsheba (2 Samuel 11) and Susanna and the Elders (Apocryphal book of Susanna); in both tales the voyeurism leads to criminal behavior. Perhaps the most famous medieval story involving the motif of spying on a woman in her bath is the tale of Mélusine (prior to 1240), where the husband disobeys his wife's ultimatum not to question her whereabouts on Saturdays, when she routinely disappears for twenty-four hours. The suspicious husband discovers that his bathing wife temporarily acquires a serpent's tail on that day. Among French wager tales, *Li Contes dou roi Flore et de la bielle Jehane* also makes noteworthy use of the bath motif.

15. The reference to Queen Florence alludes to another early thirteenth-century romance about an unjustly accused heroine, *La Chanson de Florence de Rome*, A. Wallensköld, ed. Paris: Firmin-Didot [SATF], 1901. 2 vols. The following reference to Euriaut's aunt would have pleased Marie de Ponthieu, whose own aunt Marguerite was, in fact, Queen of Hungary.

16. Aude, betrothed to Charlemagne's brave nephew, appears in both the *Song of Roland* and the late twelfth-century epic *Girart de Vienne*. There is, however, no mention in either work of the belt referred to here.

17. The medieval *vïele* (translated here as "fiddle") was a stringed instrument played with a bow while held on the performer's lap. The "zither" in question (Old French *rota*) was also a stringed instrument. Christopher Page has described the *rota* as "a triangular zither with strings on both sides of the soundbox," with a double row of tuning-pegs (123). For discussion and illustrations, see Page, *Voices and Instruments of the Middle Ages: Instrumental Practice and Songs in France 1100–1300* (Berkeley: University of California Press, 1986).

18. The heroines cited by Gerbert appear in various romances of the late twelfth and early thirteenth centuries; each is the object of a literary "portrait" extolling her beauty. They appear in the following works: Gaité, wife of Athis in *Athis et Prophilias*; Polixena, daughter of Priam in *Le Roman de Troie*; Helen of Troy, vividly evoked in the *Roman de Troie*; Dido, lover of Aeneas (*Roman d'Eneas*); Ismene and Antigone, daughters of Oedipus (*Roman de Thèbes*); Iseut la Blonde, wife of King Marc and lover of Tristan (*Tristan et Iseut*); Galienne, wife of Fergus (probably the *Roman de Fergus*); Esclarmonde, wife of Huon in *Huon de Bordeaux*. The sweetheart of Caradoc (*Livre de Carados*, part of a continuation of Chrétien de Troyes' *Conte du Graal*) mentioned in line 893, is named Guinier; she too is accused of infidelity, but later exonerated. All these heroines would have been familiar to Gerbert's aristocratic audience.

19. Medieval "portraits" usually followed strict conventions, starting with a discussion of the lady's curly blonde hair, and moving downwards to her hips. The description of Euriaut, as it occurs in the Old French text, is unusual because it does not follow the standard order. On portrait conventions, see Alice Colby, *The Portrait in Twelfth-Century French Literature: An Example of the Stylistic Originality of Chrétien de Troyes* (Geneva: Droz, 1965).

20. Euriaut's physical reactions are standard expressions of grief in medieval French literature, which have roots in antiquity. In the chansons de geste, such descriptions typically occur when a character is confronted with the death of a loved one. See Carine Bouillot, "La chevelure: la tirer ou l'arracher, étude d'un motif pathétique dans l'épique médiéval," in *La chevelure dans la littérature et l'art du Moyen Âge*, Actes du 28e colloque du CUERMA [Senefiance no. 50], Publication

de l'Université de Provence, 2004, 35–46. On the tearing of hair in medieval romance, see Myriam Rolland-Perrin, *Blonde comme l'or: La chevelure féminine au Moyen Âge* (Senefiance 57). Publications de l'Université de Provence, 2010: 171–188. In the *Violette*, Aigline tears at her hair at l. 2078, and Euriaut does so again in ll. 3944–3946.

21. Euriaut describes herself as a "femme legière," or woman of loose morals. She demonstrates a gift for extemporizing here, underscoring her unsavory connections by claiming to be a cart driver's daughter. Carts were used to transport criminals; to ride in one, or even be associated with one, was a considered a disgrace. The opprobrium associated with carts is an important theme in Chrétien de Troyes' romance *Lancelot, or the Knight of the Cart.*

22. These three Old Testament figures were often presented as a cluster of examples illustrating the perfidy of women, though in the case of Absalom, it was the murder of his sister's rapist that ultimately caused his own death. For discussion, see Susan L. Smith, *The Power of Women: A Topos in Medieval Art and Literature* (Philadelphia: University of Pennsylvania Press, 1995), 20–29.

23. As Christopher Page has observed, this passage "has often been cited as firm evidence that the ability to accompany oneself on an instrument was regarded as an exceptional skill during the Middle Ages." Page goes on to note that a slight change in Buffum's punctuation of this passage will significantly alter the meaning. He argues that Gerard is not commenting on the difficulty of self-accompaniment but, more specifically, his lack of professional training. (See Page, op. cit., 188–190.) I follow Page's reading of the line.

24. The "tale of the bull and the sheep" has not survived, though possible analogues are proposed by Gaston Paris, "Une Fable à retrouver," *Romania* 31 (1901): 100–103.

25. The Old French chansons de geste were divided into "laisses," i.e., stanzas of varying length organized according to their assonanced line endings. Gerard says that he sings four laisses of the epic *William Short Nose.* See also Appendix I, 17.

26. I.e., 2^{64}. The metaphor, a standard expression for a vast quantity, is particularly apt here, suggesting not only the severity of Gerard's suffering, but also the skill required of him to negotiate his way as a knight on the "chess board" of this adventure.

27. The words of the knight, and indeed the entire description of the desolation of Aigline's lands, are closely modeled on the description of Beaurepaire in Chrétien de Troyes' *Conte du Graal.* In Chrétien's romance, Perceval wins the hand of his beloved, Blanchefleur, by defending her city and lands. As a continuator of Chrétien's story, Gerbert knew this description extremely well. (See Introduction.)

28. Literally, Gerard "wasn't fit to be bled." I.e., he was already so pale that the medical remedy of bloodletting would have been unadvisable.

29. As M. Demaules has noted, Taulas is a minor character in various Arthurian romances, notably *Meraugis de Portlesguez* (ca. 1200), by Raoul de Houdenc (*Le Roman de la Violette*, p. 170, n. 18). The origin of the story about Gerard's sword is unknown.

30. Roland and Fernagus appear together in the *Chronique du Pseudo-Turpin.* They engage in ferocious single combat, after which the two have a lengthy conversation about Christianity. In the end, Roland slays his opponent.

31. Gerbert seems to be alluding to one of the most beautiful and poignant medieval tales of "courtly love," *La Chatelaine de Vergi.* In this story, a nobleman carries on a secret love affair with the widowed niece of his lord, the Duke of Burgundy. The duke's wife, enamored of the young man, makes advances to him, but is rebuffed; she later claims that he tried to seduce her. To regain the good opinion of the duke, the young man confides the truth about his secret liaison. When his lover discovers that he has betrayed her, she dies, her death precipitating his own. Better than any other of the period, the story dramatizes the role of discretion in courtly love.

32. Cloth (or spinning) songs (*chansons de toile*) were a popular lyric form in the twelfth and thirteenth centuries. As their name suggests, these songs were sung by women as they spun thread or

embroidered fabric. The typical subject was yearning for an absent beloved or other distress in love.

33. Wine was often mulled with pepper or spices.

34. This scene recalls the use of potions for purposes of deception in both *Tristan et Iseut* and *Cligès*. See note 10.

35. Hesbaye is a former province in today's Belgium.

36. The theft of the ring recalls a key scene in Jean Renart's *Escoufle*, where a kite steals an alms purse containing a ring given to Guillaume by Aelis. Guillaume rides off to recover the stolen objects. Aelis, who has been napping, awakes to find herself alone. She imagines that her lover has abandoned her and sets off to look for him. When Guillaume returns and finds her gone, he embarks on a quest to find her.

37. Audigier, the main character in a particularly scatological fabliau of that name, is vanquished and put to shame by an elderly female opponent who imposes a humiliating and grotesque punishment on him.

38. Guillaume Fierebras was the son of Aimeri of Narbonne; the stories about them form part of the epic cycle about William of Orange (see p. 250, n. 12).

39. Long prayers of supplication are often uttered by romance heroines. Euriaut's is among the longest and has been studied in some detail by Sister Maria Koch, *An Analysis of the Long Prayers in Old French Literature with Special Reference to the "Biblical-Creed Narrative" Prayers* (Washington, DC: Catholic University of America Press, 1940).

40. The story of Onestasse originally appears in the apocryphal Gospel of James, although the character there is called Salome. In this early version of the story, the woman's hand shrivels when she attempts to perform a test confirming Mary's virginity after the birth of Jesus. God restores her hands when she repents. In the Old French versions of the story, Onestasse (or Anastase) is, as in Euriaut's prayer, a woman without hands who wishes to hold the infant Jesus and is cured when she touches him. Gerbert may have included the reference to her here because some well-known contemporary narratives about the persecution of unjustly

accused heroines involve amputation of a hand (e.g., *La Manekine*). Amputation of a finger also occurs in some early versions of the wager tale. Various examples are cited by G. Paris, "Le Cycle de la Gageure." Florentine's earlier comment that she would willingly let Gerard cut off one of her toes if he would sleep with her (ll. 2732–36) is, perhaps, an echo of this motif.

41. The Gospel accounts state only that Herod had the male children killed; beheading seems to have been a medieval invention.

42. The Old French reads, "je ne douche mie vostre asaut ne vostre escremie / Le montanche d'un denier faus," literally, "I do not fear your attack or combat the amount of a counterfeit denier." As noted in the Introduction (10) metaphors involving money occur frequently in this work.

43. Loss of the nose signaled loss of identity. Facial mutilations were often used to punish sexual infractions, especially in the case of an adulterous woman. The punishment is featured in Marie de France's twelfth-century *lai* "Bisclavret" and also in *Le Comte de Poitiers*.

44. It seems that the duke had more than one sister! The designation signifies a particularly close blood relationship. See William O. Farnsworth, *Uncle and Nephew in the Old French Chanson de Geste: A Study in the Survival of Matriarchy* (New York: Columbia University Press, 1913).

45. The motif of "chivalric disguise" is frequently evoked in medieval romance. As Susan Crane has discussed, it was a means by which a knight could redefine or "reconstruct" his identity by directing the public gaze exclusively on the immediate situation, "without regard for lineage, past achievements, or past failures." (*The Performance of Self: Ritual, Clothing and Identity during the One Hundred Years' War* [Philadelphia: University of Pennsylvania Press, 2002], 129 and 133). Wearing a fragment of a beloved lady's clothing was also a typical practice (Crane, 138).

46. This is Guillaume III, the father of Marie de Ponthieu.

47. Literally, a thousand "marks from Tours." According to Buffum, these were worth about a quarter less than standard *marcs* (ed., 354).

48. It was typical to attempt a reconciliation before single combat was under-

taken. For discussion of historical practice, see John W. Baldwin, "The Crisis of the Ordeal: Literature, Law, and Religion Around 1200," *Journal of Medieval and Renaissance Studies* 24 (1994), 327–353.

49. The practice of swearing on relics to solemnize an oath was formalized in 803 by Charlemagne. See Patrick J. Geary, *Furta Sacra: Thefts of Relics in the Central Middle Ages* (Princeton University Press, 1978), 43–44.

50. As Buffum notes, the scribe may have made an error here, writing Gerard instead of Gerbert. On the other hand, Gerard, as the central character in the book, may be said to "finish his story" at this point. I have opted for the author's name.

The Count of Poitiers

1. The author evokes the names of several heroes of Old French epic poems (*chansons de geste*), thereby situating his story as a tale of brave deeds.

2. There were various medieval legends about Pepin's encounter with a ferocious lion. According to Gaston Paris, the oldest version, dating from 884, is found in the work of a monk of Saint-Gall (probably Notker the Stammerer), who recounts that the king, whose authority had been rejected by the Franks because of his extremely short stature, caused a lion and a bull to be brought before his throne. When the lion brought down the bull and was about to devour it, Pepin leapt forward and cut off the heads of both animals. Adenet le Roi (late thirteenth century) includes a different version in *Berte aux grans pies*. Here Pepin rescues his wife from the clutches of a ferocious lion. (Gaston Paris, "Légende de Pépin 'le Bref,'" in *Mélanges Julien Havet* (Paris: E. Leroux, 1895), 603–632; here 607–610.)

3. The meaning of ll. 17–21 is unclear. I follow the interpretation of A. Långfors, according to which it is the traces left by the horse (and not Pepin himself) that appear. (Långfors, review of "*Le conte de Poitiers, roman du treizième siècle* by V.-Frédéric Koenig," *Romania* 64, no. 255, 409; cited by Malmberg, ed., 152). The lines apparently refer to an episode from another work which the author expected

his listeners to recognize, but which has not survived.

4. Archedeclin (or Archetriclinus) was the host at the Marriage at Cana (John II.1–11).

5. The Old French expression is "joïr des menbres"; literally, "to take (sexual) pleasure in her members."

6. A proverbial expression meaning that boasting is easy and requires no valor.

7. Men who guaranteed accountability. As we shall see, this role could be very dangerous.

8. The *bezant* was a small gold coin from Byzantium in (probably) limited circulation in Europe in the Middle Ages. The term, often referred to in Old French stories, usually indicates low value, perhaps due to the gradual devaluation of the coin over the course of the thirteenth century. See Philippe Grierson and Lucia Travaini, *Medieval European Coinage* (Cambridge: Cambridge UP, 1998), 456. David Ross suggests a different explanation, i.e., that the coins were not widely used. (Ross, "Ces Deniers qui sont rouges: Le besant dans la littérature et dans la vie de la France et de l'Europe occidentale au Moyen Age," in *La Chanson de geste et le mythe carolingien : Mélanges René Louis*, vol. 2 [Saint-Père-sous-Vézelay, 1982],1063–1072). Note, however, that the term refers to high value in l. 950 below. As for the lady "Joiouse," the name is an invention; there is no such character in the Greek legend of Troy. However, the author may have intended the name as an epic allusion. It was well known that Charlemagne's sword was called Joieuse.

9. A *table dormant* was a large, permanent table, always ready to be set for a meal. Additional trestle tables were often set up just before meals were served and were taken down immediately afterwords. See Madeleine Pelner Cosman, *Fabulous Feasts: Medieval Cookery and Ceremony* (New York: George Braziller, 1976; 1992), 16. The trestle table appears in the *Roman de la Violette*, l. 488 (n. 7).

10. Old French *mua color* literally means "changed color."

11. Palatinates were geographical areas under the jurisdiction of princes or counts. These, in turn, answered to the king.

12. The term *le surplus* ("more than that") carried specific sexual connotations.

The use of it here suggests that the nurse will try to obtain even more compromising objects belonging to the countess.

13. The term used is *écu*, which can mean either "shield" or a specific kind of gold coin first minted in the 1260s. Since our text dates from the late twelfth or early thirteenth century, it is likely that the reference is to the gold paint on a shield. However, the unique manuscript copy of the work dates from the late thirteenth century; the scribe has perhaps introduced a contemporary allusion. The comparison occurs again at l. 953. We note, however, a reference to the gold on a shield in l. 1353.

14. The small gold coin is, once again, a *bezant*. The term that describes the location of the hole ("the lap of the skirt") is *giron*, which is related to English "groin." The coin-size of the hole echoes the financial stakes of the wager and the sexual nature of the bet.

15. Alotru is an unusual name. It is probably a variant of Old French *malostruz* (first attested use, 1175) which derives from the vulgar Latin *male astrucus*, meaning "born under an unfavorable star." Old Spanish *astrugo* and Provençal *astruc*, both drop the initial *m*. See Alain Rey, *Le Robert Dictionnaire historique de la langue française* (Paris, 1998) vol. 2, 2110. Rey also notes that, beginning in the thirteenth century, the term took on the additional meaning of "défavorisé sur le plan physique comme sur le plan moral." The modern form, *malotru*, is still in use.

16. The legend of Solomon's wife's adultery was apparently well-known in the Middle Ages, though its origin is undocumented. In these stories, the wife was said to feign death in order to trick her husband and run away with a lover. In an early study of the motif, Gaston Paris argues for a byzantine source ("La Femme de Salomon," *Romania* 9 [1880], 436). There are references to the legend in the late twelfth-century chanson de geste *Elie de Saint-Gilles*, ll. 1793–96; in Chrétien de Troyes' *Cligès* (ca. 1176), ll. 5796–98; and in *Le Roman de la Violette*, ll. 1294–96 and p. 244, n. 22, above. Solomon's wives are not named in the Bible but are said to have persuaded him to return to pagan practices. It is in this context that Solomon's weakness (along with that of David and Samson) is often referred to in many medieval treatises and narratives. For discussion, see Susan L. Smith, *The Power of Women: A Topos in Medieval Art and Literature* (Philadelphia: University of Pennsylvania Press, 1995), 20–65.

17. Such judicial tests or "ordeals" were a common feature in medieval stories and were considered proof of divine intervention. In *Le Roman de la Violette*, Euriaut also offers to undergo trial by ordeal (ll. 5477–5478). For discussion of the practice, see John W. Baldwin, "The Crisis of the Ordeal: Literature, Law, and Religion Around 1200," *JMRS* 24 (1994), 328–353.

18. This unexpected reference to a family tie between the countess and the king helps to explain Pepin's special interest in the case.

19. There is a lacuna in the manuscript, which reads: "and twenty... and thirty towers." "Castles" is the logical missing word.

20. The relics of saints were sometimes enclosed in the hilts of swords. The most famous example is Roland's sword Durendal, said to contain the blood of Saint Basil, a tooth of Saint Peter, some of Saint Denis's hair, and a part of a garment belonging to the Virgin Mary (*La Chanson de Roland*, ll. 2345–2348).

21. "This mighty devil" (literally, this "enemy"). The term "enemy" commonly referred to the devil and is probably used in that context here.

22. We are reminded of Pepin's unparalleled prowess, outlined at the beginning of the work. For a knight without armor to kill a lion was the ultimate in bravery.

23. A chatelain was nobleman in possession of a fief. His rank was similar to that of a viscount (i.e., lower than a count and higher than a baron). Harpin is, however, referred to as Count Harpin.

24. In Old French, the word *serpent* refers to a dragon. The Latin term *draco* is used in the Vulgate Bible to identify the seven-headed dragon vanquished by Michael and the angels in Revelations 12, where it is also referred to as "the ancient serpent who is called the devil, and Satan, who seduces the whole world" (*serpens antiquus, qui vocatur diabolus, et Satanas, qui seducit universum orbem*). With the development of the bestiary in the twelfth century, "dragons ... frequently replaced snakes, and ... gradually assume[d] the image of an elaborate hybrid beast."

(Brigitte Resl, "Beyond the Ark, Animals in Medieval Art," in *A Cultural History of Animals in the Medieval Age*, ed. Brigitte Resl (Oxford: Berg Publishing, 2007), ch. 7, 183. In medieval iconography, dragons are often depicted with stingers in their tales.

25. Literally, "wasn't worth two *deniers* to him," another example of an economic metaphor.

26. We find once again the theme of lineage as a barometer of behavior. Compare *Le Roman de la Violette*, ll. 502–511 and *Flore et Jehane*, n. 9.

27. The term *esclavine* (hooded cloak) is problematic. It is thought to refer to a type of "Slavic cloak" but may also refer to a rough type of cloth. See Takeshi Matsumura, *Dictionnaire du français médiéval* (Paris: Les Belles Lettres, 2015), 1317.

28. Saint Martin's Day marked the end of the fall harvest season and the beginning of winter.

29. Mangonels were catapults used to throw stones over city walls during a siege.

30. This is the first and only time the countess is identified by her first name, although her beauty has been previously compared to that of a rose. Her name reminds us of the floral birthmarks found in two other wager tales, *Le Roman de la Violette* and Jean Renart's *Roman de la Rose ou Guillaume de Dole*.

31. This may refer to changes in the breasts due to pregnancy. Kathleen Coyne Kelly notes a contemporary belief, attributable to Albertus Magnus, that the direction in which the breasts pointed was an indication of chastity or loss thereof. (*Performing Virginity and Testing Chastity in the Middle Ages* [London and NY: Routledge, 2000)], 31. It is likely that this belief inspired the chastity test depicted in the later portion of *Le Comte de Poitiers*.

32. A forester was a governing official appointed by the king who acted as a kind of sheriff or arbiter of justice. He was responsible for protecting the king's lands and restricting access to hunting on them. He would have been an important ally in a judicial dispute brought before the king.

33. There is an ellipsis in the manuscript here. It seems probable that the Duke *of Normandy* is intended.

34. To have assassinated a knight in the king's presence would have been an act of lèse-majesté. We remember Pepin's fury when the count strikes the duke as the king looks on (ll. 361–365).

35. I.e., the relics of the saints laid out by Pepin. It was a customary practice before a judicial battle to brings relics onto the field so that the opposing parties could swear an oath upon them.

36. Helmets worn in knightly combat were often highly decorated with family arms, precious stones, and other embellishments.

37. The following account of Constantine and his rule is entirely fanciful and bears little resemblance to the preceding narrative. The Constantine referred to here is not the fourth-century king, though various allusions suggest that the author was using him as a literary model. At least two short thirteenth-century narratives about the historical Constantine have survived; see James Coveney, *Édition critique des versions en vers et en prose de La Légende de l'empereur Constant* (Paris: Les Belles Lettres, 1955).

38. Ascension Day, i.e., forty days after Easter and ten days before Pentecost.

39. This spot refers to the place in Rome where the emperor Nero was buried. The historical Constantine's mother, Helena, garnered fame for traveling to the Holy Land and (as legend has it) returning to Rome with the True Cross.

40. As a term of address, "Master" designated any high-ranking official.

41. Dry-Tree (*Arbre Sec*) was a legendary tree said to mark the spot where Alexander defeated Darius in 331 BCE. Marco Polo situates the tree in a plain north of Persia. It came to symbolize the most distant point where East meets West. As for Uncle Noiron (Nero), there is no connection to the Roman emperor of that name.

42. Fat Bologna. A traditional nickname for the city, which is known for its abundant and rich cuisine.

43. Entertainers were often rewarded with gifts of clothing, a practice often featured in medieval romance.

44. See note 31, above. As Romaine Wolf-Bonvin has discussed, a woman "en chemise" was considered to be naked. The Count of Poitiers boasts that his wife's "skin, whiter than snow, / glows beneath her chemise of Syrian silk" (ll. 54–55); later, in ll. 934–35, her chemise is described

as "more finely spun than a spider's web," suggesting the diaphanous quality of the fabric. In the *Romance of the Violet*, however, Euriaut always wears a chemise to hide the birthmark on her breast. The fabric used for this undergarment was apparently of variable transparency. Wolf-Bonvin provides numerous examples of the depiction of the chemise in "Un vêtement sans l'être: La chemise," (*Le Nu et le vêtu au Moyen Âge: XIIe-XIIIe siècles*. Aix-en-Provence: Presses universitaires de Provence, 2001; 383–394); she does not, however, discuss *Le Comte de Poitiers*.

45. Literally: "then thought to sell herself as a virgin." The use of economic language is unusual in this context, even more so because it is a woman who is speaking.

46. Literally, "as the peasant tells us." This refers to a collection of well-known proverbs known as *Li proverbes au vilain*.

The Tale of King Flore and the Fair Joan

1. Friedrich Wolfzettel suggests that Ausai refers either to the town of Auxais or the commune of Aucey, both located in Normandy. (*Französische 'Schicksalsnovellen'* [Munich: Fink (Klassische Texte des romanischen Mittelalters in zweisprachigen Ausgaben, 26), 1986], 169).

2. Flore's extravagance reflects his nobility. The quality of "largesse," or generosity, was an important component of courtly behavior.

3. Companies (or teams) were formed at tournaments and governed by the most distinguished nobles in attendance. The right to use a banner at tournaments was tied to the number of vassals in service to a lord. Knights usually came with an entourage and these groups were then chosen to participate under the banner of one of the great lords. (Their own banner became part of the team's identity.) Tournaments could bring both glory and financial gain to the participants. As we shall see, Robin's valor helped his lord double his land holdings.

4. This is a loose translation of the Old French term *livré*. The term itself is somewhat vague and refers to the amount of land that would produce a *livre* of income.

5. The knight offers Robin his glove as a pledge of good faith. We remember that Gerard folds the hem of his cloak and offers it to the king as a pledge in the *Romance of the Violet*.

6. Literally, "I've married her." The conclusion of negotiations for marriage were considered the first formal step in the marriage process.

7. Robert is the squire's new, more aristocratic name. In medieval French literature, Robin is a common rustic name.

8. The author backtracks here, demonstrating that Joan's father knew about Robert's plan prior to the actual wedding.

9. High birth was considered a guarantee of honorable behavior; contraventions of this "norm" were deemed a shocking anomaly. We find this motif, albeit in reverse, in the *Romance of the Violet*, where Gondrée's wickedness is explained by her unsavory antecedents.

10. Hersent is the name of the wife of the wolf Ysengrin in *Le Roman de Renart*. Ysengrin is Renart's archenemy, and the fox constantly plots against him. Renart eventually cuckolds the wolf when he rapes Hersent, thus earning Ysengrin's undying enmity. The author's choice of this name hints at events to come.

11. Cross-dressing was a popular motif in hagiographic texts, where gender disguise allowed women to participate in monastic life. John Anson surveys the relevant texts in "The Female Transvestite in Early Monasticism: The Origin and Development of a Motif," *Viator* 5 (1974), 1–32. In Old French romance, the disguise served a variety of narrative purposes. In *Le Roman de Silence* (second half of the thirteenth century), an only-child daughter is raised as a son so that she may inherit the family property, while in *Aucassin et Nicolette* (late twelfth-early thirteenth century), the heroine disguises herself as a minstrel to escape an unwanted marriage and travel incognito. In both *Yde et Olive* and *Tristan de Nanteuil*, the heroine disguises herself as a man and eventually undergoes a miraculous change of gender. For discussion and bibliography, see Nancy Vine Durling, "Rewriting Gender: *Yde et Olive* and Ovidian Myth," *Romance Languages Annual* (1990), 256–262. Male cross-dressing was also depicted in Old French texts, though less frequently. See

Keith Busby, "Plus acesmez qu'une popine": Male Cross-Dressing in Medieval French Narrative," ch. 3 in *Gender Transgressions: Crossing the Normative Barrier in Old French Literature* (New York: Garland Pub., 1998; rpt, London and New York: Routledge, 2021), 45-59.

12. Ysoré was a giant Saracen who did battle in Paris with Guillaume d'Orange. Before being killed by Guillaume, Ysoré wounds him in the nose. According to the accounts in the Old French chansons de geste, this wound caused a bump (*courb*) on Guillaume's nose. The French term, eventually morphed into *court* (short) resulting in Guillaume's nickname, "William Short Nose." Guillaume's wife, Guiborc, refers to this distinguishing mark (noting that it was inflicted by Ysoré) as a "sign" or identifying feature by which her husband may be recognized (*Aliscans*, ed. Claude Régnier [Paris: Champion, 1990], ll. 2031–2038). A street called "Tombe d'Issoire" still exists in Paris. Its connection with Ysoré is somewhat vague, but it is thought to refer to the site of the battle, which is located on the route to Orléans and from there to Saint Jacques de Compostela (Ferdinand Lot, *Romania XXVI*, oct. 1897). The legend is discussed in *Guide de Paris Mystérieux*, nouvelle edition (Editions Sand, 1985), 707–708.

13. Jehan (John) is the masculine form of Jehane (Joan). Joan is consistently referred to by masculine pronouns for the duration of her disguise. Robert imagines that the similarity of the names is a sign of good luck.

14. "Livres tournois." One of many types of coinage in the Middle Ages.

15. Crusaders typically set off for the Holy Land twice a year at the most favorable seasons for travel, either in March or August.

16. White nuns were members of the Cistercian order and were particularly devoted to serving the sick and the poor. They were easily recognizable because of their all-white garb. The order became especially popular in northern France during the first half of the thirteenth century.

17. The author generally uses the male pronoun when referring to John, though when referring to Joan's actions, the female form is used. We assume that Robert had seen Raoul often, as well, though the two men do not recognize one another in this scene. This passage perhaps plays on the wager tale device of the identifying mark on the woman's body, here creating a parallel identifying mark on the body of the male.

18. This passage encapsulates the difficulty modern readers face in understanding textile imagery. The Old French text reads: "d'escarlate, de vair, de piers et de dras de soie." *Escarlate* can refer both to a color and to various fine fabrics, either silk or high-quality wool; *vair* can mean a shimmering gray-green or variegated color, or even fur; while *piers* refers to various shades of blue, often with glints of green. The construction of the clause suggests that the author is focusing here on the bright colors of Joan's new clothes.

19. The Old French text says that Robert cut through the *ciercle* of the helmet. The term is frequently found in battle scenes in the chansons de geste, though the reference is somewhat unclear. The "cercle" may refer to a band of metal on the helmet. However, flat-top (cannister) helmets were common in this period, and I have interpreted the term as a reference to the round top.

20. The beneficial effects of bathing are also noted in Chrétien de Troyes' *Perceval* (*Conte du graal*). The maiden of the tent, who is punished by her lover when he discovers that Perceval has kissed her, is ultimately rehabilitated by Perceval, who demands that the Proud Knight take her to his nearest house and see that she has warm baths, so that her beauty may be restored. The safe and beneficial quality of the baths at her cousin's house counterbalance the danger faced by Joan in the earlier bathing scene.

21. The double banneret referred to here reflects Robert's great wealth and status.

22. The text reads: "mireoirs de toutes les dames del monde." The "mirror" here indicates the lady's exemplary comportment; she represents all that is best in a woman.

23. This is an important theme in the *Romance of the Violet*, where Aiglente laments the fact that she approached Gerard first.

Bibliography

Useful overviews of aristocratic life in the early thirteenth century

Baldwin, John W. *Aristocratic Life in Medieval France: The Romances of Jean Renart and Gerbert de Montreuil, 1190–1230*. Baltimore: Johns Hopkins University Press, 2000.
Labarge, Margaret Wade. *Mistress, Maids and Men: Baronial Life in the Thirteenth Century*. London: Orion Books, rpt. 2003.

On the Wager Tale

Almansi, Guido. *Il Ciclo della scommessa. Dal* Decameron *al* Cymbeline *di Shakespeare*. Rome: Bulzoni, 1976.
Koenig, V.-Frédéric. "A New Perspective on the Wager Cycle," *Modern Philology* 44.2 (1946): 76–83.
Krueger, Roberta L. "Double Jeopardy: The Appropriation of Woman in Four Old French Romances of the "Cycle de la Gageure." In *Seeking the Woman in Late Medieval and Renaissance Writings: Essays in Feminist Contextual Criticism*, edited by Sheila Fisher and Janet E. Halley, 21–50. Knoxville: University of Tennessee Press, 1989.
Paris, Gaston. "Le Cycle de la Gageure," *Romania* 32 (1903): 480–511.
Suard, François. "Le Traitement de la Gageure dans *Le Comte de Poitiers, Le Roi Flore et la Belle Jehane*, et *Le Roman de Guillaume de Dole*." In *"Furent les merveilles pruvees et les aventures truvees," Hommage à Francis Dubost*, edited by Francis Gingras, Françoise Laurent, Frédérique La Nan and Jean-René Valette, 619–638. Paris: Champion, 2005.

Le Roman de la Violette

Editions

Buffum, Douglas Labaree, ed. *Le Roman de la Violette ou de Gerart de Nevers par Gerbert de Montreuil*. Paris: Didot Firmin [SATF], 1928.
Michel, Francisque. *Le Roman de la Violette ou de Gérard de Nevers, par Girbert de Montreuil*. Paris: Silvestre, 1834.

Translations

Demaules, Mireille, trans. *Gerbert de Montreuil. Le Roman de la Violette, XIIIe siècle*. Paris: Stock/Moyen Age, 1992.
Lespinasse, René de. *Gérard de Nevers ou le Roman de la Violette*, Nevers-Paris, 1875.
Le Roman de la Violette, renouvelé par Gonzague Truc. Paris, 1931.

Critical Studies

Baldwin, John W. "The Crisis of the Ordeal: Literature, Law, and Religion around 1200." *Journal of Medieval and Renaissance Studies* 24 (1994): 327–353.

Boulton, Maureen Barry McCann. *The Song in the Story: Lyric Insertions in French Narrative Fiction, 1200–1400.* Philadelphia; University of Pennsylvania Press, 1993.

Buffum, Douglas Labaree. "The Songs of the *Roman de la Violette*." In *Studies in Honour of A. Marshall Elliott,* 2 vols. 1: 129–157. Baltimore: The Johns Hopkins Press; Paris: Champion, 1911.

_____. "The Sources of the *Roman de la Violette*." *Romanic Review* 4 (1913): 472–78.

Burr, Kristin L. "Re-creating the body: Euriaut's tales (*Le Roman de la Violette*)." *Symposium* 56.1 (2002): 3–16.

_____. "Ringing True: Shifting Identity in *Le Roman de la Violette*." In *Shaping Identity in Medieval French Literature: The Other Within,* edited by Adrian P. Tudor and Kristin L. Burr, 53–66. Tallahassee: University of Florida Press, 2019.

Butterfield, Ardis. *Poetry and Music in Medieval France: From Jean Renart to Guillaume de Machaut.* Cambridge University Press, 2002.

Callahan, Christopher. "À l'ombre du jongleur disparu. La grammaire de la performance dans deux romans lyrico-narratifs dérimés." *Revue des langues romanes* 101.2 (1997): 211–233.

Cerquiglini, Jacqueline. "Pour une typologie de l'insertion." *Perspectives Médiévales* 3 (1977): 9–14.

Clier-Colombani, Françoise. *La Fée Mélusine au Moyen Age, Images, Mythes et Symboles.* Paris: Le Léopold d'Or, 1991.

Coldwell, Maria V. "*Guillaume de Dole* and Medieval Romances with Musical Interpolations." *Musica Disciplina* 35 (1981): 55–86.

Curtis, Renée. "The Love Potion in the *Roman de la Violette* de Gerbert de Montreuil." *Tristan Studies.* Munich: Fink, 1969: 24–27.

Demaules, Mireille. "L'Art de la ruse dans le *Roman de la Violette* de Gerbert de Montreuil." *Revue des langues romanes* 104.1 (2000): 143–161.

Doyle, Kara. "Narratizing Marie of Ponthieu." *Historical Reflections: Reflexions historiques* 30.1 (2004): 29–54.

Duval, Amaury. "Girbert de Montreuil," in *Histoire de la littérature française,* vol. 18: 760–771. [Kraus Rpt.: Nendeln/Leichtenstein, 1971.]

François, Charles. *Etude sur le style de la Continuation du "Perceval" par Gerbert et du "Roman de la Violette" par Gerbert de Montreuil.* Paris: Droz, 1932.

Galano, Sabrina. "Enchâssement des textes lyriques occitans dans les romans français: *Guillaume de Dole* et *Roman de la Violette*." *Atti del VII Convegno internazionale dell'AIEO* (Regio Calabria-Messina, 7–13 luglio 2002). 2 vols. 1: 325–341. Rome: Viella, 2003.

Haugeard, Philippe. "Preuve et vérité dans le *Tristan* de Béroul et le *Roman de la Violette* de Gerbert de Montreuil." *Cahiers de recherches médiévales et humanistes* 34 (2017): 149–171.

Keller, Hans-Erich. "L'esprit courtois et le *Roman de la Violette*." In *Courtly Literature: Culture and Context, Selected papers from the 5th Triennial Congress of the International Courtly Literature Society, Dalfsen, The Netherlands, 9–16 August, 1986,* edited by Keith Busby and Erik Kooper, 323–335. Amsterdam: Johns Benjamins, 1990.

Kocher, Suzanne. "Accusations of Gay and Straight Sexual Transgression in the *Roman de la Violette*." In *Discourses on Love, Marriage, and Transgression in Medieval and Early Modern Literature,* edited by Albrecht Classen, 189–210. Tempe: ACMRS, 2004.

Koenig, V.-Frédéric. "*Guillaume de Dole* and *Guillaume de Nevers*." *Modern Philology* 45.3 (1948): 145–151.

Krause, Kathy. "L'héroïne et l'autorité du discours: *Le Roman de la Violette et le Roman de la Rose ou de Guillaume de Dole*." *Le Moyen Age* 102.2 (1996): 191–216.

_____. "The Material Erotic: The Clothed and the Unclothed Female Body in the *Roman de la Violette*." In *Material Culture and Cultural Materialisms in the Middle Ages and the Renaissance,* edited by Curtis Perry, 17–39. Turnhout, Belgium: Brepols, 2001.

Krueger, Roberta L. *Women Readers and the Ideology of Gender in Old French Verse Romance.* Cambridge University Press, 1993. See Ch. 5 (rpt. Of Krueger, above).

Limentani, Alberto, and Laura Pegolo. "Marote ou de l'amour bourgeois." In *Epopée animale, fable, fabliau: Actes du IVe Colloque de la Société Internationale Renardienne, Evreux, 7–11 septembre 1981,* edited by Gabriel Bianciotto and Michel Salvat, 323–331. Paris: PUF, 1984.

Louison, Lydie. *De Jean Renart à Jean Maillart: Les romans de style gothique.* Paris: Champion, 2004.

Mora, Francine. "Mémoire du narrateur et oublis du héros dans le *Roman de la Violette* de Gerbert de Montreuil." In *Figures de l'oubli (IVe–XVIe siècle),* edited by Patrizia Romagnoli and Barbara Wahlen, 119–138. Lausanne: *Études de lettres* 276 (2007/1–2).

Ohle, Rud. *Shakespeares Cymbeline und seine romanischen Vorläufer, eine kritische Untersuchung.* Leipzig, 1890.

Orr, John. "Une source du *Roman de la Violette.*" In *Mélanges de philologie romane et de littérature médiévale offerts à Ernest Hoepffner par ses élèves et ses amis* vol. 1. Paris: Belles Lettres (Publications de la Faculté des lettres de Strasbourg, 113), 1949: 301–306.

Page, Christopher. *Voices & Instruments of the Middle Ages: Instrumental Practice and Songs in France 1100–1300.* Berkeley: University of California Press, 1986.

Paris, Gaston. "Le Cycle de la gageure." *Romania* 32 (1903): 480–511.

Wilmotte, Maurice. "Gerbert de Montreuil et les écrits qui lui sont attribués," *Bull. Acad. roy. de Belgique, Cl. des lettres* 3 (1900): 196f.

Zingesser, Eliza. *Stolen Song: How the Troubadours Became French.* Ithaca: Cornell University Press, 2020. Ch. 3.

Zink, Michel. "Suspension and Fall: The Fragmentation and Linkage of Lyric Insertions in *Le roman de la rose* (Guillaume de Dole) and *Le roman de la violette.*" In *Jean Renart and the Art of Romance: Essays on* Guillaume de Dole, edited by Nancy Vine Durling, 105–121. Tallahassee: University Press of Florida, 1997.

Le Roman du Comte de Poitiers

Editions

Delbouille, Maurice. "Fragments d'un second manuscript du 'Roman du comte de Poitiers,' (XIIIe siècle)." *Revue belge de philologie et d'histoire* 23 (1944): 255–264.

Koenig, V.-Frédéric, ed. *Le Conte de Poitiers: roman du XIIIe siècle.* Paris: Droz, 1937.

Malmberg, Bertil, ed. *Le Roman du comte de Poitiers Poème français du XIIIe siècle.* Lund: Gleerup, 1940.

Michel, Francisque. *Roman du Comte de Poitiers* (Paris: Silvestre, 1831).

Translations

Demaules, Mireille. *Gerbert de Montreuil: Le Roman de la Violette, XIIIe siècle.* Paris: Stock/Moyen Age, 1992. Partial translation (ll. 23–1237) into modern French, 175–203.

Critical/Historical Studies

Durling, Nancy Vine. "Women's Visible Honor in Medieval Romance: The Example of the Old French *Roman du comte de Poitiers.*" In *Translatio Studii: Essays by His Students in Honor of Karl D. Uitti for His Sixty-fifth Birthday,* edited by Renate Blumenfeld-Kosinski, Kevin Brownlee, Mary B. Speer, and Lori J. Walters, 117–132. Amsterdam: Rodopi, 1999.

Fahlin, Carin. "Les sources et la date du *Roman du Comte de Poitiers.*" *Studia neophilologica* 13 (1940–1941): 181–225.

Paris, Gaston. "Le cycle de la gageure." *Romania* 32 (1903): 480–511.

Le Conte dou roi Flore et de la bielle Jehane

Editions

Michel, Francisque. *Le roman du roi Flore et de la belle Jeanne, publié pour la première fois d'après un manuscript de la bibliothèque royale.* Paris: Techener, 1838. (Republished in *Théâtre français au Moyen Age (XIe-XIVe siècles)*, edited by L.J.N. Monmerqué and Francisque Michel, 417–430. Paris: Firmin-Didot, 1839.

Moland, Louis and Charles d'Héricault, "Le roi Flore et la Belle Jehane." In *Nouvelles françoises en prose du XIIIe siècle*, 83–157. Paris: Jannet (Bibliothèque elzévirienne), 1856.

Translations/Retellings

"La Belle Jean." In *Medieval Legends,* adapted and edited by Philip S. Jennings, 53–65. New York: St. Martin's Press, 1983.

Le roi Flore et la belle Jeanne, Amis et Amiles, contes du XIIIe siècle, adapted by G. Michaut. Paris: de Boccard (Poèmes et récits de la vieille France, 2), 1923.

Romances of Old France, retold by Richard Le Gallienne. New York: Baker & Taylor, 1901:-11–32. Rpt. Freeport, NY: Books for Libraries, 1969.

"The Story of King Florus and of the Fair Jehane." In *Aucassin & Nicolette and Other Mediaeval Romances and Legends*, translated, with an introduction by Eugene Mason, 99–138. New York: E.P. Dutton & Co., 1910 (rpt. 1958).

Wolfzettel, Friedrich, trans. *Französische "Schicksalsnovellen" des 13. Jahrhunderts. "La Chastelaine de Vergi," "La fille du comte de Pontieu," "Le roi Flore et la belle Jehanne."* Munich: Fink (Klassische Texte des romanischen Mittelalters in zweisprachigen Ausgaben, 26), 1986.

Studies

Delany, Sheila. "Flore et Jehane: A Case Study of the Bourgeois Woman in Medieval Life and Letters." *Science and Society* 45:3 (1981): 274–287.

Durling, Nancy Vine. "*La bielle Jehane* and the Body of the Text." *Romance Languages Annual* 2 (1990): 93–99.

_____. "Le Parchemin souillé: traces d'une lecture érotique dans un manuscript tournaisien, vers 1300." In *La Souillure*, edited by Danielle Bohler, 29–37. *Eidôlon*, no. 92. Presses Universitaires de Bordeaux, 2011.

Lefèvre, Sylvie. "Roi Flore et la belle Jeanne." *Dictionnaire des lettres françaises: Le Moyen Âge*, edited by Geneviève Hasenohr and Michel Zink, 1298. Paris, Fayard, 1992.

Levy, Raphael. "Le roi Flore et la belle Jehane." *Philological Quarterly* 14.3 (1935): 253–262.

Söderhjelm, Werner. *La nouvelle française au XVe siècle.* Paris: Champion (Bibliothèque du XVe siècle 12), 1910. 532–534.

Trotter, D.A. *Medieval French Literature and the Crusades (1100–1300).* Geneva: Droz, 1988.

Index

255